NAKED, DRUNK, AND WRITING

Writing Essays and Memoirs for Love and for Money

PRAISE FOR *NAKED, DRUNK, AND WRITING*

Tracy Johnston, author of *Shooting the Boh*:
Your insights are terrific and so is your voice: funny and self-deprecating, ballsy and enthusiastic.

Janis Newman, author of *Mary*:
This is a really wonderful book. One of the best (and most helpful) books on writing I've read. And unlike most practical guides, never pedantic or boring.

John Leland, professor:
WOW! You've got a treasure chest here that's just brimming with jewels!

Mary Patrick, author of *Family Plots*:
Adair's keen editorial eye and sharp sense of story arc helped me pare a 500- page manuscript into a tighter, plot-driven read. Her coaching and enthusiasm opened doors to locating an agent that had previously been bolted.

Ruth Chambers, author of *The Chinaberry Album*:
Thanks SO much for sending *Naked, Drunk, and Writing*. I started underlining, highlighting, tagging pages. What a gift to writers every-where! I'm struck by your conversational voice. I feel that I'm there in the room with you, watching you fold and unfold your glasses as you share your experiences and wisdom with us. Your material is never dry, but interesting, funny, instructive, and memorable. I just wish I could open the top of my head and pour all this good stuff inside.

Gregory Peebles, soprano:
I read your book and was inspired to apply some of your techniques to my writing. I've gotten very good feedback from readers. Your voice is so true that it encourages me to listen deeply to my own. Thank you, thank you, thank you!

Barbara Olson:
Every time I read something by Adair Lara, I feel like drawing something.

NAKED, DRUNK, *and* WRITING

Writing Essays and Memoirs
for Love and for Money

BY ADAIR LARA

BOOKS BY ADAIR LARA

The Granny Diaries, Chronicle Books (2008)

The Bigger the Sign, the Worse the Garage Sale, Chronicle Books (2007)

You Know You're A Writer When, Chronicle Books (2007)

Oopsie! Ouchie!, Chronicle Books (2004)

Normal is Just a Setting on the Dryer, Chronicle Books, 2003

Slowing Down in a Speeded-Up World, Redwheelweiser (2002)

Hold Me Close, Let Me Go, Broadway Books (2001)

The Best of Adair Lara, Scottwall Associates (1999)

At Adair's House, Chronicle Books (1995)

Welcome to Earth, Mom, Chronicle Books (1992)

ABOUT THE AUTHOR

Adair Lara started her career writing for local magazines — first *San Francisco Focus,* the city magazine, and then *SF,* a design magazine at which she passed herself off as someone passionately interested in interior design. She wrote freelance humor pieces for the *San Francisco Chronicle* Sunday section, and in 1989 joined the staff as a columnist, where she won a number of awards, including the Associated Press award for Best Columnist in California. She writes for a number of national magazines, including *More* and *Reader's Digest.* Her essays have been anthologized upwards of fifty times. May 17, 2002 was declared Adair Lara Day in San Francisco by proclamation of Mayor Willie Brown.

Adair Lara
97 Scott Street
San Francisco, CA 94117
Adair.lara@gmail.com
Adairlara.com

· ·

Copyright © 2009 by Adair Lara
All rights reserved.

Library of Congress Cataloging-in-Publication Data available.
ISBN 978-0-578-01245-2

Scottwall Associates, Publishers,
95 Scott Street, San Francisco, Ca. 94117

Cover and book design: Katie Heit

· ·

The lesson that one's own experience matters, that it provides the best line to truth, is knowledge we were born with, and then taught to forget, and then learn anew.

— from *Secret Paths* by Terri Apter

TABLE OF CONTENTS

FIRST PERSON SINGULAR

What Gets in the Way
I Was Just Another a Blocked Writer

> I should not talk so much about myself if there
> were anybody else whom I knew as well.
>
> — Henry David Thoreau in *Walden*

If you have picked up this book, then I think I already know something about you. You are already a writer. You wrote a sonnet about pores in high school. Your mom said, "Now I'm ironing the placket" and you stood beside her thinking, "*Placket.*" *Good word.* You know where the outlets are at the coffee shop. You keep a notebook by the bed. Stories crowd your head waking and sleeping, and demand to be set down. You get an idea and stay up writing until 3 a.m. while cups of cold coffee and bowls encrusted with cereal pile up on your desk. You close down your laptop, allow yourself to give it a small pat, and tremble into bed next to your twitching mate. You feel exultant. Dreams of chatting on the *Oprah Winfrey Show* about the day you began your bestselling novel fill your head.

WHAT GETS IN THE WAY

You are already a writer, which means you already know that the will to *not* write is strong in all of us. If I even think about writing, I find myself in the pantry eating cereal straight from the box. Writing is a scary, vulnerable, and in a way conceited act, one that says the words you set down are worth a stranger's time to read, and that this is a worthy use of your own time. There are those twin delights on every writer's shoulder, despair and self-loathing. *You're kidding yourself about this writing thing*, they whisper. *You're just whining on the page, no one will want to publish your ramblings or even read them.*

No one is free of them:

> Can I write? Will I write if I practice enough? How much should
> I sacrifice to writing anyway, before I find out if I'm any good?
> Above all, CAN A SELFISH EGOCENTRIC JEALOUS AND
> UNIMAGINATIVE FEMALE WRITE A DAMN THING WORTHWHILE?

If you're wondering who stole that thought out of your head, it was Sylvia Plath. And she had early success—she already knew her poems pierced the skin.

Believe me, I know about all the ways there are to keep yourself from writing. My story begins as that of just another blocked writer with a trail of crumpled paper balls littering her wake.

I WAS JUST ANOTHER BLOCKED WRITER

I grew up in the San Geronimo Valley, twenty miles north of where I live now in San Francisco, a bookstruck little kid sitting on a stump writing stories. Writing was easy then. I used my dad's square carpenter pencil to cover sheet after sheet with stories of dogs that rescued families from a flood or a fire. Faithful dogs, faithful horses — it all caught in my throat. I tore holes in the paper in my haste to get it all down. One of my stories was read aloud to other classes at Lagunitas Elementary, my little adobe-styled school, and at recess Debbie Nelson eyed my home haircut and baggy brown plaid dress and accused me of copying the story from a magazine. I raced home and told my mother I was going to be a writer when I grew up.

Then I did grow up, and nothing happened. I didn't even dare take creative writing in college and felt it was putting on airs even to call myself an English major. I felt I had no talent and nothing to say, which was especially painful because I couldn't stop dragging out a pad and pen, or screwing paper into a typewriter, trying again. When my confidence petered out, I'd stalk off to read a book, which made everything worse. I'd write, "I wish I could set things down the way I see them in my head." Then I'd read Flaubert's version of the same thought: "Human language is like a cracked kettle on which we beat out tunes for bears to dance to, when all the time we are longing to move the stars to pity."

I had the cracked kettle — he had the stars weeping. Yet books sang down my nerves, made me want to write. Even as a kid I read everything — tags on pillows, the backs of cereal boxes, the tiny brochure that came with our new freezer, the moldy novels that lined the high shelf in our shadowy living room. I never got confused about the difference between real life and books: real life was what happened in books. The cold that raised goose pimples on my own arm as I walked to school in the frosty morning was nothing to the cold in the books with tattered cellophane covers that I checked out of the little Forest Knolls library seven at a time.

I moved across the bridge to San Francisco, finished college, married, had kids, unmarried, all the while continuing to punctuate my life with attempts at writing. At night, in my railroad flat high up on Dolores Street, I'd tap away at the kitchen table after I'd gotten most of the dirt off my kids and had thrown them into bed. My son Patrick's newts would watch dubiously from their smelly tank on the refrigerator as I punched out a page, or two, or three, read them over, and cringed.

I tried other things: I bought a stack of romance novels at the Goodwill — "The Silken Web," "Sweet Anger," "A Nurse to Marry"— and tried to write like that. Every English teacher in America was doing the same thing. We all had the idea that anything we thought ourselves too sophisticated to read would be easy to write.

Wrong. My every attempt fell over into parody. Sighs became pants, pants screams. Square jaws became—anyway. I also tried my hand at writing greeting cards.

> *You have bedroom eyes. Can I see the rest of the house?*
> *Your new baby is beautiful. Is it adopted or what?*

By the time I passed 30, I decided if I couldn't be a writer, I could at least get a job in a related field. No one hired writers — I knew that much, and when I was interviewed for a job as a copyeditor at *San Francisco Focus*, the local city magazine, I swore to the managing editor that I wasn't one, that my happiness lay in making sure that the absence of "h" in Natan Katzman's name in the KQED masthead was not an error.

The magazine had an office in a modest building set amid the warehouses, factory outlets, and coffee shops south of Market Street, a few blocks from my apartment. Pleased to my rope sandals to be hired at a real magazine, I proofread, fact checked, and coded manuscripts for the typesetter. I sweated over the captions that came my way as if they were *War and Peace*, and wrote headlines like "Swell Wines at Swill Prices" (which they rejected, the cowards). I called writers to say things like, "Listen to this sentence and see if you can live without the comma." I'd remind myself it was terrific to be an editor, enjoying all those lunches out and wearing all those black outfits. All the time, though, I yearned to be one of the writers who came into the office, who looked as if they had tramp streamers moored outside, or had just left wintry palaces, and came and went at odd hours.

My friend Cynthia, the production editor, wanted to be a writer as much as I did. She was as thin as a butter knife and wore her sweaters down to her knees. Some days after work, hung over from a long day of polishing other people's sentences, we'd go to the bar across the street to drink huge round glasses of red wine, overcome with sorrow at being destined to slave over the tortured scribblings of hacks while we went unpublished and unrecognized.

One day at the bar after a long day of compiling restaurant listings for the annual August restaurant issue, she and I started a writing club. The idea was simple: we'd write 500 words every weekday and give them to the other person. We'd mark the parts we liked in the other's pieces with a yellow highlighter before returning them. I got the idea from a teacher at San Francisco State ten years before. He marked passages that caught his eye with a yellow highlighter so that when the papers were turned back, everybody in the class had something — at least a paragraph or two — to feel proud of.

Cynthia and I scribbled a list of topics on a bar napkin: parking, rain, first dates, and father. And we were off. We handed our 500-worders to each other over the cubicle walls at work, fished them out of our purses at the bar, and brought them with us in our gym bags to our Friday night Rhythm & Motion class in the Haight. It didn't matter what the 500 words were — we could copy them from the Yellow Pages or the back of the Cheerios box if we wanted to. I'd rarely shown my work to people before, outside of school, because you only showed people stuff you thought was good. Now I gave Cynthia any old piece of dashed-off thing — not because it was good, but because it was *due*. When Cynthia gave my pages back, I'd read the sentences

she'd highlighted with swooning admiration. Even if there was one sentence
bathed in yellow, suddenly my head was too big to fit through doorways. *I
wrote that!* I could rewrite the whole piece, now that I knew I had it in me
to come up with that sentence. Her scrawled, "I love this!" gave me back the
confidence I'd had as child. In those dark years before I discovered writing
partners — I went on to have many — I'd been missing the necessary other
half of the writing process: the pleased reader. It was as if I'd been trying to
tell myself I was a good cook, but without ever asking anyone to dinner.

I kept showing up at the magazine to check proof galleys and call headline
meetings, but with a new song playing in the back of my head: I was a writer.

That's how it started. I was 33. I would seize my pieces back from Cynthia,
rewrite them, and send them to the *San Francisco Chronicle* Sunday Punch,
which then published freelance articles, and they began to be accepted. I
was so excited at having a byline in the section that got more jam stains and
crumbs on it than anything else in the Bay Area that I'd talk the proprietor
at the corner store into selling me the Sunday paper early. "The sports page
not here yet!" he'd object and I'd have to practically jerk the thing out of his
hands. I'd stand there on the sidewalk, forcing people to go around me, while
I read my own piece — or rather my own name — over and over, with a joy
that seemed to start in my toes.

Cynthia sent pieces out too, selling them to Sunday magazine sections as far
away as Wisconsin.

That first writing club, as we called it, changed my life. It made me a writer
by giving me the confidence to be one. And it led to my job as a columnist.

At a party I met Rosalie Wright, features editor of the *Chronicle*. Rosalie
greeted me warmly and said she'd been following the humor pieces I'd been
publishing in the Sunday section. "She's better than Anna Quindlen," she
said to her companion, who rattled the ice cubes in his glass in bored answer.

Three months later, dopily dressed in a velvet-jogging outfit (it was 1989), I
drove my beat-up VW convertible to the historic old Chronicle building at
Mission and Fifth streets and parked in the garage nearby. Rosalie met me
in the lobby, tiny and neat in a pale blue suit, and we took the elevator to the
third floor office of Bill German, the editor-in-chief who had to approve my

hire. Nervously, I followed her into a large office paneled in dark wood where a grey-haired man in shirtsleeves sat reading at a desk in the middle of the room. German had a large square face that he swung around on his otherwise stiff shoulders like a club. He asked how many columns a week I thought I could write. Rosalie and I hadn't talked about that. I said, "Three?"

Thank god we settled at two.

I still had a question. German was already turning back to the papers on his desk. He was hard of hearing, so I had to shout.

"What should I write about?" I yelled.

He waved impatiently. "Write about your life."

I drove home in a daze to my latest crappy apartment, this one on Waller Street. The kids were at their dad's next door. I was so happy that I kept walking from room to room, from the tiny kitchen overlooking a dime-sized back yard to ten- year -old Morgan's room down the hall, with its sea of garments covering the floor (she liked to be able to see all her clothes at once). I had to call Neil, the boyfriend I had just broken up with, so I could tell him — thus providing myself with several months' worth of material before we came to our senses and split up again.

For the next twelve years, I wrote two columns a week. What a crucible for a writer! I learned so much. It was a wonderful, terrifying gig. When I got that column I had nowhere to run, nowhere to hide. If I wanted to talk about teenage smoking, I had to mention the thin tendril of smoke appearing in the blue sky above the heads of my own two kids. If I talked about mistakes, I talked about my own. I wrote about everything that happened to me — about trying to pass off my little kids as friends when renting an apartment, about being a twin, about driving a car. When my husband Bill switched me to decaf coffee without telling me, I wrote a column about marital lies. When my dad, drugged by a prescribed tranquilizer, landed in a nursing home and almost died, I wrote about medications and the elderly. If I made pancakes for my boyfriend, and he said, "Kind of thick, aren't they?" I wrote a column on nagging. I kept saying to Rosalie, "You're sure this is what you want?" And she kept insisting it was.

It was a personal column, which meant that I wrote about whatever touched my own life. This was disconcerting to longtime newspaper readers, not all of whom understood why I was telling the world how it felt when the smell of yet another smoked clutch filled my Toyota, about the new iciness between my mother and me, about having an ex-husband living upstairs. One reader said mildly in a letter, "I wish you would explain the purpose of your column. When you are not occupying that space, others write of similar personal experiences and I just do not understand what place they have in a newspaper." Another helpfully clipped my columns and mailed them to me with the "I's" and "me's" circled in red, to let me know I was doing it again.

It *was* odd to be reciting the events of my own life in a paper. I clung to Jung's idea that, ironically, the more intensely individual a person's thoughts are, the more uniquely applicable to him or her, the more they have meaning for the rest of us. "That which is most personal is most common," he said.

I have to admit it suited me, writing about family, and relationships, and knocking about in the world. Since my beginning with the column, I have made a little cottage industry out of writing about, well, myself, though I could hardly be more ordinary — a middle-aged married woman living in San Francisco. While I was still at the paper, I published a memoir called *Hold Me Close, Let Me Go: A Mother, a Daughter, and an Adolescence Survived*, about how my Cabbage-Patch-doll-loving daughter Morgan morphed into a beer-soaked, class-cutting, thrill-seeking, lying-is-like-breathing teenager from hell. When Morgan, by some miracle, became a lawyer and not a jailbird, and had two little girls, Maggie and Ryan, I wrote a little book about being a grandmother called *The Granny Diaries*.

When I began teaching writing classes in essay and memoir at schools and bookstores and in my living room, I also made notes for this book — in which, you notice, I don't trouble to keep myself off the page.

The first course I taught was at a converted army base south of the Golden Gate Bridge in San Francisco. I was so terrified that I spent the half hour before that first class at a restaurant across the street trying to get drunk. Today at least half my friends are people I met in my courses, which I hold at colleges and bookstores, in addition to the ten-week course I often have going in the San Francisco flat I share with my husband Bill, a cookbook editor.

Linda Robinson came to my house knowing she had less than a year to live. She was 36, with thick blonde hair just growing in again, married and living with two small sons in Belmont, on the peninsula south of San Francisco. She wrote a piece about her visit to a funeral home to arrange for her own burial. Her face still puffy from chemo, she read it to the hushed room:

> Joe, the manager, showed me various combinations of options, from the Lenin-lying-in-state model on down to the shoebox-in-the-backyard version. I had a pleasing vision of being buried in my jewelry box. When Joe got back, I asked him if you could provide your own container for cremated remains. He said, "Yes, but you'd be surprised how many people neglect to bring a lid." I said, "I guess Saran Wrap would be tacky?"

The laughter started when she was only halfway through, and by the time she was done the class was roaring and my dog was barking.

"You *laughed*," Linda exclaimed gratefully. "I'm so glad you laughed."

In the discussion that followed, Linda's classmates suggested she drop the paragraph about driving into the funeral home parking lot, for sure keep the part where she fogged the shiny rich wood of a coffin with her breath, and asked her to make the bit about the incense clearer.

No one had the poor manners to express sympathy. Linda wasn't the dying woman here, as she was in other rooms: here, she was a writer. In this room everything that happened, however terrible, was material. Just as the Plains Indians used every part of the buffalo, so writers, too, use everything. If it doesn't kill you, you can use it in your writing. Even, as Linda showed our class, if it does kill you.

And writing makes you a writer. Lolly Winston wrote essays for me, and then discovered she is a novelist — with *Good Grief* and *Happiness Sold Separately* so far. Midwife Peggy Vincent's pieces full of blood, and mucus, and babies being delivered in the backs of cars and on the floor and in waterbeds was later published as *BabyCatcher*.

Susan Parker, author of *Tumbling After*, had never written anything until her husband Ralph broke his neck in a bicycle accident while pedaling down

Grizzly Peak near Berkeley, California. Ralph was a retired nuclear physicist; she was in her early forties, thirteen years younger. The accident left Ralph a quadriplegic and Susan a caregiver, with instructions to catheterize her husband every four hours 24 hours a day.

> My life was wrecked after Ralph's accident. There was nothing left of it. Writing about that experience in class, and then later in a book, gave me a new sense of self worth, new friends. Ralph was proud of me. I'm in an MFA program. My life is so much richer than it was before.

Jackie Winspear first took my essay class, then began coming to my house once a month with a new piece. One day she arrived to say she'd been stuck in a traffic jam by the Pennzoil station in San Rafael, and used the time to conjure up a character named Maisie Dobbs, investigator and psychologist, for a novel she didn't even know she had in her. She began bringing me pages of that book, which became *Maisie Dobbs*. All I said during those monthly meetings was, "Keep going." (At book readings she tells the story of how after she broke her arm falling off her horse, I said, "You have another hand, don't you?") She'd been a life coach, struggling to get by. Now she's living the dream life of a writer, with seven novels in the prize-winning Maisie Dobbs series.

Hundreds of others have had essays published in newspapers and magazines, on radio, in columns. Rita Hargrave, a psychiatrist by day, publishes her pieces on salsa dancing in music magazines and writes about her work in trade publications. Stacey Appel writes a monthly essay for *Skirt! Magazine*. Janis Cooke Newman has numerous articles and two books out, the second one a widely reviewed novel on Mary Todd Lincoln called *Mary*. Published books by my students also include *The Water Dancers* by Terry Gamble, *Now Breathe*, by Claudia Sternbach, and a shelf of others.

My book is called *Naked, Drunk and Writing* because I like that title, and because somebody at a party once remarked to me over the sushi that books with "naked" in the title always sell. And writing about yourself *is* like stripping down to your Bali bra in the middle of a crowded party, so that everybody can see the stretch marks on your belly (and be reassured about their own). And writing is a kind of word-drunkenness that makes you want to do that — to take off your clothes and turn your experiences into art, despite who may be watching, despite your own embarrassment, despite anything the world and your own self-doubts throws against you.

In it I've put pretty much everything I know about writing essays and memoirs. My credentials are not that I'm a natural talent myself, but the opposite. I had to learn how writing worked before I could do it well, or well enough (I imagine that you can make a parlor game out of all the places in this book where I fail to take my own advice). I had to learn by writing 100 pages I didn't need, or listening to my husband saying, "Stretch it out," when I couldn't write a scene over 30 words long.

This is a book about writing down what happened to you — call it autobiographical writing, or personal writing, or writing from life. In the next chapter we'll talk about what makes both essays and memoirs succeed, and then in succeeding chapters take on first essay, then memoir, always keeping in mind that the principles of good writing pretty much always apply to both. A lot of books encourage you to skip around, and fine, do that, but I'm writing this as if you're reading it front to back.

....

NOTE TO THE READER
Many of the writing examples in this book are from my students. I have sometimes taken the liberty of referring to them by first name only, or by giving them an alias.

....

CHAPTER TWO

ESSAY AND MEMOIR

Change
Is It About You?
What if Mom Reads It?
The Hot Heart and the Cold Eye

The word "essay" may remind you of what Mrs. Bernardicou with the baggy arms made you write back in high school, and in truth the word covers a lot of ground. In this book I talk about only one kind: a short piece, about 800 to 2,000 words long, that you write in the first person about something that happened to you. Over the years of writing the column, I wrote hundreds of these, although of course mine were all the same length, about 700 words.

A memoir is longer—a book, in fact—but similar. You can think of the short personal essay as an extremely short memoir, and of the memoir as a very long essay. A memoir is more complex, with a story that unfolds over months and years. The two have the same relationship that the short story has to the novel.

Successful personal essays and memoirs share these four elements:
1. They are about change
2. They are about you (this is less of an obvious point than it may seem to be)
3. You write about real people
4. They are well-crafted — put together in a way satisfying to a reader, rather than just blurted out

Let's take this list one by one.

CHANGE

Whether you're writing a short essay or a 100,000-word memoir, you aren't required to find a new universal truth — a weighty topic that has never been addressed before. That's impossible. Humans have spent centuries documenting such truths. What you do is share your personal, eccentric struggle with one of them and tell us how it changed you.

By changed you I mean altered your behavior, your choices, your understanding, or your relationships with others. Knowing that you will be writing about change helps you choose which of your stories will have meaning for others.

Some life events feel huge, but do not necessarily change you. You and your mother haven't spoken in six months. You got fired, you got dumped, you got cancer, or you got treated unfairly. These stories affect you deeply, and feel as if they have meaning for that reason. But many upsetting events come up under the heading of Shit Happens. You can lose a lot of time trying to write about them. Practically everybody who gets fired sits down to write a book about it — but what's the story? Getting fired makes you mad, but that's not change. The change may be in what happens next: after you were fired, you realize you never meant to spend your life cooped up in an office anyway, and go to Guatemala to rescue street children.

Let me give you an example of a vivid event that nonetheless doesn't show change. My sister Nora told me about taking a cab down a dark back street to a business meeting at a hotel in Taipei when suddenly the driver jumped out and ran off. Nora was left with her suitcase and little blue overnight case in an empty cab. She couldn't even read the street signs, and had no idea where she was. In the end, though, she found her way back to the hotel without much trouble.

"Did that experience change you?" I asked her.

"I found out I could take care of myself when I needed to," Nora replied.

"Before that cab ride, did you think you *couldn't* take care of yourself?" I asked.

"Well, no," she said. "I always knew I could."

No change. She was the same confident person after the experience as she was before it. She didn't find out anything new about herself. She remembers that night because she was alone in a strange city, with street signs she couldn't read.

Nora's story is an *anecdote* — a short recounting of an interesting or humorous incident. Anecdotes have a strong role to play, but they don't always add up to an essay no matter how much time you spend on them. It's funny that your old mother bought a BB rifle to kill her squirrels with, but that's all it is — funny. An anecdote is just something that happened. Running into Mick Jagger in a sports bar in New York was exciting, but where's the struggle, the change in you? Belinda Hulin, an editor at *Skirt! Magazine* who took a workshop from me, put it this way:

> If there's no catharsis, no growth, no change involved, then you're left with an anecdote — a part of some larger whole — rather than a self-contained essay or story. Like that of most women, my life has been full of hilarious-in-hindsight incidents. But alas, my accordion body, my landfill approach to housekeeping, my bizarre divorce, my cradle-robbing second marriage, my unseemly yearning to become a born-again trust fund baby and the myriad instances in which my slow-to-rehabilitate smart mouth have gotten me into trouble, are just not going to write. Why? Because I've happily, gloriously learned nothing from these romps.

THE CRAFTY WRITER
You want to write about your anecdotes anyway, because they're so vivid or shocking or funny. Everybody says, "You should write about that." Group them with other anecdotes to make a story: "My Brushes with Celebrity," "Disasters That Didn't Happen," or "Three Things That Happened That Led Me to AA."

Not all experience reveals, but all revelation comes through experience. Find the points of change (turning points, learning points) in your life, and you will find your material: the time you realized you were gay, that your mother was not going to get better, that it was a mistake to move to the country, that you are not going through with the adoption. Or the day you threw your estranged husband's nail gun into the bushes, and realized that the worst part of divorce for you was not how badly your spouse behaved, but how badly the process made *you* behave. The time your Volkswagen filled with twenty pairs of expensive shoes was stolen in Mexico, and to your surprise you were glad. The time you discovered you had a twin who died at birth, and decided to become a pediatrician.

Everybody's life is filled with such moments. When you sat on the steps in your wedding dress and realized you had made a mistake. When the friend who'd annoyed you every hour of your trip together in Ireland saves you from a gypsy and you realize it is not the first time she has saved you, that she has always been your protector.

I remember a turning point in a graduate seminar at San Francisco State. I'd been a shameless grade-grubber: my idea of getting ready for a discussion of a book in class was to streak over to the library to look up what other people had thought of it. I wasn't about to be caught thinking that *Moby Dick* was actually about a whale, or that *Women in Love* wasn't really a very good novel.

One day my classmates and I were assigned a paper on a poem the professor handed out. As usual, I tried to crib the answer from the library but I couldn't — the poem was unpublished. I studied that poem for days, carrying it around in my purse on the N Judah streetcar, puzzling over it at meals. I couldn't make heads nor tails of the thing. Finally, I wrote something or other and turned it in. When the papers were returned, mine had a scrawled red D on it, as did most. What was the poem about then? we demanded to know. The professor said, "This poem is an extended metaphor about the act of writing."

I sat there with that D paper in front of me. I unfolded the poem, wrinkled from my many readings, covered with my notes.

The turning point would be something like this: I must have read that poem 20 freaking times. I have normal intelligence and I was paying attention. If I didn't get that the poem was about writing, then *the poem deserved the D, not me.* That moment came late in my formal schooling — I left the next semester — but it was the beginning of my education. Before that day in class, I went to the library to find out what I was supposed to think. After that day, I thought, what do *I* think? I never again looked up the critics.

IS IT ABOUT YOU?

You are the subject of the personal essay or memoir, the one to whom the experience is happening, the one who undergoes the change.

Is a piece you're writing in first person about something that happened in your life automatically about you? Not necessarily. You may just have been in the neighborhood, or in the family, or in the way. If your best friend's mother just committed suicide, how is that your story? If the memory of that kept you from later taking your own life, it's important. If it was just something shocking that happened when you were around, it might not be. A story about the scheming hospice nurse who got herself written into your mother's will and ran off with your inheritance still has to be about you changing. Being the victim of a swindle, or suddenly being poor, is not change, but bad luck. Finding out that people can be rats is not change, either.

This may sound obvious. It's not, really. One student wanted to write about being conceived after her father had a vasectomy. But she wasn't there. (Her father might have a story to tell us, though.) I wrote the whole first draft of my memoir about my teenaged daughter Morgan without grasping that a memoir written by somebody's mother has to be about being a mother — not about having an at-risk teenager. In fact my early drafts were not so much a story that built to anything so much as an annotated list of Morgan's escalating escapades: "And then she cut class and lied and got in stolen cars with boys who went to other schools. ... And then she met a boy who introduced her to speed and got her pregnant. ... And she refused to go to the drug program and I kicked her out. ..." In between each of her adventures you were treated to some shots of me sobbing on the bed or wetting her stepdad's shirt, the ocean air blowing in from the window Morgan had so recently disappeared out of.

I didn't even know that a memoir had to be about *me*.

If you're writing about your stepdaughter's severely disabled child, the essay is still about you — how you feel about that child, perhaps how you have tried and failed to accept him. If your father shouts at you, it's not about him. It's about why you put up with him, how this affects your life, what choices you make because of it.

(If the story is not about you, by the way, that's fine — it just means it's a different essay than the one we're talking about here. It might be humor, or a first-person piece about another person, or any of a number of first-person forms that are not the personal essay.)

Your writing is not only about you, but about you not exactly at your best. Personal writing works best when it has a rueful aspect — illusions shed, wrong turns taken. You got something wrong, did something wrong, thought something wrong. Thus your bad moments are gold. (If your life has been one of ping-ponging from triumph to triumph, keep it to yourself, thanks). It's much easier to write about trouble, because you are vulnerable and we like you when you're in trouble. As J.P. Donleavy said, "Writing is turning your worst moments into money."

My friend Steve Rubenstein, a reporter and columnist, was riding across the Golden Gate Bridge once when the handlebars snapped off his bike. "I had the first line written," he told me, "before my head hit the pavement."

George Orwell said that many writers never mention the humiliations that make up seventy-five percent of life. Write about what you really think and feel, and how that's different from what you're supposed to think and feel, like the day your friend left a telephone message saying she had cancer, and you waited until the next day to call her back. Cop to things: you don't want your ailing mother to live with you; you backed your SUV into a Miata when it was raining and didn't leave a note. Write about the "I Hate Sarah Club" that you and Shirley Matson formed when you were eight.

Philip Lopate said in his wonderful introduction to *The Art of the Personal Essay:*

> The real possibility of the personal essay, which is to catch oneself in the act of being human ... means a willingness to surrender for a time our pose of unshakable rectitude, and to admit that we are, despite our best intentions, subject to all manner of doubt and weakness and foolish wanting.

That doubt and weakness and foolish wanting? That's your material. My dad's mother died when he was five, so that as a child he went from house to house, and stayed sometimes in orphanages. He said to me once, "I ever tell you about sneaking down to the cellar at about sixteen, to study not a corset ad, but a bloodied fighter held in the arms of a woman in his dressing room? You can believe I never told no headshrinker that. That gave the whole show away, and I've always known it."

Your aim is to give the whole show away. Rip the curtains from the windows. Describe what you long for, because your mother died when you were five, and no one held you in her arms like the woman in that picture.

TRY THIS:
Did you ever do something that you knew was wrong? Been wrong about someone? Been surprised by your own behavior? Write about it.

TRY THIS:
Write about the contents of your closet. Who did you buy that rabbit shearling fur coat for? And those tall, spiked black boots, the ones that were going to change your life? How many of the clothes fit you, or fit who you are now? Be specific.

WHAT IF MOM READS IT?

You can say anything you like about yourself, blab to the world that you drank morphine from a straw or did the Macarena on your father's grave. But what about the other people caught in your flashbulb? Will your sister be enchanted that you told the world she threw tampons over the neighbor's fence? Surely you won't be mentioning your mother's abortions? It used to be that writers presented their experiences in the "thinly disguised autobiographical novel." Relatives depicted in them, however transparently, could say airily, "Oh, me take a bath in champagne bought with the baby's milk money? What an imagination that girl has!"

Now we call it a memoir (or essay). And say it happened. To me. Uh, to us. There's a lot of family underwear hanging out on the line.

Every writer has to decide how much underwear she wants up there, and whose. Sometimes, truth will win out, sometimes the demands of privacy.

One thing is for sure: in the first draft, put it all in. If you're writing each word with your mother looking over your shoulder, lips pursed, her sharp little fingers digging into your ungrateful shoulder blades, you will censor words you haven't even written yet. Later you can read it through to see what you've said about other people, and how it will make them feel to read it, and which you want: a published book or a mother who speaks to you.

I am reading a manuscript now in which the author has declined to state not only any identifying details but even what *country* she grew up in. That approach unfortunately might guarantee her no fallout from outraged relatives, as the resulting memoir is at present too murky to be published. That's what happens when you withhold identifying details rather than change or disguise them.

On the other hand, if an anecdote will hurt somebody, and it's not crucial to your story, I'd say take it out. Why say your brother spent time in prison if the story is about the six years you spent in Nepal? Your brother, like all of us, works hard at trying to have some say over the self he presents to the world, and he wants to keep it that way. Then a writer pops up in his family, armed with a notebook and a habit of leaving the room to scribble down what he said.

In the essay collection, *The Writer on Her Work,* novelist Gail Godwin relates a moment when she and her sister and mother are sitting around talking about a novel she had written:

> Franchelle was saying, "She'd better never put me in a novel again. I don't like being frozen in print for the rest of my life, forever wearing those silly panties and short skirts; and I'm not big like that, she's made me into some sort of Amazon-freak."
>
> "Darling," our mother said, "the sister in *The Odd Woman* wasn't you. Gail just took parts of you, the parts she needed. Writers work that way."
>
> "Well, I wouldn't know. I'm a lawyer and they don't work that way, Besides, it hurts."
>
> Tears filled her eyes and she ran from the room.
>
> "It's unfair," I said. "She's being unfair by not trying to understand."
>
> "It's difficult when you haven't written," agreed my mother. "Now I understand why you had to make Kitty a more passive mother than I am, also a little stupid, that was necessary to your overall plan."

That's something you can hope for in fiction: people often don't recognize themselves. People who behave badly are particularly unlikely to have a lot of self-knowledge. In memoir, though, Mom is called Mom, not Kitty. Dad is called Dad. You can't say, "My father, let's call him Ned." Call him what you like, he's gonna recognize himself.

Author Sue Shapiro said she tells students that the first piece you write that your family hates means you've found your voice, then cautioned, "Also if your identity revolves around being thought of as a nice person you might want to do cookbooks instead."

My own mother was great when *Hold Me Close* came out. She knew perfectly well she was in it. She worked in a bookstore, and offered to sign my book when people came in. But she didn't read it. She had by then logged more than a few hours as the mother of a writer. She didn't want to get mad at me.

Other relatives might take the long view, see what you've set down about them as, well, writing. My twin sister Adrian read *Hold Me Close*, which had a subplot about our father, and wrote this to our mother:

> While I was reading Adair's book, the one thing that struck me was how different events were in my mind than in Adair's. It was weird reading in a book about myself from a point of view not my own. I started out by saying to myself, 'Hey, that didn't happen that way,' but after awhile I realized it wasn't my book. Adair made herself the hero in places about Dad in ways I didn't think were accurate. But it's her book — I guess she can make herself the hero. When I write a book, I can make myself the hero too.

I imagine that if Iris Murdoch had read *Elegy for Iris*, her husband John Bayley's memoir about her sufferings from Alzheimer's disease, she would have understood. She was a writer, and knew that the agonizing incongruity of a brilliant intellectual novelist who now did not know her own name would make a terrifying and poignant book.

But we all can't hope for the maturely detached reader, the flattered one (yes, there are plenty of those), or the absent one.

Kirk Read, author of *How I Learned to Snap*, a memoir about growing up gay in a southern town, told me some members of his family were so offended when it came out that they wouldn't return his phone calls. Given the chance now, he says he would change some things.

The truth about my own memoir, *Hold Me Close*, about my daughter's fitful navigation of adolescence, is that if I could go back, I would not write it. Yes, Morgan gave me permission, and yes, she is still okay with it, but it wasn't my story to tell, not when it was all about Morgan during the worst period of her life. Now she is a lawyer, and her past is, literally (if someone is reading that book at this moment, which despite all I'm saying I hope someone is) an open book. As Joan Didion famously said, "The writer is always selling somebody out."

You Can Be As Delicate About This As Possible

1. Let the Reader Know You are an Unreliable Narrator
Suggest in an author's note that you are relying on memory, or that some relatives would disagree with your account of things. This will give Dad a way to tell all and sundry that you made the whole thing up, even if you didn't.

2. Disguise Them
You can change the names of friends, and sometime omit names of relatives ("My aunt told me"). Your husband's brother can appear as a man called Don, "an engineer in his 40s." Or you can assign a story you heard from one person to someone else. Give people details that don't affect the story, but are odd enough to throw readers off the scent. Change where they live, give them unusual habits — going home to play the trumpet at lunchtime. If the gender doesn't matter, you can even change the sex (the therapist you thought was a loon could be changed to a man). Novelist Anne Lamott always says to give a male character a very small penis and he'll never claim it's him. In my memoir only the names of my immediate family and of my siblings are real — the rest are changed. (Morgan's boyfriend had a perfect name — it killed me to have to change it).

3. Ask Permission
Novelist Annie Dillard says she lets her relatives read her books and take out anything they don't like. (Dillard's last novel was a description of the landscape.) Dave Eggers sent the manuscript of *A Heartbreaking Work of*

Staggering Genius to people mentioned in it and let them make revisions. "You have to choose who you're ok with pissing off," he said. He even put phone numbers in the first edition, though he took them out in later editions.

Caveat: Sometimes asking the permission of someone who loves you is emotional blackmail. In an essay called "Other People's Secrets," memoirist Patricia Hampl recalls how a poem outing her mother as an epileptic rid her mother of a guilty secret. Then Hampl learned that her mother always hated that poem, and allowed it to be published anyway only because she wanted to help her daughter succeed as a writer.

"I am trying now to remember if I cared about her feelings at all," Hampl said in an essay written years later. She had argued with her mother into letting her use the poem by saying, "I will cut it if you really want me to," then, beat, "But it's the best poem in the book."

You ask permission, but can they say no? "Here, I wrote this whole book, is it okay to publish or should I throw it away?" (I was certainly uncomfortably aware of that when showing the manuscript of *Hold Me Close* to Morgan.)

4. Bribe Them
You're getting paid—spread the loot around.
In his memoir *Family Man*, Calvin Trillin said that when his daughters were five and eight, he asked them to sign a standard nondisclosure agreement. "Nothing fancy. When they didn't understand why they were doing it, I said, 'Trust your daddy.'" David Sedaris wrote in *Naked* about his mother's death from cancer and his sister's first period. He told *The New York Times*, "The publisher made everyone sign a waiver saying they wouldn't sue me. At Christmastime, I took a big stack of gifts and said, 'Everybody, these are your presents and this is the release form — just sign here.'"

I discovered the power of bribery early, when I first got the newspaper column. When my son Patrick was nine, I drove him on a date with a classmate — both of them stiff as dolls in the rearview mirror. She wore a Walkman and did not trouble herself to remove the earphones during the ride. I wrote about the date and gave it to Patrick to read. "Is it okay to put this in the paper?" I asked him.

He scanned it at the kitchen table, his pajama-ed leg swinging. "No way," he said when he was done.

"Ok," I said. But I was only a few months into the job, and reluctant to throw away a column I knew worked. I let a couple of days go by, then found Patrick tending his turtle in the wading pool out back. "How about if I gave you 20 bucks?" I said.

"Done!" said Patrick. He changed the girl's name, took out the word "hussy," and let me print it. And that was the deal from then on: if a column was all about one of the kids (no payment for the occasional mention) they got a twenty. Morgan got ten percent of my advance for the memoir I wrote about her. (Her brother Patrick said he should get some money, too: "If I hadn't been so good, your book would have been a pile of psychotic scribblings.")

5. Use a Pen Name?
Publishers hate pen names. They want you to promote the book, go on tour. If nothing else will keep the world from knowing that your mom had gentlemen callers while Dad was preaching his Sunday sermon, and not migraines as she said, as a last resort you can legally change your own name. Lisa Michaels, whose dad was a Weatherman whom she had reason to believe the FBI were still interested in, changed all the names in *Split*, her book about being a child of radical 60s parents. Including her own! She legally changed her name to Michaels — and then her husband took her pen name. They're the Michaels family.

6. The Law
Not walloping people in print is a matter of conscience and decency, but it does have its legal aspects. Augusten Burroughs's family sued him for certain details in *Running with Scissors*, including saying that his father burned his forehead with a cigarette when Burroughs was six.

For a portrait to be "actional," as they call it — meaning it is libel — it must be so accurate that a reader would have no problem linking the incompetent doctor in the story with the one who actually treated the narrator for breast cancer. My publisher asked my ex-husband, husband and both kids to sign releases. (Not my mother, thank god — she'd say, "I don't think so, Adair," and I'd end up with two covers and nothing between them).

7. The Real Solution

The main protection for your relatives, though, is one that has nothing to do with drawing mustaches on them or changing names. It's your own honesty in the writing. You write about other people, yes, but you're the one screwing up, the one taking responsibility for what happened. If you are attacking other people, justifiably or not, then the writing fails—because you're too angry, or too much a victim, or too unreflective.

THE HOT HEART AND THE COLD EYE

> Whatever may be our natural talents, the art of writing is not acquired all at once.
>
> — Jean Jacques Rousseau

So we've said that the story you tell should be about a change, and that it should be a change in you, not in Aunt Matilda, or in your bank account, or the state of your health. We've discussed about the never-quite-resolvable issue of having to invade other people's privacy in order to tell your own truths.

Now we talk about how overall structure of what you write is a lot more important than any of that — more important than the beauty of your individual sentences, or the originality of your insights, on how "literary" you sound on the page.

I certainly started out thinking just that — that writing was literary. I was like a lot of beginners who are, as novelist Marilynne Robinson said, "At first less in love with structure or pattern and more in love with the words in a foolish but sweet way."

I was an editor at a couple of magazines that often published the kind of writers I would have called "bad" (no tone, interesting images or language) on health and weekend retreats in May and guides to Hawaii in September. The blindness of the editors astonished me. Why did they not publish the literary essays they received from snotty English majors like me instead of dry little features on pet adoptions? Could they not tell the difference?

They could, as it happened, but they preferred well-structured pieces to pain-fully wrought masterpieces. The writers they hired did not spend two days trying to find the perfect way to describe the movement of palm trees in the breeze. They knew how to put a piece together, where to start, when to end. They knew to quote people, and how to make the reader want to visit the little inn in Mendocino or be interested in the story of a jazz player they had never heard of. They had a set of skills that could be learned: they had *craft*. Tip: Do not have contempt for commercial success, yours or anybody else's. Study them for what they often are: a triumph of a well-told story, whether you think the story or characters or sentences are crap.

No one sits down to write a screenplay without familiarizing himself with how to do it, but when you write about yourself, you figure you'll just write what happened. I taught a semester at a private college, and the girls who signed up for my advanced creative nonfiction class were incensed that I was "telling us to write the way she wants us to write," as one of them put it to the dean. They didn't want to learn about setup and epiphany and so on, but to pour their raw experience onto the page. I didn't blame them, of course, but it was my job to equip them with the skills they would need.

Writing a column twice a week for 12 years taught me the value of craft. People saw the two columns a week, and asked what I did the rest of the time. (When I told my mother I was going on vacation, she said, "From *what?*")

But I worked all the time. Like an essay, a column wasn't a blog, a blurt, a blast. It had to have several elements: a story to tell, a way to tell it, a reason for telling it now. And a reason to tell it — a way to transform the story from being about me to being about the reader.

All that took time. I'd want to talk about why I still listened to bad rock music and ate hot dogs, but hadn't found a reason to do so, a point to make. I had a story about getting Norplant installed in my arm, but didn't know yet what I was doing with that story. Was it about my both wanting and not wanting another baby? I usually had nine or ten columns marinating all over the apartment, like pans full of beans, waiting for one missing element or other.

I was learning that writing is a craft, a set of skills, not something you do blissfully, sitting in a garden with birds tweeting overhead. You start with inspiration, sure, but then you *work*. Many memoir authors write a first draft in under a month, and then spend the next two years revising.

As a writer, you need your hot heart, the one that spilled a book out in mere weeks, raining the smoky truth down any old way on the page. That's what you do when you stay up until 3 a.m., writing until your wrists hurt. Putting down thoughts as they come in no particular order without censoring or holding back is necessary if your unconscious is to inform your writing.

And then you need a cold eye. The cold eye knows that the piece must begin somewhere and end somewhere, and satisfy the reader with a sense of progress in between. It knows the raw writing you do will be jumbled, contradictory, and random at first, and that you want to impose a pattern of cause and effect on it. You want to lift from the raw material of life a tale that will shape experience, transform event, deliver wisdom. And the way to do that is structure. I just right-clicked on that word in my Microsoft Word file and called up this definition: "a system or organization made up of interrelated parts functioning as a whole."

In writing, you can think of it as the skeleton that holds up the work. Imagine your body without its skeleton. You would still have all your lovely parts, but in a heap on the floor. The skeleton tells you where the head goes, where to stick the anklebone (connect it to the leg bone).

Structure is not sexy — there will be no woman with tear-stained cheeks grabbing your sleeve at a bookstore reading to say how much she was moved by your use of setup or that tieback ending. You won't get letters from readers grateful for all the digressions you took out. But structure will get you into that bookstore. Essays and memoirs may read like inspired outpourings, but if they've been published, chances are they were painstakingly rewritten in many drafts until, as the above definition says, the many parts function together as a whole.

Doctorow and others have compared creative writing to driving a car at night on a country road. You don't worry about anything but what is exposed in the glare of your headlights — the listing mailbox, the blur of a surprised deer, the gun (or divorce papers, or empty pack of Little Debbies) in the purse on the seat beside you.

Writing this way has benefits: it keeps you from being overwhelmed by your task, and it forces you to slow down. But you can't make a whole trip that way. You can get where you're going only if you know the road. Otherwise you might drive until the headlights give out, and end up sitting there in the dark car, feeling like an idiot for having come so far and then not bothering to stop at the 7-1l to get a map.

In writing, structure is the road map. (Ok, I switched metaphors, from skeletons to road maps. Shoot me.) You achieve it with techniques, from deciding on a focus, to using setup, to starting with the action and putting in the back story later, to bringing things to a neat close with a tieback ending. Learning them can be discouraging at first. You loved to write and now find out it's so hard! It's like correcting your tennis serve: for a while neither your old serve nor your new one will seem to work.

Then the new, better serve becomes part of you. You produce pieces that are both true and aesthetically satisfying, and this brings you checks and bylines and other forms of appreciation.

CHAPTER THREE

THE PERSONAL ESSAY

Telling a Story

Outlining the Essay

The Epiphany

> In the end, it is my belief that words are the only things that can construct a world that makes sense.
>
> — Kate Atkinson, author of *Behind the Scenes at the Museum*

Anyone can write a personal essay, or at the very least write sketches of considerable charm and promise. But how do you bring that essay home, nail it? As a lifelong reader you can go a long way on instinct and talent, but you can go a lot further on skill. In this chapter and the next we'll look at some techniques for putting an essay together.

Let's agree we're talking about a piece of about 1,200 to 1,600 words. It's the kind of essay that newspapers and websites and magazines are mostly interested in. I leafed through some magazines recently to find some examples: a man writing about his 16-year-old son dying from inhaling computer duster underwater in *The New York Times*, another woman talking in that paper's Sunday magazine about her daughter's anorexia: "I stood in the kitchen looking at the mess and thought of how our lives had shrunk to the confines of these four walls."

A woman in *Alternative Medicine* recalled how she began taking naps: "The first time I did it, I wondered what was wrong with me." Pauline Chen wrote a piece for the "Lives" section of *The New York Times* about a night harvesting organs from cadavers that was routine until she found herself working on a woman who looked much like herself.

What are a personal essays about? The irritations, jubilations, aches and pains, and humorous flashes we experience as we go through life. They're about the barking of the dog next door, being alone, bad nerves, sloth, learning to live with the pettiness of your own craven soul.

They're written in first person, in a conversational style, and provide a surprising point of view on some element of ordinary life. Ideally a short essay is small in scope, though large in the implications of the truth it tells. "Great subjects," said V.S. Naipaul, "are illuminated best by small dramas." You can show the strains in the marriage in the fight over how to stack the dishwasher. The hospice patient's insistence of really *hot* hot chocolate may show the reader his real feeling: fear of dying.

You know those nesting boxes they make for kids, where you start with a large box and take out smaller and smaller ones? With an essay it's the opposite: you start with the smallest box. Begin with the day you asked your father to teach you to paint, and he set you up with a still life of a lemon and a crème de menthe bottle and when you drew it, heard him say to your mother, "See?" Work toward the larger: the day you realized you were an artist. Talk about the day the movers came to pack up your belongings to move to your tiny new apartment, and we will get the story of your divorce without your having to jam in all the details. The avocado tree that served you as a Christmas tree can be the way to show your new life in California.

The more specific your topic is, the easier it will be to tell what goes in and what doesn't, and the fewer drafts you'll have to struggle with. The broader it is, on the other hand — "the two years I spent taking care of my grandfather" or "my interesting experiences in Saudi Arabia" — the more you're forced to use abstractions and make statements we have to take on faith, and the duller the read will be.

We need a central focus, which means that in many pieces you have to take perfectly good ideas out and save them for another day, lest they distract. Try to focus on one thing, one story, one thing you are trying to say. It's like clearing a choked up waterway. You hack and tug until the water trickles through.

My student Scottie Ross's piece takes place in a ten-minute period when she sits in a waiting room. It begins with Scottie asking herself why she thinks of her psychiatrist as "this white woman" when the doctor is late:

> Where the hell is this white woman? Whoa, who said that? Good
> grief, I did. Ok, so she's 20 minutes late. But still, that's no cause
> for me to be mind screaming 'White woman.' I've never called her
> that, never thought of her that way. Let's think about this.

The rest of the essay catalogues Scottie's experiences as a black woman growing up in America, including answering an ad for a babysitter, only to be
handed a rag and told, "You can start in the dining room."

As it is in Scottie's piece, often a question is at the heart of a personal essay. In
his famous essay, "Death of a Pig," E.B. White asks himself why he felt so bad
about killing a pig when he raised it for slaughter. In "Shooting an Elephant"
George Orwell puzzles out why, as a British officer at an Indian outpost, he
had to kill an elephant even after it was finished with its rampage through the
village and was harmless. The question that drives your essay can be small:
Why can I not stand to watch my husband lolling in the tub for thirty minutes? Why did it take hundreds of wrong exits off the freeway for me to get
contacts? Why, when I have been content to follow my husband from job to
job and city to city for ten years, am I so unhappy about the move this time?
My student Catherine Shepard-Haier published a piece in *The Denver Post* in
which her question was: Am I going to take the toiletries? And if I am, *why*
am I?

Also, when you're asking why, ask *why today*? If you found yourself driving
to the social security office to add your husband's last name to your own, tell
us why. You were married for five years, and swore you would never take his
name. What's different about today? What's changed?

Here are some examples of changes that would make good essays. First, this
one from a student paper about a dinner date that ended less innocently than
it began:

> We walked out of the restaurant and while waiting for the valet to
> bring my car around, Steve asked me if we could have dinner again.
> Immediately, I knew it was more than dinner he wanted, and I was
> shocked as the word "Yes" came out of my lips. At that moment,
> I changed from a committed, solid wife to someone who was will-
> ing to flirt with, well, flirting. I had crossed my own line. I found it

exhilarating. My self-image was shattered and a sexy, dangerous woman emerged.

My student Kristin Lund changed the moment she found out she and her husband were expecting twins:

> I discovered I was not in control of the universe. I know it sounds crazy. But I was a control freak. I thought I could see everything on the horizon before it got near me. Twins! I never saw that coming.

Notice that she is not talking about a change in her circumstances — having twins is a change in anybody's circumstances (as anybody who's tried to wedge a double stroller down the aisle in Target knows). It's a change in *her*.

In another example, a friend of mine told me her colleagues at *Sunset* magazine threw her a ten-year anniversary party. As they paraded around the room with every story she'd done for the magazine taped together in a banner — thousands of words about redwood decks, blue jays, table arrangements — my friend thought, *Enough*! And quit the next day. That's a change.

A problem drives every personal essay. What makes them interesting is that very often the narrator is unaware of the problem. Almost every essay about getting a *thing*, from a promotion to a big screen TV to a big splashy surprise birthday party, is really about something deeper. The essay is never about the in-laws, or the new house, or getting to go to Italy. This surface concern may mask the true problem, one the writer is at the time unaware of.

The problem that the writer begins with may be a seemingly trivial one: I need a car. I want to lose ten pounds. I got stuck with a cat. I can't find the swimming hole my friend drew me a map of. It may just be what was going on the day you had the epiphany that changed your life: a piece about you trying to evade an irritating boyfriend at a weekend retreat can end with you kissing another girl in a hot tub — and liking it a lot more than you ever liked kissing with a man.

A good way to define the problem to yourself as you write is to say, "What did I want?"

EXAMPLES:

I wanted my son to get the guitar I wanted, not the one he wanted.

I wanted to propose marriage to a canoe instructor I met fifteen minutes
    before.

I wanted to get through a routine operation harvesting human organs from a
    cadaver without feeling much of anything, but the cadaver looked like me.

I wanted to understand being dumped by a man I was dating out of pity.

I wanted a car.

You'll see that all these will be fleshed out in the actual writing, as my student
Robert Doane did when he wrote:

> I wanted a car. I wanted a car that belonged in the after-school
> traffic jam, that row of chopped-down Chevy coupes and shiny
> waxed hot rod Model Ts that clogged Mission Street from Jefferson
> High all the way to the light at the top of the hill. I wanted the
> thrill of blasting out "Blueberry Hill" and "Love Me Tender" on the
> Motorola. I wanted to have a cheerleader sticking so tight to my
> sweaty thigh that she left room for two or three more to her right.

In a short essay, we should get to the problem by about the end of the second
paragraph, which means not as much leisurely scene-setting or back story as
you might be inclined to include. If your piece is about how you overcame
your shyness by studying acting, your need to overcome your shyness should
come up by the second paragraph.

TELLING A STORY

For all its charm and sometimes apparent aimlessness, an essay has a skeleton,
an underlying structure that makes it work. Often it's the age-old structure of
a story. By "story" I don't mean "something that happened," but a story in the
formal sense of the term: somebody (in this case, you) wants what they can't
have and tries to get it. The end resolves the problem. Almost every movie,
every novel, every short story, has this structure, and no wonder. A story is a
world where every character, every action, has meaning and purpose. A story
is why we read: it's life arranged to fill the basic human need that life have
purpose, that events lead somewhere, add up to something. A story takes random events and gives them meaning. It takes *life* and gives it meaning.

An essay that tells a story (called a narrative essay) has these elements:
Character
Problem
Struggle
Epiphany
Resolution

The *character* is you—which is why we want to know and like you.

You have a *problem*: you are, say, stranded at home because you don't have a car.

You *struggle* to solve your problem. This can be several actions: You take a part-time seamstress job to get the money for a car. You take driving lessons.

Epiphany: You realize something that changes you. For example, you realize you wanted a car so you can leave your husband.

Resolution: You do something that shows you really did change. You get the car anyway.

In between these major story elements, we get image and detail, tone, fantasy, memory, style and language and the other elements that draw us into any pleasurable reading experience.

Character

You are the "I" voice of the book. Cells snapped into something singular when you came along — and that's what you want to get on the page. It's not enough to tell us what happened — let us know *who it happened to*. This is where tone comes in, and images, both of which I deal with in future chapters.

In the rest of this book, by the way, you will find that I sometimes say "you" and sometimes "the narrator." Once you hit the page, you are the narrator, the one telling the story, and the one to whom, in autobiographical writing, it is happening.

Problem

In an essay that appeared in the *Chronicle*, my student Marilyn Penland's problem appears in the first paragraph: "I have hundreds of images of her from our nine years of life together, but the sound of my mother's voice eludes me." The middle of the story gives us the only four sentences she can remember her mother speaking. At the end, she realizes that she sounds just like her own mother, and her daughter sounds like her. "I hear my daughter's voice and know my mother is speaking to me from across the years ... I no longer wish I had more words from my mother."

Struggle

If the beginning (also called a lede, or lead) of your essay describes the problem, then the middle shows you trying to solve it: you try something, you react, and a new obstacle pops up. These two — action, reaction and new obstacle may be repeated several times, depending on the length of the essay and the complexity of the struggle. (If this process is long and complex, you have a memoir.)

Some obstacles will be external: you want a car, but don't have the money, your husband doesn't want you to have a car, or you can't drive. If you stay with purely external obstacles, though, it won't be as interesting (we can read a how-to article on how to buy a car). The interesting obstacles will be internal: you are afraid of driving because your parents died in an automobile accident. You hesitate because you sense that once you get the car, it will help you steer a course out of your marriage.

Here's an example of an action and reaction in "Without Me, I'm Nothing," an essay that San Francisco writer Bonnie Wach wrote about her post-partum depression. One of her many actions to make herself feel better is to join a baby support group. This is her reaction, which shows us that she will have to try something else:

> Even in places where I should have felt some kind of kinship — new mom's classes, support groups — I was an outsider. Happy new mothers made my flesh crawl. Trust me when I tell you that nothing can drive a depressed mom to the bottom of a shame spiral faster than a circle of blessed-out breast feeders happily comparing burping techniques, smug and satisfied in the certainty that they are exactly where they're supposed to be, doing exactly what they're supposed to be doing. Saying that your infant feels like one of those animal leg traps, and that you're contemplating chewing off your own foot to get away from it, isn't exactly the stuff of baby chitchat.

Bonnie's paragraph also shows how you get yourself across in an essay — become someone with such an interesting voice that we want to follow you around as you wrestle with your problem. In *The Art of the Personal Essay*, Phillip Lopate refers to this as "the need to assert a quite specific temperament."

OUTLINING THE ESSAY

Before we go on to epiphany and resolution, let's look at outlining the essay. It's a handy way to get a quick sense of where the piece is going, what to put in and what to leave out. (Later we'll see that drawing an arc does the same for the memoir writer.) You can try to outline it like this:

I wanted _____
I wanted it because (back story) _____(this is where character comes in)
To get it, I _____ (action)
However, something got in my way: (there may be several actions/reactions sequences depending on length) _____
I had to try something different, so I _____
All the time I was thinking that _____
The turning point came when_____
When that happened, I realized _____
Resolution: After that I _____

My student Rita Hargrave, a psychiatrist by day who now carries dance shoes in the trunk of her car, used this exercise to plan an essay on how she got into salsa dancing:

I wanted to go salsa dancing
I wanted it because I was bored and alone and it seemed as good an idea as any.
To get it I headed for a salsa club recommended by a hotel maid.
But some things got in the way: The cab driver did not want to drive to a Latino neighborhood, and once I got there the bartender at the club was hostile, and there were no empty chairs or tables.
So I asked one of the women who was seated with friends if I could use the empty chair.
But I couldn't dance.
So I told myself not to worry about it.

The turning point came when An elderly man embraced me, danced with me, and I passionately connected with him. When the older man clasped my hand and started dancing with me, I realized that what I really wanted was an emotional and physical connection with a man and to be seen as desirable and seductive, and that I could do that as a salsa dancer.

Resolution: I found the passion and caring that I was searching for in my life. I have been a salsa dancer ever since.

An outline will sketch the story in the order it happened, but an essay doesn't necessarily have to be written in chronological order (in fact it's often better to start at a point near the end). A *story* is a series of events recorded in the order they happened, but a *plot* is that same story rearranged for maximum effectiveness.

THE END/EPIPHANY

If you're having trouble with one of your stories, it could be missing an ending. If your story is about buying a house in remote Mono Lake, for example, and you are still torn over whether moving there is a good idea, you can't yet write an essay with a conclusion. You want to avoid such unresolved, ongoing stories — your conflict with your sister, your penchant for picking the wrong men, your patients with their same old stories.

TRY THIS:
Summarizing your story in 200 words or less will help you see if you have an ending or not.

EXAMPLE:
My father was going to die. I knew that if I didn't confront him with all these angry feelings I had that I would be stuck with them after he died. I confronted him at his house in Minneapolis, MN, told him how angry I was at him, and threw a Polaroid camera on the floor. He was amazed. Not mad — amazed that I felt that way. He had no idea. I felt much freer after that. AND THEN...he didn't die. So we had around ten years after that in which we had a nice relationship with most of the baggage just dropped overboard...

The end of the essay must in some way resolve the problem brought up in the beginning. Since the problem will be internal — the narrator in conflict with herself or himself at least as much as with outside forces — the solution will be internal too. The solution won't be getting the car. It will be deciding to get the car.

You can think of the essay in its simplest terms as problem-solution.

Problem: My husband makes unrealistic marital demands (clean house, sex four times a week, wife stay in shape) one month before the wedding.
Solution: I realize that his demands are the result of cold feet and marry him anyway.

Problem: I hate the large, ugly dining room furniture my mother insists on hauling from small apartment to small apartment.
Solution: One day while dusting the French sideboard I see how it forms a link to our family's story.

In an essay, the solution is the moment of change that's called an *epiphany*. This was James Joyce's word for the moment where things change irrevocably in a flood of new understanding. Magazines, more prosaically, call it the payoff, or the take-home point. The epiphany is what turns a mere story — or what might have remained an anecdote — into an essay.

You may have heard teachers stress that the point of an essay is to show, but showing is not enough. The reader knows you actually lived through the experience you're describing — he expects you to understand what happened and have reflected on what it meant.

Let's look at an epiphany April Martin wrote in *The New York Times* in a piece about taking up ice skating in her forties:

> Skating has helped me to reclaim the body with which I spent too many years at war. I stop briefly to reflect on the apparent contradictions: I have deepened and matured as a woman in a sport geared to little girls. And I am now nourished and replenished by a sport whose standards of femininity were once a form of bondage. Though I bring to the ice the painful bunions and chronically

stiff muscles of middle age, I also bring one of its benefits: the increased capacity for living comfortably with contradictions.

I've read that a hundred times, and am still moved every time I read it. That last phrase is even alliterative: "the increased *c*apacity for living *c*omfortably with *c*ontradictions."

Admittedly, some epiphanies give the whole business a bad name, like the one a guy wrote in a *New York Times* piece about how he had his girlfriend's smelly dog foisted on him, and then how he got to like the dog. He concluded: "Because their emotions are so pure, dogs can often touch the deepest part of us. And in so doing, they might in their own way prepare us to understand ourselves."

That's the kind of epiphany that makes a reader go, "Huh?" You can substitute anything as the subject of that sentence and it will make about as much sense: "Because their emotions are so pure, angry geese can often touch the deepest part of us. And in so doing, they might in their own way prepare us to understand ourselves."

(It's a good idea in fact to avoid the "we" sort of epiphany altogether, as it tends to make the reader growl, "Speak for yourself, buddy.")

A good epiphany is surprising, not cloying or trite. It doesn't condescend, or offer a predigested insight. My friend Wendy Lichtman had an awful thing happen to her: a doctor told her that she was dying of liver cancer. Days later, she learned that she wasn't: the "cancer" the X-ray was seeing were harmless birthmarks on her liver. At the end of the essay she wrote about that scare, she said:

> I know people might expect me to say that the experience taught me to better appreciate my life, to savor every moment. But it doesn't seem to have worked out that way. What I appreciate, in fact, is that I don't have to feel as if each moment is a treasure. Now when I watch my children do their homework, it's not a particularly touching experience; it feels, instead, like the normal business of a school night. That normality is what I'm most grateful for.

The epiphany transforms your story from a window into your life into a mirror where the reader sees himself. You can test this out: If you write a piece about your mother, and your reader starts talking about *her* mom, the piece works. I often wrote columns about my wreck of a dad living in a truck in the Mohave Desert. If someone came up to me at a party and started to talk to me about my father, I'd be embarrassed. Was I writing a soap opera? But if someone read the column and then told me about how he flew across the country to see his 87-year-old father, how the two of them sat up late, drinking scotch, and that he blurted out to his dad, "I think I came here to tell you I love you," and then burst into tears — then I'd know the column worked.

Let's return to April Martin's piece about ice skating. You say, Fine. I'm so glad this Martin person found meaning in her new hobby. But I don't live in New York, am not middle-aged, was not once a feminist, and don't skate. What does Martin's experience have to do with me?

Well, nothing maybe. But you might recognize a truth in what she says — a truth for yourself, as well as for her. Maybe you too have done something out of character that's surprisingly satisfying, like a student of mine who was violently anti-gun until she discovered the local shooting range.

If there's any justification for telling personal stories, it's that every person, every selfish little clod of ailments and grievances, including you, including me, contains within himself the entire human condition (as Montaigne pointed out). If you can tell me you made sense of something in your life, it can give me a moment — a fleeting flash — where I get the distance necessary to understand my own struggles. That connection between Martin's experience and your own? It's what you get to keep when you put the article down. It's the door prize, the booty bag.

By the way, not all pieces need epiphanies. Humor pieces don't. I discovered this when I sent a piece on my son Patrick's birth to *Parenting* magazine. They wanted me to put in the epiphany (you will find magazines are big on this: they want the reader to have that "take-home point"). I tried to put it in — magazines pay well — but it kept sounding stupid. You can't write a piece in which you crack jokes ("I was going to give the doctor one more chance to give me drugs, and then I was going to try to get somebody with real connections, like a screenwriter"), and then suddenly stop and say in a completely different tone, "Until you have a second child, you don't know how you can love another the way you do your first."

Opinion pieces don't have epiphanies either: opinion pieces are not about change. You start out in favor of the return of the martini and end up in favor of it. They're rants, or arguments.

WRITING THE EPIPHANY

There are two kinds of epiphany. An *implicit* epiphany shows us the change wordlessly. This kind is what you see in fiction, and especially in movies, which can only show, not tell. In the scene at the end of "The Paper Chase," Timothy Bottoms, after sweating through a year of Harvard law school, even taking a motel room to cram for finals, doesn't even open his grades when they come, but throws the envelope into the waves: we get it that he no longer cares about his law-school grades.

An *explicit* epiphany, on the other hand, spells out the realization, as in this piece by a woman who lost her parents when as an infant she was thrown from the car that killed them both:

> We were together for only a few months, I want to tell them, but I am grateful for what memories I can collect, even if they are secondhand. Looking at you now from across the years may not tell me what kind of family we might have been, but it reminds me to treasure the life I've made, even if I was not the fairy tale princess I once imagined myself to be.

Make it Universal

Draw back from a piece now and then and ask yourself: What am I saying about human nature, about how we all are? What transforms this story from being about me getting arrested at 16 to being about all of us? The epiphany must have meaning for other people, which means it must be some degree universal. The topics that are not universal (about you, yes, but not about us) include fame, riches, and, unfortunately, writing. When I gave my boss at the paper a piece on being a columnist, she said, "Ok, but you can do that only once in your career." Being a columnist is not universal.

Neither are psychological explanations:
"I realized my father didn't love me."
That's about your father.
"I realized I had been deluding myself into thinking my father loved me, because I needed him to."
That's an insight that could have meaning for the rest of us, who may have done that too.

It doesn't take much to tilt a piece in the direction of the universal. In a column about growing up poor, I said, "But then the poor are always putting on airs. We Daly kids with our Bargain Box rags looked down on the Wilson kids with their indoor plumbing and on our own cousins because they had a television set. If we couldn't rise, then it was necessary for others to fall." The phrase, "but then the poor are always putting on airs" was enough to make this a more universal piece about being poor in America.

Show The Moment Of Change and What Led to It

The reader wants to be there with you, experiencing the change with you. A student of mine wrote a pretty good piece about how time is getting away from her: the microwave clock ticks too fast, her daughter is turning 10, she's turning 35, and her husband has cancer. Then on the last page, she says, "So I've decided to make peace with the passage of time. I'm going to stop letting it beat me up when it's already got my attention."

It's a good epiphany. But what made her go from being someone hyper-aware of the manically ticking microwave to someone feeling peaceful, maybe sitting quietly in a rocker on the porch? The piece needs the transforming moment, the event that changed her.

If, for example, you decide to leave your husband and go into hiding with your child, saying, "I decided I should take off that night," isn't enough for such a crucial turning point. Give us a scene in which you make your decision — when you see the court document awarding the abusive father full custody, or hear your child say that he never gets enough to eat at his dad's.

This is how essay writers and memoir writers take the chaos of life and turn it into art — by letting us be there when a change happens.

My student, Evelyn Strauss, reminded me that sometimes you have no trouble coming up with the dramatic moment of change, but you don't know why it happened when it did. A woman stands in the hospital room of her dying father listening to the hissing of the machine he's hooked up to and suddenly realizes he always loved her. We see the change in her — she tenderly straightens his covers and erases the Groucho Marx mustache she drew on him (kidding). What made her realize it?

What makes things crack at any particular moment is often hard to understand even after it happens. Evelyn said:

> I can identify so many moments of epiphany in my life. The flashes
> of insight and meaning are true and dramatic, but they tend to rest
> on months or years of hacking away at some internal issue. That
> can make it difficult to capture what happens in the moment of
> epiphany. I can identify the exact moment I finished coming out
> of the closet, for example — the moment when I let go of the last
> vestiges of wanting to be straight. Something really did break inside
> of me. I slumped to the floor, I cried, I shook. But I have no idea
> why it happened after that particular trip with the woman I was in
> love with then. We had known each other for eleven years.

I know what she means. Why did I decide to leave my husband Mike Lara after he insisted on bowling one more game at San Rafael Bowl when I wanted to go home? Why not earlier? I was already spending part of every Saturday morning crying.

It helps to keep posing yourself the question and trying to answer it. "Why did I stop wanting to be straight at that exact moment? Was it because …?" Was it because …?"
Your fingers can type things you didn't know were in your head.

The epiphany can be dark, speaking of disappointment, or diminished expectations. The point of the piece does not have to be Pollyannaish. It may show that you can win by losing and lose by winning. The best writing reflects life, in showing that while there may be few permanent solutions, there are moments of clarity, moments when the change we undergo is simply an expansion of our understanding. My friend Joan Frank, author of the novels

The Great Far Away and *Miss Kansas City*, who began writing essays at the age of 40, has this to say:

> By talking about acknowledging isolation, by acknowledging a frag-
> mentary life, an incoherent life, you are making contact with other
> people who might feel equal isolation. A good essay is a communal
> act, though I never think of that when I'm writing: I'm just trying to
> get things right. To get experience right, whatever the experience, is
> to make a communal gesture. Even if getting it right is an expres-
> sion of disappointment or failed expectations.
>
> There are Hallmark cards that talk about apparent happinesses
> and joys. It seems to me to be affirmative to take on the darkness.
> To do so affirms that you can talk about almost anything unpopular,
> unsavory, dark, and if you get it right, and have embodied it, you
> have affirmed at least the difficulty of living, and that affirmation
> is solace to me. Always if you get it right, it's solace to someone —
> and its solace resides in precisions, not in its pleasing sentiments.

As Joan says, you can offer the reader an ambiguous or indeterminate ending that mirrors the complexity of real life, or one that affirms the difficulty of living. A young woman found that several wolves were attacking her cattle. Her story told the story of the struggle she faced as she made the choice of saving the cattle or saving the wolves. She shot the wolves, but learned that whatever her choice had been, she would not have been comfortable with it. One of life's lessons is that sometimes there is no right choice, and that was the point of the essay.

My student Sharon, who is childless, had a similar experience when she got a tubal ligation. She convinced herself she was fine with that decision. Six months later she was moved to tears by the sight of a friend's new baby, and admitted to herself that her heart wanted a baby even if her head did not. She experienced not simple regret, but the more complicated knowledge that you may not regret a decision and yet not be fine with it, either. An epiphany can be something bleak:

> I told my mother I loved her and she said, 'Well, I don't feel loved.'
> All of a sudden, I saw that I couldn't fix that hole. I could send
> something to her but if she didn't want to receive it, there was
> nothing I could do. This allowed me to get some much-needed

emotional distance. We still talk to each other at least once a week but we have a difficult relationship.

TRY THIS:
1. Choose a story about a personal experience that changed you.
2. Show us how you were before the epiphany
3. Show us the transforming moment
4. Write an explicit or implicit epiphany
5. Resolution: show us what you do differently afterward as a result of the epiphany

Work Backward from the Epiphany

Choose topics in the first place by finding the turning points in your life. That gives you your structure, because once you know your epiphany, you know how to write the essay: by starting with you as you were before the epiphany that will change you. Start by showing us you cowering at heights, end with you diving off a rock.

Let's consider a change that happened to John Fogerty, once chief songwriter for Credence Clearwater Revival. He was so bitter about signing away the rights to many of his songs (including "Born on the Bayou," "Who'll Stop the Rain," and "Proud Mary") to Fantasy Records that for years he refused to sing the songs at his appearances. Then one day he visited the Mississippi grave of legendary bluesman Robert Johnson. He stared at the name etched in stone and found himself wondering who owned Johnson's songs now. He thought to himself, *It doesn't matter. Johnson owns those songs.* At that moment, Fogerty realized he, too, was the spiritual owner of his songs. If he wrote an essay, that moment in the graveyard would come near the end. The resolution (what the narrator does differently as a result of the epiphany) would be that he starts singing his own songs again.

If he ends by playing his songs again, he might begin with the first day he refused to sing any of them at a performance. If you know the end, start with the opposite.

Where to Put the Epiphany

The whole essay aims itself at the epiphany. It must occur close to the end, because once it happens, you're about done. This is why you often find the epiphany in the next to the last paragraph of a piece.

It's sometimes followed by a more lighthearted ending to bring things back to a less portentous vein. In the last paragraph of the ice-skating piece, Martin dives back into the story and lightens the mood: "My coach bellows across the ice, 'You call that speed?' My dead grandmother can move faster!' "

RESOLUTION

Then there's *resolution*. Often in the last paragraph, after the epiphany, we'll see the narrator do something he would not have done before the epiphany. Noah Lukeman said in *The Plot Thickens,* "A character can feel remorse, and think kind thoughts, and have a powerful self-realization, but at the end of the day, when it comes time to make a judgment on this person, we are left only with the trail of his actions, like dots on a map. Indeed, one would even argue that a realization is not a true realization if it is not followed by action." In other words, life-changing realizations must change lives.

If you realize your boyfriend's a jerk but go on seeing him, you may have had a genuine epiphany, but we'd be more convinced of that if we see you dump him. If you realize that your mother is never going to change and decide to accept her as she is, let's maybe have a little scene where your behavior changes: where you *don't* bristle when she tells you you'll never succeed at anything. Maybe you are detached enough to joke about setting up your homeless tent in her backyard.

This is not essential — many fine essays omit that final event showing resolution — but it sure is nice.

I remember a moment that changed my own life forever. I was 31 and had been married for seven years. I was hurrying home from the library to meet my husband Jim at home so we could take our three-year-old son Patrick to the doctor. We'd moved to Petaluma, forty miles north of San Francisco, when Jim bought a country house to restore as an inn. We missed the city after three years and came back, but by then the marriage was over, thanks to that moment.

When I stopped at a light near the little green park in the center of downtown Petaluma, a series of images filled my head: a stormy night, a knock on the door. I open it to a highway patrolman with rain dripping off his hat above his shadowed face. He tells me, "It happened so fast — nothing anybody could do — he died instantly." He means *Jim*.

A pickup behind me honked, and I came out of my reverie to see the light was green. As I drove on, I realized I'd been fantasizing the death of my husband — and not for the first time.

I had to switch off the radio to let my next thought fill my head. *He doesn't have to die. I can leave him.* I had never thought that before. I had put my unhappiness down to other causes. I entered the intersection as a young married woman heading home to meet her husband. I left it well on my way to being single.

I might end the story by saying that the following night I asked my husband out for a drink and told him I wanted a divorce. That would make a satisfying resolution, and has the additional benefit of being true.

Formulas?

So that's the narrative essay. I see those raised eyebrows. "How nice! All these formulas! Did I wander into a science lab?" My student Katherine Brennan told me, "I can't seem to wrap my head around writing this way. I prefer imagining a story I want to tell, or a scene I want to share, and just writing it. I let the piece itself determine a path, a trajectory." Well, she's right, of course, and it makes me feel bad to suggest less poetic ways of looking at an essay, but, in defense of myself, I argue that personal writing can be overwhelming. It has all the complexity of real life, with its many things happening at once, and every idea leading back to the past. Often the story you want to tell is so fused with other memories that a lot of the time spent in writing narrative is in the prewriting stage. Guidelines or formulas or outlines help you think about what you're doing, and thus save you a draft or two.

I read that Frank O'Connor talked about reducing a story to four lines (or less) and committing it to paper in skeletal form, using algebraic terms: "X marries Y. Y dies. X visits Y's parents in Ireland, but does not mention that Y is dead." And Frank O'Connor was famous for his ripping Irish short stories. At least *I* haven't given you math problems.

....

THE CRAFTY WRITER:

Useful "formulas" exist for other kinds of short writing as well. In newspaper writing the structure can look like this:

Anecdote

Nut graph

Evidence

Why

History

Reaction

Future

Also, I read that the formula for a children's story is, "Once upon a time" (the situation) then "One day..." (the complication), and then "Luckily..." (the resolution).

Sorry. Digression. In the next chapter we'll look at other useful techniques that are helpful to the narrative essay, and that also provide a deft structure when you are not telling a story, but taking a different approach.

....

CHAPTER FOUR

WHAT'S YOUR ANGLE?

Angle Equals Surprise
How to Find an Angle
Using Setup

There may never be anything new to say, but there is always a new way to say it.

— Flannery O'Connor

A theme, a thesis, a subject, is in most cases little more than a sort of clothesline on which one pegs a string of ideas, quotations, allusions and so on, one's mental undergarments of all shapes and sizes, some possibly fairly new, but most rather old and patched; and they dance and sway in the breeze and flap and flutter, or hang limp and lifeless; and some are ordinary enough; and some are of a rather private and intimate shape, and rather give the owner away, and show up his or her peculiarities. And owing to the invisible clothesline they seem to have some connection and continuity.

— Kenneth Grahame, *My Dearest Mouse*: *"The Wind in the Willows" Letters*

What do you want to write about? Falling in love, flat tires, dental surgery, strange engine noises, notices from the IRS, making mistakes with your kids? Whatever it is, it has been said before. Your job is to find a new way to say an old thing, and for that you need your wonderful voice and details that could have come only from your life. And you need a surprise approach: an angle.

ANGLE EQUALS SURPRISE

An angle is to the essay what a premise is to a book, or a handle is to advertising, or high concept is to a movie (dinosaurs brought back to life for a theme park!). It's a gimmick or twist or conceit that grabs our attention long enough for you to say what you want to say. Like the outline of a narrative essay, the angle tells you what to put in, what to leave out.

An angle can be how your mutual loathing for the couples counselor brought you back together. Or how Halloween was the one day you could out-shine the rich kids. How dating never ends, because when you're a couple, you have to find other couples willing to go out with you. It can be how great your hair always starts to looks on your way to the hair salon (and how suddenly better you feel when you're sitting in the doctor's waiting room).

Think of the angle as the Christmas tree. Once you have that six-foot pine standing up next to the piano, it's pretty easy to see where the decorations go. Without the tree, what have you got? A lot of pretty balls on the floor.

Let's look at the angle my friend Stan Sinberg used for a piece when he was a columnist for the *Marin Independent Journal*. Stan had a big birthday coming up, and he wanted to write about it. Of course Stan could have just blurted out to his readers that he was about to be forty and realized many of his dreams remain to be fulfilled. That would be the direct approach. In life, directness is good. In writing, not so good. It's said that when Henry James received a manuscript he didn't like, he'd return it with the dry comment, "You have chosen a good subject and are treating it in a straightforward manner."

Having your dreams unfulfilled at forty is a common reaction to a common experience, which means Stan needed an angle. Here's what he came up with in his humorous twist on the subject. "Listen," his piece began, "I can't spend a lot of time on today's column because there's a lot I have to do. See, today's the last day I'm 39 years old, and there're all these things I always wanted to accomplish before I turned 40. Like get married. Always wanted to be married before I turned 40."

Stan's angle was that he had to realize all his dreams on that final day of being 39. No problem with the marriage thing — "I'd had my eye on this woman who came into the health club most mornings at eleven" — but he also had to write a novel ("Fortunately, I have a couple of ideas"), and acquire kids, a house, a horse, a piano … He was going to have a busy day.

Notice that Stan's account of all the things he needed to do before turning 40 is a *list*: he could start with the piano, and then talk about kids, and the piece would still work. What follows an angle is in fact often a list (in the sense that you can make your points in any order). It's one way a good angle gives you a easy way to structure the piece: set up your angle, give us your list.

EXAMPLES OF ANGLES

A *New York Times* piece came up with an audacious angle when it compared Staten Island's refusal to accept New York's garbage to the breakup of a marriage. It began: "It is generally advisable to start rethinking your marital relationship if you come home one evening and find your belongings in a heap outside the door. This is more or less the situation between Manhattan and Staten Island."

Elizabeth Rapoport souped up a piece on insomnia with this terrific angle:

> I've figured out the dirty little secret of women's fantasy lives. And it's got nothing to do with thumbing through herotica or fondling Brad Pitt's backside or soaking in a penthouse Jacuzzi with Richard Gere. Sleep has become the sex of the 90s.

Sometimes an angle is conflict — an element that all pieces must have. (Readers want trouble.) But what if there is no trouble? The trip to Paris was wonderful in every respect, the new boyfriend is heaven-sent, you are floating in a sky-blue pool in a Caribbean resort and your only source of distress is that the tiny umbrella from your drink fell in the water.

Once I had a tedious few pages on how weird women are about food, and another few on how weird men are about money. I needed conflict, so I put the two of them together, and wrote the piece as a scene at a restaurant:

> I figured out why first dates don't work any better than they do. It's because they take place in restaurants. Women are weird and con-fused and unhappy about food, and men are weird and confused

and unhappy about money, yet off they go, the minute they meet,
to where you use money to buy food.

Another fix is to bring into the piece something or somebody who's prevent-
ing you from doing what you want to do.

If I want to arrive hours early for a flight, maybe even get a hotel room at
the airport the night before just to make sure, and I am free to do so, I don't
have a problem. My piece would be: "Hey, everybody listen while I tell you
that I need to get to the airport early." So, in the column I wrote about that, I
brought in someone with the opposite point of view — in this case, my husband Bill, who gets to the airport for that last-minute swan dive into the 747
as it pulls away from the gate.

This is why, incidentally, columnists are always bringing in their mates as
straight men —to be the "You can't do that" obstacle. You can use the same
technique. Bring in a friend, a boss, or a mother (mothers are always good) to
oppose you.

ANGLE VS. SUBJECT

When I wanted to write about mothers and their middle-aged daughters for
More Magazine, I had a *subject*. When I proposed a piece to them on how
daughters start to take it easy on their mothers in middle age, I had an *angle*.
When a writer talks about having an idea for a piece, he usually means not
that he has found a subject to write about, but that he has found an angle
for his subject. Even when an essay is a chronological narrative — here's my
story of life as a black woman in America — finding an angle will sharpen it,
as Zora Neale Hurston did when she began, "I remember the very day that I
became colored."

A friend of mine wrote that she was determined to lead the same life she did
before she had her baby, Tanner. That's the direct approach. But she found
her angle when she pretended that she thought she really was leading the
same life as before. She could say that everybody had warned her that her life
would change when she had the baby, but she declares to the reader that tra
la, it hasn't, she still does all the things she ever did. The reader, however, sees
her breasts leak in yoga class, the baby squalling at a Mexican resort, how

she takes the baby along skiing and when they're furthest from the resort he poops and has to be taken back for changing.

Once I assigned my class a piece on Barbie dolls, and everybody returned with a different angle. One woman said *she* was a Barbie doll, another talked about how keeping Barbie well dressed turned her into a shoplifter, a man said he pretended to hate Barbie —burning her hair off over the gas jets — but was more drawn to her than he let on. A student named Lisa found her angle in a wonderful remark she happened to make in her first draft:

> Barbie is regarded to be the standard of feminine perfection, yet Barbie isn't perfect at all — her arms don't even bend! She carries out a tray of frosty beverages, balancing it on the two bamboo poles they've given her for arms. She can't even curl her fingers to keep the tray from sliding onto the yellow flowered Kleenex box that Ken is reclining in.

Note that the angle governs the whole piece: Now that Lisa knows that her piece will be on Barbie's imperfections, she will focus the next draft on that, and only that. If she talks about Barbie's stunning array of careers, she'll do so from that point of view (maybe by observing that a flighty resume hardly demonstrates seriousness of purpose).

HOW TO FIND AN ANGLE

An angle can come from something you hear yourself saying aloud. I was having Thai food with my friend John when I happened to remark to him that my husband Bill and I kept all our finances separate. "We don't even have a joint banking account."

My friend stared as if I had lifted a door in my skin and revealed a howling wilderness where sunshine and a lawn should be. "It doesn't sound romantic, but it is," I rushed to assure him. "We've practically never had an argument about money." When I heard myself saying that, I jotted a note on my napkin: "Divvying up finances like college roommates can be romantic."

Angles are half the battle, so when you find one it's often almost not an exaggeration to say you are practically done, except for the typing. Stand up, stretch, and go look for something to eat in the fridge. After my lunch with John I went home and read a novel before writing the column because I knew exactly what I was going to write.

You can find an angle by talking the piece through with someone. If you don't have a writing partner, follow that other human you live with around the house. "See, I'm trying to write about this brother I never met who died when he was a few days old, and the fact that I became a pediatrician keeps coming into it, and…"

Your housemate can yawn, or keep folding the towels, or shaving, or even watching TV — it doesn't matter. It's what you hear yourself saying that does the trick, not what the person you're talking to says back. We know things that we don't know we know.

A few years ago I'd been trying to find a way to write about a dark painting my mother made that showed the seven of us kids at the swimming hole in Samuel P. Taylor Park. I talked to my husband about it. "She painted in all the shadows," I commented to him as I hung the painting in the hall, "but I remember all the sunlight."

Bingo. Angle.

You might find the angle in a remark you made somewhere in one of your early drafts. A student of mine set down some thoughts about her and her sister being confined to an apartment in Iran all one long summer when their father was on assignment there. When she wrote, "The closer we were kept together, the more we grew apart," she had her angle.

Similarly, my former writing partner, Ginny, who teaches college up in Sacramento, said in a piece about lesbian potlucks, "It's like so many other things in the lesbian community. For many lesbians, putting a lot of energy into something that is traditionally female seems wrong." Angle! If she used that angle, she'd talk about the potluck, but also add other examples of lesbians balking at makeup or housekeeping or fancy clothes.

In a first draft, where you set things down any which way to see what you have to say on a subject, you may come up with several ideas for angles, as my student Liz Dossa did in response to an assignment to write about cooking. I took these sentences out of her piece; notice that she could develop almost any one of them as the angle:

1. The wonderful thing about cooking for me is that you don't have to keep up to date.
2. Reading the recipes in the newspaper food section has always been like reading tiny novels for me.
3. I don't really imagine tastes together very well. I guess a lot.
4. When I follow a recipe, my attention will lag. I won't measure carefully.
5. I like to evaluate my friends' response to the food during the meal, which my husband thinks is rude.
6. How we cook reflects our personalities.
7. I heard on the radio this morning that the prime minister of Thailand has to resign because he continued to host a cooking show on TV. I understand. He can't help himself.

You can sometimes coax out an angle by writing a final paragraph. I do this often. In this paragraph you say, "I don't know what I'm trying to say here. What am I saying about my high school reunion? Am I trying to say this? Or that?" As when you talk a piece through with someone, if you force yourself to wonder aloud what it is you're driving at, you find you know — or your typing fingers do.

USING SETUP

Your angle can be to start with the opposite of where you want to go. I call this *setup*. Here's an example of how it works: One day *San Francisco Chronicle* columnist Jon Carroll was at a wedding reception when he realized he was boring the bride he was talking to. Naturally any such bad moment has potential, but a major metropolitan paper doesn't hire people to write columns that say, "I had a troubling experience the other day that I'd like to tell you about." In order to write about that moment of humiliation, Jon set it up by starting with the opposite: how nice it is, as a celebrated Bay Area columnist, to be recognized and admired.

Nice wedding last weekend. Very fine pizza; always a plus at a wedding. Lovely couple. Sweet music. Chocolate wedding cake — why doesn't everyone think of that? Fans. I don't mean to be immodest, but try to stop me. I am standing there in my extremely lovely Italian suit (the kind that causes people to involuntarily finger the sleeve and say, "I had no idea that you owned a suit like that, or at all"), eating a nectarine and gazing benignly into the mystic ...

Then the fall, as it appeared near the end of the column:

> I look into Shana Morrison's eyes. [The bride was Shana Morrison, the daughter of Van Morrison.] She is looking at me with devastating politeness. She is waiting for my rap to end. She's done this before — her father has a lot of really old fans with obscure enthusiasms. I am the old guy at the wedding. My face is close to hers, and I'm sure my breath smells of whiskey and cigarettes and denture cream, though I've stopped using the first two and have not yet started the third.

Betsy Carter wrote in *Glamour* magazine that she liked to hang onto people in her life. She started the piece by talking about throwing things out. "When in doubt, toss it. That's pretty much how I live my life. I have been known to throw away paychecks and dump IRS forms. The only thing I seem unable to shed is people."

There's no reason for us to know Carter threw out her checks — what do her feckless accounting methods have to do with anything? It's there for the contrast — throwing out vs. keeping — that gives the piece its structure. Without it you have a writer tugging on your sleeve and telling you how she likes to hang on to people, from ex-husbands to dentists.

Another example? In a piece called "Professions for Women" Virginia Woolf began with how easily she became a writer: "When I came to write," she said, "there were very few material obstacles in my way." Writing was a reputable occupation, the scratching of a pen disturbed no family peace, and paper was cheap. She quickly sold a piece about a Persian cat that brought her into disputes with her neighbors. "What could be easier," she said, "than to write articles and to buy Persian cats with the profits?"

A lot, it turns out. That was the setup. The rest of the piece lists the harsh obstacles that impeded the woman writer in her day.

When you become aware of setup you see it everywhere, especially in the movies. When Bill and I watch war movies, and a weary soldier leaning on his rifle starts talking about that little farm he's going to buy when this is over, we look at each other and say in unison, "He's dead."

Setup: The dream that shows how much the character has to live for.

Payoff: Oops. Where'd that grenade come from?

Okay, that's a joke, but it's one that leads neatly into our next topic, which is tone and humor.

CHAPTER FIVE

TONE AND HUMOR

Using Humor in Essays
Flip the Script
If You're Right, It Will Not Write
Voice

WHAT TONE IS

Consider how many ways a person can say, "Where did you get those pants?"

Where did *you* get those pants?
Where did you get *those* pants?
Where did you *get* those pants?

The difference is tone. Tone in writing is like tone of voice. It can be amused, wry, serious, pedantic, outraged, sad, sarcastic, bitter, angry, mocking, whimsical, jocular, awestruck, facetious, admiring, or joyful. Tone, more than anything else, determines how the reader responds — whether we laugh, bristle, sit up, yawn or leave the room and forget to come back.

We've all read writing that is clear, well-organized, and thoughtful. We pick up an article that says, "Ten Easy Things to Do to Become Rich by Thursday." We want to become rich by Thursday. Yet before we finish the article the magazine slips under the bed, and we forget we were reading it. I know that I keep buying self-help books on things from digital photography to good posture but never open the books. I didn't even use the posture book to balance on my head. Why? Reading them is work.

On the other hand, we devour writing on subjects that don't interest us simply because we like the tone. Many of the readers of Anne Lamott's books on faith are unbelievers, but they charge down to the bookstore every time she has a new book out because they will follow that wry, warm, funny tone anywhere.

Tone is feeling. In fact tone can be whatever a human being can feel. In a piece on breaking up with his girlfriend, San Francisco writer Ethan Watters used a tone of regret: "As Sarah collects her books upstairs, I look around the living room. I spot a lamp from our old apartment and run my hand over the arm of a sofa I used to nap on."

Tone can be rueful: "It's raining on the island this morning, the last day of an impulsive vacation, and when I woke up and heard rain I felt instantly cheerful."

USING HUMOR IN ESSAYS

Humor is of course a tone. It can provide needed distance on searing subjects in both essays and memoirs. In her *New Yorker* piece, "Cancer Becomes Me," Marjorie Gross used a casual, humorous tone where we'd expect despair: "So I'm sitting in the doctor's office, he walks in, just tells me straight out, "I was right — it's ovarian cancer, so I win. Pay up."

This tone might be too abrasive on many subjects, but it works here, because the writer wins our sympathy by being so ill. (Later in the piece she says, "I hope with all this negative talk I haven't painted too bleak a picture and therefore discouraged you from getting cancer. I mean, there are some really good things about it.")

Humor is established by word choice, among other things. When essayist Laura Blumfeld began a piece by saying, "I was speaking with two female friends recently, and in an instant came face to face with the odious beast that is my soul," the humorous, self-deprecating words "odious beast" established the wry tone. Daniel Ben-Horn struck that same tone in a *San Francisco Chronicle* piece when he began a camping story by saying, "We were three men being Manly Men on a winter weekend in the Sierra two years ago." My student Ellie Spencer adopts a great tone as a pious little brat in this sentence: "I proudly wore a medal of the Holy Virgin pinned to my undershirt. I made sure that the communion wafer melted in my mouth, lest I accidentally cause pain to Our Lord by having His Body come in contact with my teeth."

Listen to how Nora Ephron establishes a self-deprecating tone in her novel *Heartburn*, a book that for my money is all tone: "My father's apartment was empty, my father having been carted off to the loony bin only days before by my sister Eleanor, who is known as the Good Daughter in order to differentiate her from me."

TRY THIS:

Look at the first line of your essay. Does it establish tone? What is the tone? Can you find another sentence in the piece that's livelier, and move that up to the beginning?

A surprising tone is one we don't expect. It can make a piece work all by itself. Once I wrote a grumpy column once on how I wanted it to rain, starting now. I wanted those sailboats off the bay and those garage sales off the corner sidewalks, those people off the beaches, and those parks empty. Since it makes no sense to tell the rain to stop, the tone is surprising. If I'd said, "I want those homeless people off the streets starting now," it would sound strident and off-putting.

You can use an inappropriate tone to keep a sentimental tone out of a sentimental subject, as my student Bernadette Glenn does below.

> I cried when I handed in my ID card. There went my whole identity. Home to the greedy sucking jaws of my kid. I had to face the misery of filling the day with a boisterous, self-centered little bully who had no control over his own bowels, never mind his emotions. I had imagined a small period of rest everyday, but he was outgrowing naps and he drooled on the newspaper and punched me if it looked like I was not paying attention to him.

Better than her whipping out a billfold of photographs of her little darling, isn't it? A sentimental subject is always a challenge. I wrote a book about grandmothers because I found the ones already out there mawkish and treacley ("Grandmothers are mothers with frosting"). The writers love their grandchildren and say so, which leaves the reader with nothing to do except get an insulin shot. Okay, now what I just said sounds a bit superior, doesn't it? Bad tone ...

In a piece called "Seeing the Sights in San Francisco," Kay Boyle employs the lighthearted, slightly ditzy tone of Sunday magazine travel writing to describe San Francisco's Golden Gate Cemetery filling up with dead Vietnam veterans: "Last year I frequently suggested to sojourners in these parts that Sunday was the best day of the week to make a tour of the fabulous Golden Gate Cemetery which lies in all its verdant beauty in the rolling countryside."

My friend Mark Hetts, a handyman who lives around the corner, made use of an inappropriate tone in a different way when he started an advice newsletter called Mr. Handyman that offered suggestions on such topics as picture railings, spackling, and best brands of paint.

Look at the engaging Miss Manners-like tone of exasperation — which is not at all what we'd expect from a man advising us about mildew — that made Mark, scant months later, a syndicated columnist in 30 papers.

> The worst thing that can be done (and one of the most common) is to get one of those prepared tub and tile caulking kits, and smoosh out white caulk all over the mildewed places to make everything look clean and pretty again. For about three weeks. This is compounding the original personal slothfulness that allowed the mildew to appear in the first place with gross misconduct, since the caulking compound forms a perfect protected environment under which the mildew can flourish into a tile-removing, paint-cracking, corner-splitting dragon that will eventually cause your house to collapse around the bathroom.

Using an inappropriate form can be funny, too. In "Audio Tour," a piece in the *The New Yorker*, Patricia Marx talks about an old boyfriend as if she were a tour guide to his apartment:

> Hello, and welcome to the rent-stabilized apartment of Todd Niesle. I'm Debby, a specialist in Todd Niesle, and I'm going to be your guide. Before you begin your journey through the World of Todd Niesle and His Stuff, may I ask you to reduce the volume on your Acoutstiguide player to a polite level? Todd Niesle does not know you are here. Moreover, the woman in 12-A has had a bee in her bonnet about me ever since I, Debby, while, O.K., yes, a tiny

bit drunk, mistook her door for Todd Niesle's late one night and jimmied it open.

You are standing in Todd Niesle's foyer. The faux faux-marble table on your right is attributed to Todd Niesle's mother, circa last Christmas. It's a fine example of a piece that I, Debby, do not like …

In *The New Yorker's* Shouts & Murmurs page, Robert Sullivan wrote a business memo to his family: "As your father, I am happy to report that our family had a marvelously successful first quarter this year . . ." Then, later: "Let's begin with Jimmy. I've been reviewing your contribution to the family, and I'm afraid we're going to have to let you go."

THE CRAFTY WRITER
Tone can slip around on you. When you write a paragraph that sounds the way you want the whole piece to sound, clip it to your computer. Also, when you are after a certain tone, watch what you read before you sit down to write, as you unconsciously pick up the cadence. It's like being in England and finding yourself saying, "I'll just put this in the car, shall I?" which is not an American way of speaking. When I want a funny tone, I read some Calvin Trillin before sitting down. In doing this book, I kept picking up Anne Lamott's *Bird by Bird* in the faint hope of coming off as funny and personable as she does.

SOUND LIKE SOMEBODY IN A MOOD

When you're writing humor, you want to sound in some way unreasonable (unless you're Jonathan Swift writing "A Modest Proposal," in which case you want to sound reasonable to balance the outrageousness of offering to solve the famine by eating Irish babies). Somebody exasperated, or silly, or whatever. Someone compelled to speak, unable to keep quiet anymore.

My writing partner, Ginny, was an excellent college dean, able to see all sides of a question, to qualify her statements, to avoid taking extreme positions. She had to knock all that out of her writing before she could be a lean, mean writing machine. Reasonable and nice: good qualities in life, rewarding, get you promotions, boyfriends, seats on the aisle, maybe even a bottle of champagne sneaked to you from first class. But all those "prettys," "rathers," and "kind ofs" suck the soul out of writing. Writers are not nice. They are maniacs, gripped by unreasoning desires, driven by passions, consumed by jealousy. They are drama queens. And drama kings. In the process of becoming civilized, a person naturally learns to conceal strong feelings, fight down irrational responses, and look at all sides of a question. This is socialized behavior. In writing you want to ramp feelings up. Let's not have you being vaguely unhappy in Vermont. If you have the flu, you are not merely feeling unwell: you are near death, and in fact have become anxious that whoever handles your funeral will get everything wrong.

My favorite use of the unreasonable tone is the rant. Rants can be heard on NPR's "All Things Considered" and "Morning Edition." Fran Leibowitz OWNS this form (get any of her collections: *Manners, Metropolitan Life,* or *Social Studies).*

Nancy Franklin began a rant in *The New Yorker's* "Shouts & Murmurs" like this:

> While the rest of you loudly and meaninglessly celebrate the New Year — I'm not judging, I'm just making an observation — I prefer to reflect quietly on the lessons I've learned or partially absorbed or once thought I heard someone talking about as I was going down the street trying to get to the hardware store before it closed.

That's pretty silly. I love rants. Women writers need to use them more. Here's the beginning of one my student Lisa Pongrace did in class on what she calls the "The Holy Grail of Black Shoeness."

> I mean, sure, I could be a sensible, contented cow and wear the old strappy, flat black sandals from three years ago with the black skirt and the chartreuse top, but it would be more fashion forward to wear the newer, higher, chunkier ones. Unless I have to do any walking whatsoever in them, in which case I'd have to glue them to my feet on account of their idiotic slide-in, no-strap-around-the-heel design, so that when you walk you have to squinch up your toes just to keep the shoes from falling off, and if you squinch for too long you get cramps in your feet and after all, good heavens, I am NOT a slave to fashion; I will NOT have crampy feet just for the sake of a little style..." (And so on)

TRY THIS:

Take a very small incident, such as your flapping shoelace, the failure of your co-workers to notice your stunning ten-pound weight loss, or your husband's insistence of going for a bracing walk in the sunshine when you want to slouch on the couch, and make a huge deal of it.

OTHER WAYS TO USE HUMOR IN ESSAYS

1. Take a statement literally. When I asked my nine-year-old where his homework was, he said, "Somebody stole it. It was right in my pocket." In the piece, I say that his statement made me shiver. "We live in the Duboce Triangle in San Francisco. With several schools nearby, it's a favorite turf of the dread spelling-homework gangs."

2. Adopt a fake tone of sympathy. When comedian Jackie Mason filed a lawsuit in the New York State Supreme Court after he didn't win the Tony award, Brendan Gill skewered him in the "Shouts & Murmurs" column of *The New Yorker*: "I see the lawsuit as a characteristically unselfish gesture on Mason's part," he said. "Mason was striking a blow not only on his own behalf, but on behalf of all those of us who have spent their lives longing in vain to be awarded a prize." My student Marsh Rose did the same when she riffed about a neglectful landlord:

> Dear Zoë,
> I would like to introduce myself to you. In fact, I often sit in this dim living room — cross-legged on the floor furnace, praying for warmth — and imagine what that might be like ... to introduce myself to you. I see myself racing into the street, flinging myself at your noisy green Camaro as you drive by with your gaze averted, and shouting out the truth about you. "A landlady!" I would cry. "A landlady!"
>   You know me by sight. I'm the woman in the muddy boots and rubber gloves who stands in the driveway of this rented hovel, leaning on a rake and peering up at the porch roof, gauging with my eye how much farther it's tilted to the left. On some early mornings when I'm about to leave for work and I'm at the threshold with my purse over my shoulder, I imagine I hear a whoosh. When I open the door, there on the ground would be the porch roof in a mound

of debris with a still-settling cloud of dust, mold spores, old sparrow feathers, pine needles and squirrel droppings.

3. Use unlikely comparisons. I once compared having a boyfriend unfavorably to having a fern: "If you leave town for a day or two, the fern will simply use the time to put out new fronds, or to see many leaves it can drop on the rug, or experiment with leaning over in arresting new postures. It will not call up an old girlfriend and get itself invited to dinner."

Another time, I compared teens to cats:

> While children are dogs, loyal and affectionate, teenagers are cats. It's so easy to be the owner of a dog. You feed it, train it, boss it around and it puts its head on your knee and gazes at you as if you were a Rembrandt painting. It follows you around, chews the dust covers off the Great Literature series if you stay too long at the party and bounds inside with enthusiasm when you call it in from the yard. Then, one day around age 13, your adoring little puppy turns into a big old cat. When you tell it to come inside, it looks amazed, as if wondering who died and made you emperor. Instead of dogging your footsteps, it disappears.

FLIP THE SCRIPT

As a writer, as much as seventy-five percent of your energy in revision will be devoted to getting the tone right.

Most of the time, in personal writing, the tone is going to be fine, because you are being honest, and vulnerable, and because if anybody in the piece is screwing up, it's you. The confessional tone gets the reader on your side. A bad experience makes you vulnerable, and vulnerability is necessary.

The tone gets trickiest when you're writing about those nasty other people rather than your shining golden self. Attacking another person, even the insurance company that towed the wreck to your house instead of to a garage, or the girlfriend who stole your Nikon as she left, makes the reader take a step back from you, as we would from any person in a rage.

If what you're writing is your chance to inform, or set the record straight, or get revenge on that asshole you married, though, the tone will suffer. Your account of what happened must be fair, or we'll be wondering what your mom's side of the story is. To guard against portraying yourself as the victim of the story, or unconsciously seeking sympathy, *flip the script*. Make yourself the one who is getting something wrong. Write about the mistakes you made in your friendships, rather than how you were treated by your friends.

If you write, "Growing up in the fifties, a repressive time for women, I decided very early cooking pot roasts and raising children in the New Jersey suburbs was not for me," the tone is too confident. Better to flip the script — show yourself trapped in a life you will never find fulfilling, rather than you feeling superior to your surroundings.

Whether you're describing the sexual abuse you suffered from your older brother, or a teacher's cruelty to you, be calm and dispassionate. Assume that everyone was doing his best, according to his nature. Write with forgiveness, understanding, and humor.

Write as if you're filling an old friend in on events he missed in your life. It's a trick for keeping an accessible tone, remembering to explain the necessary background of all characters and events, and being emotionally open and honest with someone you trust.

Often you can't avoid sounding snooty, or pissed, or aggrieved, or sarcastic or outraged until time and perspective (and many revisions, and perhaps the tiniest amount of therapy) do their work. Frank McCourt said it took him decades to detach from his anger toward his feckless father enough to give *Angela's Ashes* its non-judgmental tone. He has said:

> The voice came one day. It was miraculous. One day I just wrote the sentence. "I'm in a playground in Kassen Avenue in Brooklyn. I am three and my brother, Menachie, is two. We're on a seesaw. Up down, up down." I wrote in the present tense, and I wrote as a child and felt very comfortable. And I was on my way after that.

You can see this resulting unjudging tone of a child throughout the book. His father comes home drunk on the dole money, blubbery sentimental about the siblings who have died (through his neglect) and yet the child narrator is not angry.

> He staggered to me and hugged me and I smelled the drink I used to smell in America. My face was wet from his tears and his spit and his snot and I was hungry and I didn't know what to say when he cried all over my head.

A number of people I know couldn't bring themselves to read Frank McCourt's *Angela's Ashes* because it was too grim: alcoholism, humiliation, poverty, dirt, disease, untimely death. But for me the dry humor throughout the book tempers the meanness and provides hope.

IF YOU'RE RIGHT, IT WILL NOT WRITE

Some stories won't write because the tone problems are built into the situation. Let me give you a painful example. I flew from San Francisco to Portland once to spend a week with my sister in her little house near the Willamette River after she came home from the hospital following an operation for pancreatic cancer. Her son had refused to come, and she had no one else. On my second night, she and I fought over something trivial — I was irritated that she wouldn't let me use her bike, she was nervous that I was moving around in her kitchen as if I owned the place. When she blew up at me for running her silverware through the dishwasher even though she'd asked me not to, I muttered that I might have to leave before the week was up. She said, "If you're leaving, leave right now." Stung, I said no. I didn't have a flight.

She called the police.

Half an hour later I found myself trembling, packing my suitcase under the gaze of three policemen while my sister, her robe folded over a fresh, long, half-moon-shaped slice in her belly, lay on an antique sedan chair in the next room, talking to the officer assigned to her while the others talked to me. Exciting story, but no way can I tell it: I flew to Oregon to help a sick sister, and she threw me out of the house with the help of Portland's Finest.

So I have a story that was upsetting when it happened, and has plenty of action, but it won't write. Even if you accepted my version of events, and found it interesting, you would find yourself in the middle of a family quarrel that offers no real insight into behavior. I don't change in that story. It falls under Shit Happens.

The only way it might work would be if I could show myself in the wrong. I could, for example, say that I realized it was intolerable for my sister Nora to be so helpless, and have me barging around in her house — that I should have found a way to let her be the boss, even when she was ill. That I suspect I liked bustling around, being so strong and healthy and so great about coming up to help her. Or I could say the experience could make me accept that there are some things that can't be helped. With either of those approaches, though, I come off as a little too saint-like.

It's best to avoid that subject. Sometimes this is the best solution. My student Jean, a therapist, wanted to write about taking care of her demented mom, but everything she wrote sounded bitter, one-sided. The rest of us in that class didn't know what a nice woman Jean was until she started writing little columns, and then we wanted to hear everything she wrote, including how she went to a nursing home to recruit voters for Barack Obama and found herself pinning campaign buttons on people in various stages of coma. Her mom was just not a good topic for her.

With some topics, the tone problem can't be overcome. I ran into a problem with tone when I sent my mother a draft of a piece about the mobile home park she lived in. I thought the piece was an homage — I loved that park, with its pool and duck pond and a pretty marsh running up one side. But she was livid. I live in a large Victorian in San Francisco. No way can I write about the trailer park. (I've been forced to confine myself to jokes to my sister who lives in the park, too, saying, "Shall we walk over to the store or take the house?")

KNOW IT ALL

Opinions are not good for tone. When you're on the side of truth and justice, or you take an obvious stand (Anna Quindlen comes out against spousal abuse!), your tone can be dull or ponderous. In general, if you're right, it will not write.

I've learned to be wary whenever I'm expressing an opinion (you know you're doing that when the writing starts to feel like a breakthrough, as if you are bringing the tablets down from the mountain). Your job is to show the experience that led to that opinion, not to bore the readership with your views.

It isn't as if your views will not creep in anyway; as someone said, "You put your opinion into all your art or it ain't art." Self-assured types can be wonderful at opinion, criticism, and op-ed pieces, but they don't make good personal essayists.

The know-it-all tone is a problem I have with this very book, as you can imagine. I have had to figure out how to shoehorn into it what are — no bones about it — bits of advice, without making you, the reader, feel lectured to. In fact that very use of "you" just now might be dicey. I noticed that Anne Lamott in *Bird by Bird* took care to say, "I tell my students" to avoid lecturing the reader directly. I hate that it when authors say "we": "Now we apply the eye shadow to the upper eyelid." But my saying "you" makes me the expert, you the receiver of the expertise. *Hmm.* Did I solve that tone problem in the pages of this book? You're reading it. You be the judge.

VOICE

Your voice is the personality of the writing, which is your personality. "Finding your voice" means sounding like yourself on the page. It means discarding the unnatural pitches you experimented with along the way, and letting your natural voice out, that low, thrilling voice you were born with.

It's you sounding so much like you, and so much unlike anybody else, that we know it's your story without seeing your byline. Get voice-recognition software to talk your stories into the computer and capture the directness of your voice. Did you know that blind Milton chanted "Paradise Lost" to his daughters? If you have a laptop with a microphone, you can dictate as you drive. Write your way to work!

Part of finding your voice is knowing whom you're talking to. Imagine a reader who loves every word you write, is your biggest fan, but is easily bored, who'll gag if you say something sentimental, and won't blanch at a swear word or at what you did behind the hardware store with Bill Hawkins. Jane Jacobs (*The Death and Life of Great American Cities*) would try her ideas out on a series of astute imaginary companions. Sometimes she addressed her thoughts to a Celtic novelist called Alfred Duggan who was familiar only with fire and the sword. Everything else had to be explained to him. She'd talk to Thomas Jefferson while she was out running errands, and then switch to trying her ideas out on Benjamin Franklin, trying to put difficult ideas in simple terms that he would like. "Like Jefferson, he was interested in lofty things, but also in nitty-gritty, down-to-earth details," she told a reporter, "such as why the alley we were walking through wasn't paved, and who would pave it if it were paved. He was interested in everything, so he was a very satisfying companion."

Novelist Lynn Freed described finding her voice in *Reading, Writing and Leaving Home: Life On The Page.*

> The opening paragraph was the hook of my story. More than this, it was the paragraph in which I had fallen into a voice both new and, at the same time, completely familiar to me. It had taken me back to myself as a child, perhaps, to the sort of provocative behavior practiced at the far end of the dining-room table. Whatever the case, it had brought with it a new and completely familiar way of considering the world — a way of seeing, a way of knowing, that I had never before been able to translate onto the page.

Next we take up the element of writing that is the most easy to master, and the one that can make your writing a thousand percent better almost immediately.

CHAPTER SIX

USING IMAGES AND DETAILS

The Five Senses

Using Image And Detail to Slow the Pace

Specific and Surprising Details

Give Examples

The Dread Necessity of Inner Emotional

     Landscape

A writer wishes — indeed all of us wish — to speak about profound matters that are, like it or not, general and abstract. We wish to talk to each other about life and death, about love, despair, loss and innocence. We sense that in order to live together we must learn to speak of peace, of history, of meaning and values. Instinctively, we go to our private store of images and associations for our authority to speak of these weighty issues.

—Patricia Hampfl

Writing is turning your thoughts, abstractions, generalizations, and opinions back into the experiences you got them from. Not "women my age become invisible," but "they handed drinks around and forgot me, again."

Here's what happens when you write in images. One of my students wrote a piece in which she described her troubles with a gang at a Catholic grammar school this way: "The girls in the gang roll their white socks down around their ankles, instead of folding them over, like we're supposed to. They never polish their Oxfords either — there are always gray, metal-looking scuffmarks on the sides. It makes their feet look like ice-skating blades, sharp and thin."

Does the narrator have a chance against a gang so brazen that they roll their white socks down around their ankles? No. How do we know? Because we see that she is so nervous that she overpolishes her own shoes: "I polish mine every morning, leaving crusts of white chalk around the lace holes and the seams."

The writer brings her camera in close — right to the shoes! — and keeps it there. Look what happens when she does: "Their shoes look like ice-skating blades, sharp and thin." "Sharp," "thin," "blades," and "metal." Put those together and what do we have lurking just below the level of consciousness in that sentence? *Knives*!

Did the writer intend all this — the accumulation of menace with each succeeding image? I doubt it. When you trust images to do the work for you, much of what gets on the page is unconscious. That's why you are so often astonished to see what you said (and why you have to write things out so you can see what surfaces).

Think of how much better the above is than, "The other girls at school were really mean to me. I was scared of them because they weren't afraid to break the rules and I was."

Here's a good habit to get into: every time you write a sentence, ask yourself, *How can I show this?* Try to get image and detail into every sentence. You'll be amazed at what comes up on your screen. Instead of saying, "My mother was untidy," show us your mother in her laddered nylons, her shimmering slip with the lace coming off, the lipstick hastily slashed on. Parachute your reader into your pages so completely that he won't hear his own phone ringing because he's hearing the porcelain clink of your mother's compact on a vanity in Kentucky in 1974.

You can start with a statement: "The house burned down when I was ten." But don't leave it there. Ask yourself questions about that day (Where was I when it happened? What did I see?) until a scene emerges of a boy trembling in a cornfield, watching his mother come out of burning house with a baby in her arms, kicking a rolled-up Persian rug in front of her.

My writing partner Ginny McReynolds wanted to say that her mother was older than the other mothers. To show that she wrote, "By the time all of those other five-year-olds were reaching across sheets of creamy butcher paper for yellow and brown paint to give their mothers' hair, I was the only one mixing black and white to make gray."

I read that, and I'm leaning over a child's shoulder in a classroom — practically getting chalk on my blouse from the nearby blackboard. I am not being *told* that the narrator feels set apart from the other kids because she has the wrong sort of mom. I *feel* it.

We want experience, not information. "Joan was distressed" is information. "Joan looked away" is an image. The reader notices Joan looking away, and has the pleasure of concluding for herself that the Joan is distressed.

THE FIVE SENSES

The word "images" sounds like a word for a picture, but it's used to refer to all five senses: sight, hearing, smell, touch, and taste. Use them all:

The tiny brown splotch where a cookie has been filched from the tray

The gloves that still have the shape of your father's hands

The high-pitched hum at Thanksgiving dinner that turns out to be your father's hearing aid

The sticky pads you put on your shoes so you wouldn't fall down on the dance floor

Your school friend drawing an eyebrow pencil across your forehead to mark where your bangs should end

Smell might be the most important sense of all, at least for memory. It unlocks the past. You smell your Aunt Caroline's cologne on the person next to you and you're eight years old, sitting on her bed, trying on her pearl earrings, your little fingers fumbling with the screw to tighten them. It can produce great literature. Sven Birkerts, in *The Art of Time in Memoir*, pointed out that before Proust had his famous cookie epiphany, he spent much time collecting the facts of his experience for a more straightforward sort of book. Then:

A single taste swamped him with charged-up sensations of childhood, and in the light of this visceral reaction, his earlier reaching
for remembered experience seemed irrelevant. The vital past,
the living past, he realized, could not be systemically excavated;
it lay distilled in the very details that had not been groomed into
submission.

Proust and his cookies have nothing on the smell of diesel gas. I smell exhaust
from a passing Muni bus on Market Street in San Francisco and for an instant
I am nine again, standing in front of the post office with my thin white socks
already disappearing into my shoes, as the school bus whooshes up in a cloud
of exhaust and wavy air. I can use that flashback in writing as the first of a
series of connected memories, intensely re-experienced more than remembered.

Flannery O'Connor said it takes an appeal to at least three of your five senses
to make a scene real. "If you are deprived of more than two of your five
senses," she said, "you almost aren't there." She referred to this example from
Flaubert's *Madame Bovary*:

She struck the keys with aplomb and ran from top to bottom of
the keyboard without a break. Thus shaken up, the old instrument,
whose strings buzzed, could be heard at the other end of the village
when the windows were open, and often the bailiff's clerk, passing
along the highroad, bareheaded and in list slippers, stopped to
listen, his sheet of papers in his hand.

Instead of telling us that Madame Bovary was playing the piano, Flaubert gets
strings buzzing, the piano shaking, and the camera moving past Bovary out
the window and past the town to a bailiff's clerk who has stopped to listen.

How do we know a bailiff's clerk really did stop to listen? Because we know
what he had on his feet. "It's always necessary to remember," said O'Connor,
"that the writer is much less immediately concerned with grand ideas and
bristling emotion than he is with putting list slippers on clerks."

Say you work for a big New York magazine. They send you to the Midwest to
cover a concert, and you come back with an accurate, nicely punctuated story
that says something like, "It was really hot and really loud at the concert."
You would find yourself collecting images from the experience of landing on

a Manhattan sidewalk with the pages of your opus settling in a picturesque manner all around you.

This is what Alec Wilkinson actually wrote in his *New Yorker* piece on a Midwest concert by Sophia Ramos, a glam rock singer from the South Bronx:

> On this blistering day of sullen farm heat, the needle on a thermometer worn on a string around the neck of a white boy like a piece of jewelry reads a hundred degrees. The expressions on the faces of the everywhere kids are flat and abstracted, as if they had just been yelled at. [sight] The band they're listening to is playing so loud that the sound stirs the surface of a glass of water on a table in a room a hundred yards away. [hearing] Three white boys wearing shorts and no shirts stop Sophia, and one of them asks for an autograph. He extends his arm and Sophia writes with a black felt-tip marker on his biceps. [touch]

That's three, we're there. Wilkinson found those images because he looked for them; he went through that crowd hoping, consciously or not, to find a way to show how hot it was, how loud. That's why writers carry notebooks.

TRY THIS:
Build images by adding appositives. "Apposition" means that one thing is put beside another; an appositive is a word or group of words that add detail to the original. The italics below show appositives added to the original sentence:

"I moved back to Kansas *with its flat plains and harsh winters.*"

"I gave away the household furnishings we'd used the two years we'd lived together before marriage, *the towels from Goodwill in shades of 70s earth tones, the brown comforter with the burn hole that had become a tear, the odd-lot silverware with the bent fork tines and dull-edged knives.*"

"Her apartment was messy, *tank tops hanging off the oven, pizza boxes stacked in the open bottom dresser drawer, a fuchsia bra wrapped around a lampshade and forgotten.*"

"Within fifteen minutes a new scent began to waft its way through the kitchen, *edging through the other, more pleasant odors like an impatient man pushing his way through a crowd.*"

"He turned the car to the right, *the plastic bobblehead Jesus on the dash nodding as if to say, 'Hard call, son, but you made the right choice.'* "

Remember to tell us what people said. In her memoir, *The Facts of Life*, Maureen Howard writes:

> "Ah, did you once see Shelley plain," one of my mother's beloved lines, delivered on this occasion with some irony as we watched Jasper McLevy, the famed Socialist mayor of Bridgeport, climb down from his Model A Ford.

That's the way to quickly sketch your mother. A mother who ironically quotes Shelley on seeing the mayor isn't everybody's mother—she's a particular person.

TRY THIS:
What did your own mother say?
" 'Nice girls don't jiggle,' Mom informed us as we obligingly, with the help of a liberal dash of baby powder, forced ourselves into Playtex girdles." (student Cheri Doege).

" 'You look like a fullback,' " my mother said when I put on the dress." (Carol Costello)

Another student of mine brought her mother to life in one sentence: " 'I love you way too much to send you to summer camp,' said my mother. 'Only parents who do not love their children and want to be rid of them send them off.' "

STAY CLOSE TO THE EVERYDAY OBJECTS OF THE WORLD

Start with where the chairs were in the room. Write about the empty pool, or the shoes your mother threw off the ferry. Or focus on an object — the pot-bellied stove, or the picture dangling lopsidedly from a nail — and gradually enlarge the view to show you and others in the room.

We saw earlier that Frank McCourt, whose bestselling memoir *Angela's Ashes* helped set off the memoir craze, tried all his adult life to write about his childhood. He and his brother even had a stage play based on it in New York. We saw that it wasn't until he was 66 that he found the unjudging tone of a child that he needed to tell that horrific story.

McCourt found that tone through an ordinary object. It was during a classroom exercise at New York University, in which the students were asked to write about their childhood beds. "I wrote about the bed we slept in, we — my three brothers and myself," McCourt has said. "It was a great half-acre of mattress with red hair sticking out of it, no blankets, sheets, or anything like that. And the professor said, 'Oh, that's vivid, would you read it to the class?'

"And I wouldn't," McCourt said, "because I was ashamed of my background, my poverty. But I put it away, and I remembered what he said about how vivid it was. I started writing little things, keeping notes about growing up in Limerick."

TRY THIS:
Look over a piece of yours and rewrite a sentence, adding detail and image. My student Jean Shiffman's original was, "On trips, my mother reads, which she always does anyway at home, and my father drives." Her rewrite: "On trips, my mother reads Agatha Christie novels rapidly and hungrily, one after the other, leaving the finished books behind in motel rooms for other kindred spirits. My father drives silently. My mother says he is thinking of mathematical formulas in his head."

TRY THIS:
Tell a story of a room from your childhood. What did the room see? What were its secrets? Who spent time in this room? Who was not allowed in this room? What did the room feel like? Look like? What did you feel like when you were in this room? How did your body feel? Whom did the room belong to? What does the room remember?

TRY THIS:
Write a page each on the themes of:
My mother's house

My father's hands

My father's house

My mother's hands

USING IMAGES TO SLOW OR INCREASE THE PACE

Add more images where you want to slow us down, fewer when you want to speed up. This is called pace. When you want the story to move fast, confine yourself to a single image or two: "For the next two weeks, we crossed the country, discarded McDonald's wrappers eddying behind our seats."

The more important the person mentioned is to the story, the more you describe them. The person who hands you your paper can be a blur, but when you open the door to see your dead husband grinning on the doorstep wearing the Stanford sweatshirt he wore on the cruise ship he supposedly fell off, slow down.

My student Janna Denig wrote this funny example of too much detail:

> At the sound of the gunshot, he ran to her, his unknotted blue silk paisley tie (the selfsame tie his mother had given him the Thanksgiving two years before when his Uncle Sal suffered a massive coronary at the table and face-planted in Aunt Mae's famous mashed parsnips) flapping loosely in the delicate September breeze, slipping from around his thick neck to drop leisurely to the oil-stained asphalt like an exhausted ballerina at the gripping conclusion of *Swan Lake*, and knelt at her side, cradling her bleeding head in his arms.

The more important a scene or character, the more image and detail it gets. After all, when you watch a horror movie, the camera doesn't zip straight to the kitchen to show the pills scattered on the linoleum and the woman in a bathrobe slumped across the table. It goes first to the hallway closet, then creeps down the hall, then lingers on a burning cigarette in an ashtray, then lets us hear a siren in the distance.

If your readers missed something that is right there in the story — you said your father was holding a pistol — you didn't use enough detail to slow down the narrative down and draw our attention to the gun.

Here is the crisis in George Orwell's famous anti-imperialist essay, "Shooting an Elephant," that I mentioned in an earlier chapter, in which the narrator shoots an elephant simply because the crowd expects him to. The whole essay is aimed at the moment, so Orwell takes his time with it:

When I pulled the trigger I did not hear the bang or feel the kick —
one never does when a shot goes home — but I heard the devilish
roar of glee that went up from the crowd. In that instant, in too
short a time, one would have thought, even for the bullet to get
there, a mysterious, terrible change had come over the elephant.
He neither stirred nor fell, but every line of his body had altered.
He looked suddenly stricken, shrunken, immensely old, as though
the frightful impact of the bullet had paralyzed him without knocking him down. At last, after what seemed a long time — it might
have been five seconds, I dare say — he sagged flabbily to his
knees. His mouth slobbered. An enormous senility seemed to have
settled upon him. One could have imagined him thousands of years
old. I fired again into the same spot. At the second shot he did not
collapse but climbed with desperate slowness to his feet and stood
weakly upright, with legs sagging and head drooping. I fired a third
time. That was the shot that did for him. You could see the agony
of it jolt his whole body and knock the last remnant of strength
from his legs. But in falling he seemed for a moment to rise, for as
his hind legs collapsed beneath him he seemed to tower upward
like a huge rock toppling, his trunk reaching skyward like a tree. He
trumpeted, for the first and only time. And then down he came, his
belly towards me, with a crash that seemed to shake the ground
even where I lay.

Beats saying, "I shot the elephant and it fell down dead," doesn't it?

DETAILS

The terms "image" and "detail" are often used interchangeably. A concrete
detail, for example, is said to be one that appeals to one of the five senses. I'm
using the word "detail" here to refer to a particular and specific piece of information: "She wore a size 36c bra." Or: "My first car was a hot rod, a red Ford
Fairlane with a 428 Cobrajet engine. It would go an astounding, whiplash-
producing 3 m.p.h. when my college pals and I pushed it to the gas station for
repair, which was 99% of the time."

Here's a passage by former *San Francisco Chronicle* travel editor John Flinn
that shows how deftly to insert details:

What started in 1912 with 122 sturdy young men huffing from
the Ferry Building to the Cliff House — and dodging traffic along
the way — has evolved into what it is today: 350 seeded and elite
runners being pursued across the city by a churning, panting sea of
humanity looking like a mass audition for a Village People reunion.

The details are "1912," "122," "Ferry Building," and "350 seeded and elite
runners." We get that information in the midst of lively images, such as the
conceit that the lead runners are being chased rather than leading.

Images let your reader experience what you experienced. Details prove it
happened. If you say you are late because you hit traffic, the boss may squint
at you, but if you say some bozo in a Mini-Cooper tried to drive along the
margin of the road on the Waldo Grade and hit a gravel truck, spilling rocks
across the road and blocking all the lanes in both directions, you have a shot
at being believed.

TRY THIS:
Write a list of details from your childhood. (My own list would include milk
delivered in glass bottles, metal ice cube trays with levers, cap guns, hula-
hoops, linoleum flooring patterned to look like bricks, and clothespin guns.)

TRY THIS:
Select a memory from your childhood (between ages 5 and 15, say). What did
you feel at the time of the event? Go through the senses of touch, smell, sight,
hearing, and taste. Describe the colors you remember, and how the event
made you feel. What impact has this memory had on you? Invent the details
you don't remember.

The Best Details Come Straight From Life

 My student Joan Murray wrote in a class essay, "If your protesting is serious,
don't wear your Birkenstocks. Be sure to wear something with a reinforced
toe so that you don't scrape your toes when you go limp and the police drag
you away."

Has she really been to a protest at an abortion clinic? That detail proves she
has. Another student wrote, "Dad gave me the most inappropriate gifts for
Christmas. When I was eleven he gave me a deep fat fryer, and at 13 it was
a vacuum cleaner — used." No way had this essayist made up the deep fat

fryer. That's what he gave her. Another writer mentioned that after years as a masseuse she couldn't get a passport: her fingerprints were too worn down. You, too, will find great details that say a lot fast: the time in the Depression when all your relatives lived with you, and there was only one bathroom, and you got stuck on the toilet because somebody had painted it without telling you. The time you fell down the stairs at school and a nun looked up, and said, "Maureen. I see FLESH."

Clothe your story in those eccentric details that could have come only from you. You may not be relating a situation we haven't heard before, but you are giving us that situation with the details and images and offbeat characters straight from a frontier that no one else has ever been to: your life. You say what happened to you using images and details that could have happened to nobody but you, and magically your story is transformed into a story about the rest of us.

You think that Cream of Mushroom soup's aftertaste resembles the taste of Cap'n Crunch cereal? Tell us. You like the drool spots on a cool pillow? We want that. The most neurotic details resonate like a tuning fork. Who can forget the story about a jealous astronaut driving from Texas to New York to intercept her lover's new girlfriend — and wearing a diaper so she wouldn't have to stop to pee? A *diaper*! It's the strange detail that makes the story. And it's enough — we don't need to know what she did to shorten her time in gas lines, for example.

During the 2008 Super Bowl, bananas were rushed to the bench after a coach decided the players needed more potassium. "There are the bananas," the announcer said, as if we home viewers could not pick them out. Of course we could: we were riveted by seeing bananas appearing in a championship football game. It was the kind of weird detail you notice.

SPECIFIC AND SURPRISING DETAILS

Don't get carried away and start describing everything in sight, of course. Go for the significant, the surprising and the fresh observation. The impressionistically rendered scene tends to hit us harder than the one photo-realistically reported — perhaps because we fill in the rest from our imaginations and thus participate in the writing. A photographer for *The New York Times* said, "When you stand in Baghdad with the sand under your feet, you're in the middle of a civil war." What better image to show a city breaking up, return-ing to desert under the destructive force of battling factions? You don't have to add the block after block of collapsed buildings — they're implied.

Give us a woman wearing a single, brilliant diamond necklace, not one draped in jewelry from head to toe. Take out the doctor's white coat — they all have white coats — but leave in the nervous jiggle of his foot. If the church pews are more or less what we would expect to find in a church, describe something else. A coffee cup being rinsed will give us the kitchen, a glance at a bedroom clock the bedroom, a dying geranium the deck. A Japanese paint-ing shows you a bamboo branch and you have the whole tree. You develop a sense, in time, for what the reader needs to know, and what he doesn't.

(By the way, even when you need a lot of detail, feed it to us a little at a time, rather than in one great epistolary lump.)

In one story, the writer describes the nurse's feet when she learns of her still-born daughter. This tells us, without telling us, that she can't look up.

In a story about a missing child, mention the light on the porch taped over so that no one can turn it off, ever. This will tell us more than anything else can how that family is feeling.

Those writing about the Irish famine said the mouths of the peasants were green from eating grass. Of all the thousands of Gold Rush diaries that survive, we remember those with vivid detail, like the one by the captain of a ship coming around Cape Horn who told how he periodically came into the galley and leaned over the teapot to defrost his mustache.

Notice the details of sun lotion strength Kathy Alimac gives us in a paragraph about the tanning process.

> We started with Coppertone SPF 20, working our way down to 8, then 4 as the months wore on. During the first two weeks I turned down the edge of my bikini bottoms every five minutes, feeling a triumphant rush when my skin started showing a clear line between the exposed part and the shaded marshmallow underneath. Once I had turned five shades darker, I got to break out the triumphal bottle: Coppertone Oil, SPF 2.

Details tells us all sorts of things without you having to spell them out for us. Someone who warms Dinty Moore stew on the radiator of a '54 Olds has a different lifestyle than someone spooning up beef bourguignon at the Paris Ritz. The fan of "Bonanza" reruns is different from the "Antiques Roadshow" enthusiast.

NAME THINGS

Not a box of cereal, but a box of Wheaties. Not a tree, but an aspen. A car didn't pull into your space: a green Mini-Cooper did. A certain ex-president's affectionate intern wore not just lipstick, but Club Monaco Glaze lipstick and Club Monaco Bare lip liner. "Adopted a cat from outside a darkened Walmart storefront," is better than "brought home a stray."

Detail locates us in time and space. You can give us the era by telling us what song is playing on the radio: "'Sugar. Ah, honey, honey. You are my candy girl …' sang the Archies over and over the summer I was seven." Or, "My parents lived in a small brick ranch-style house in the suburbs, with a big picture window and a tiny cement slab in front."

The details also allow the readers to bring their own experiences to the page. Mention a Suzy Homemaker Oven and a female reader of a certain age will be rocketed back to the time when she was nine years old and cooking tiny pies with the heat of a light bulb.

Notice the specific names of things in this passage from my student Marsh Rose's piece about being a drug therapist in a county jail:

> There was only one place in town where Tammi Lynn could have gotten her tattoo. Donatello's Skin Design was on the lower end of the main drag, between a Harley-Davidson chopper shop and an adult bookstore. I elbowed my way past the small group thumbing through a rack of catalogues, past a silver-haired executive type in a Tarzan T-shirt with a young thing in black leather plastered to his side. I saw the two problem children of Doreen O'Reilly, the Dolly Parton wannabe checker down at Tiny's Market.

Notice how much more interesting this is than, "There was a tattoo shop on the lower end of the main drag. I walked in." Of course, if the tattoo shop was not important, this would be too much detail.

GIVE EXAMPLES

Whenever you make an assertion, back it with an example. When you tell me that he stopped at a water fountain when you said you wanted a drink, I'll get that your boyfriend's cheap.

When you say, "My grandmother tried to hide the evidence of her marital problems," add an example: "Every morning the covers on the twin bed in the spare bedroom were smoothed and tucked and flattened with precision, even if she had just risen."

One of my students wrote, "I didn't come from a drinking family," and then added this example: "For twenty years my father saved the annual bottle of scotch he was given at Christmas against the day my oldest sister Marcia married. When that day came and she married an Englishman, he distributed the booze frugally, exactly one bottle per table of twelve."

In "Out of Reach," a *New York Times* essay, Nancy Davidoff Kelton begins a paragraph with a general statement about her mother: "Her illness turned me to my father, whose presence in my life grew."

She follows this assertion with numerous examples: "We played casino and gin rummy every evening. When I went to overnight camp he stood at the bus window crying. He wrote to me every day. In the fall, we perfected my Ping-Pong game."

Want to convince us that your boyfriend's messy? Tell us you can write your name on the back of his toilet. If he's neat, say he aligns the pot handles on the stove. Don't tell the reader that your sister was artistic; say that, "She painted the outside of her claw-foot tub like a Rousseau jungle, tacked post-cards of Matisse and Klee paintings on the walls, walked around barefoot and dyed her hair black."

If you say, "I had to help my mother when she started dating," we have an unsubstantiated assertion. Give us examples, as my student Kathryn Kefauver did when she said: "At home I showed my mother how to control the spray-pump on her Chanel No. 5, to fluff her hair with a round brush, and to purge her speech of terms like 'necking' and 'going steady.' " (Notice she gives three examples — for some reason, humans like examples that come in threes.)

THE DREAD NECESSITY OF INNER EMOTIONAL LANDSCAPE

Jonathan Safran Foer, author of *Everything is Illuminated*, said that for him the key to good writing was, "Let me slow down and tell you exactly what I'm feeling."

If something happens in a piece and no one reacts, it almost didn't happen. You say your house burn down, taking with it everything you owned, and if you don't feel anything, we don't feel anything. An essay, like a memoir, is an emotional story. If it matters to you, it will matter to us. Let us feel what you're feeling. Have you ever noticed that in movies, every action is followed by a shot of someone's face, registering a reaction? If a child says to a stranger, "I'll go with you," a mother looks worried, or drops a tray. If a guy kisses another guy on the rooftop, the camera pans next to the shocked expression of his fiancé watching from a door. Even in a televised basketball game, every time something happens — a muffed shot, a foul, a score, a missed free throw — the camera moves to the coach so we can see his expression. Those feelings and reaction shots are called the *inner emotional landscape*. You have to describe what is producing the anger, joy, the fear in you so that we can feel it, too.

You show feelings by stating them directly, or by letting us pick them up from images and description. My student Anne Kaiser could have said, "I was worried as I drove to meet my son at the emergency room." Instead she gave us an image: "I chewed my fingernails again, getting the polish off in little sharp pieces of red, spitting the bits of nail on the floor of the car."

As the poet Stephane Mallarme said, "Paint, not the thing, but the effect which it produces." You are translating inner feelings to actions we can see (and thus pick up those feelings for ourselves). Let us see what you are feeling by whether you stand too close or look away. Shrug. Refuse to meet someone's eyes, paste the smile expected of you across your face, exhale between parted lips. Drawing lips back shows fear; dismay is revealed by pressing finger-nails to the lower lip, insecurity by sticking them in the mouth. You can anxiously scuff your shoes against the floor, nervously smooth your hair or fiddle with buttons, angrily spit your toothpaste right where you know your husband wanted to spit his, or flinch at his hand on your shoulder. If you're upset you may forget to use soap in your shower, or even forget you already took a shower. If you're scared you may find your fingers too weak to dial a telephone, or you may collapse on a chair.

Putting in feelings does not come naturally to me. When my agent, Fred Hill, sent several chapters of *Hold Me Close, Let Me Go* to New York, many of the editors who read it said they wanted more "inner emotional landscape."

I hated that phrase from the first time I heard it. I'm from a beer-soaked family background, which, according to a therapist I saw (for about a minute), means numb. My writer friend Wendy Lichtman, who was in my writing group when I worked on that memoir, had a teenage daughter herself. She'd stir impatiently as I read my pages aloud about allowing sixteen-year-old Morgan's boyfriend to sleep over. "What's the mother feeling when that happens?" she wanted to know.

I thought it was enough to say what my hell child was doing — skipping out of the house when she was already grounded, say — for readers to know how I felt. It seemed unsubtle to spell it out. I was like the late columnist Molly Ivins, who said: "I tend to treat my emotions like unpleasant relatives — a long-distance call once or twice a year is more than enough."

But — no emotion in the writer, no emotion in the reader. I had to learn to think like an actor: what do I feel in my body when I'm sad, or worried, or joyful? How can I express those feelings through action? It's like method acting, only you're playing yourself, making those interior feelings visible to an imagined audience beyond the footlights. Here's what I came up with to show what I felt when the boy slept over:

> We all went to bed, exhausted from the move. Some of us anyway: I kept hearing loud sounds of lovemaking coming from the room next to mine, groaning and bedsprings, and then a bed banging against the wall, and laughter. I found a pair of earplugs in my dresser drawer, stuffed a pillow over my head. Still, the sounds penetrated, and I comforted myself by imagining her hanging out on some street in another city, asking passersby for cash, her

unwashed hair stringy on her pale forehead. I imagined her sitting beside a car on a deserted road with her head in her hands, bloody from a car wreck. I thought of my niece Erin, off in Texas somewhere.

She was not any of those things. She was warm and dry and safe, and, from the sound of it, happy.

USE DESCRIPTION TO REVEAL EMOTION

A child's train left out on the rug can bring a fond smile or a surge of exasperation. You can show tenderness or impatience in the act of brushing an insect from a child's mosquito netting.

What you notice and what you don't also conveys feeling. If you describe a house as having empty cabinets and uncurtained windows that make it seem larger than it is, this description lets us know that you don't want to be there.

A burg you long to escape from will be full of eyes, old-timey stores, and a movie theatre that plays corny old movies. A town you left unwillingly will have friendly faces, a wonderful old five-and-dime, a movie theatre you could count on to screen *It's a Wonderful Life* for the entire month of November.

TRY THIS:
Describe a setting that has changed over time — a family home sold to remodelers, a forest or farm turned housing development, a city block demolished for a freeway. Focus on the details of the place, including weather, geography, people, and machines, letting those details imply your feelings about the change. Or describe a setting that has remained the same, but let readers see how your description of it reflects changes that have occurred in you over time.

In a draft of a memoir about her anorexic daughter, my student Eva Williams relates how she sent her child to Langley Porter, a psychiatric hospital in San Francisco. We know how she feels about the place from her description of it:

> It was a big brick building that I had walked past many times on my way to the nearby medical center. I had never been inside, but I'd pictured what went on behind the big double doors, behind the overgrown pine shrubs that seemed to be wrestling for dominance

with the aggressive ice plant chewing up the front lawn. Even the big oak tree in front of the hospital looked gnarled and twisted, more sinister than the oaks in front of the buildings on either side.

In *Tiger's Eye, A Memoir*, Inga Clendinnen shows how she feels about being in the hospital when she describes the gown she was made to wear:

> Social trappings are surrendered along with clothes and other valuables at the door of the ward. Abruptly naked, you are thrust into a vestigial smock. Starched, snowy, it rises high to the chin, but stops, incredibly, at the crotch, and at the back the little ties end with the ribcage. When you move, your buttocks show. It is at once lewd and sexless. An outfit designed for depraved choirboys. When you climb into the bed the bottom sheet strikes cold on bare skin, you feel thick tucked stuff under you, and chill with forgotten shame: rubber sheeting.

Let's look at my student Kat Brennan's memory of her parents on the beach:

> When my father bent forward to let her get his back, his gray-furred chest collapsed on his belly. He looked old and soft. He had on the felt hat he always wore at the lake, the one with the speckley quail feather tucked in its band. Mom capped the Coppertone, sat back down in her stubby plastic-webbed beach chair, and took a swallow from her gin-and-tonic. Her short, bleached-blond curls were so stiff with hairspray they remained rigid even in the wind that puffed up off the lake's surface. She might have been happy or sad or angry behind her sunglasses.

Notice how the details tell us what the narrator is feeling: This is a vulnerable dad, one who might not be around forever. Is Mom sad and vulnerable? No. The tension builds. Later the choice of verbs add to the bleak feeling we get — waves *slap*, a brother *stumbles* along the shore, his swim trunks *sag*, the minnows *spin* in furious circles. Every image does much more than paint the scene: it adds emotional complexity and foreboding.

TRY THIS:

Expand paragraphs from pieces you've already written, adding images, details and the narrator's emotional response to what is happening or being described.

Speaking of inner emotional landscapes, let's take a break from the how-to for now, and talk about ways to get your reluctant little self sitting down at the desk in the first place.

CHAPTER SEVEN

HOW TO TRICK YOURSELF INTO WRITING

Finding A Time And Place

Ways to Sneak Up on Writing

Lower Without Standards

Partners, Groups and Classes

Feedback: How to Give It and How To Take It

> I write when I'm inspired, and I see to it that I'm inspired at nine
> o'clock every morning.
>
> — Peter De Vries

Oh, boy. So much to think about, right? I've spent years learning and teach-
ing this stuff about writing and here I am throwing it at you all at once.
If I were you, I'd be feeling overwhelmed, like one of my students, Hank
Martinson, who emailed me after one class to say:

> Yesterday morning, as I was happily cranking out material, I was
> thinking, "It's about time I got an agent." This morning, after class
> last night, all I can think is, "It's about time I got an angle." An
> *angle*! Son of a bitch! Who even knew about an *angle*?

Forget angles and all that for a moment. Too much thinking about techniques will freeze you, ice over the well of your unconscious. You want to
know this stuff, but not all at once. Let's go back to the hot heart — getting
words on paper. I don't have to tell you how much gets between you and this
apparently simple goal. Writing is scary. It always will be. So we won't try
to face that beast. We'll tiptoe around it by changing the goal. That's what I
did when I broke a lifelong writing block by writing 500 words a day for my

friend Cynthia, my first writing partner. My goal wasn't to write something good. It was to write 500 words.

APPLYING PART (A) BUTT TO PART (B) CHAIR

Since you probably don't write standing up, let's get you sitting down regularly at a place where writing can occur. In other words, get in the habit of showing up at the same place at the same time in order to write. Habits are not only for nuns. If you don't have a habit, you have to decide all over again every morning that you are going to write. And how many times will the answer be yes?

They say it takes six weeks — or is it three? — to form a habit. Force yourself for that long to go from your warm bed to the computer at 6:30, so you can write for twenty minutes before work, and soon you won't have to force yourself.

Begin, as always, with a goal anyone can accomplish: just show up. March your sleepy pajama-clad self over to the computer at the agreed-on time. Don't require yourself to do any actual writing: you can clean out your junk drawer, play computer games, change the color on the screen, go through your pens and throw out the ones that don't work.

Develop a routine

Dame Edith Sitwell apparently did not sit well: she liked to lie in an open coffin for awhile before writing. Stendhal read two or three pages of the French civil code every morning before picking up his pen; Schiller kept rotten apples under the lid of his desk and would inhale the pungent scent for inspiration. Hart Crane liked to warm up by throwing a loud party, putting Ravel's "Bolero" on, and disappearing to write a poem that had come to him in the midst of the bedlam.

A PLACE

Where should you go? Doesn't matter. The library, a coffee shop, the park, a card table in the hall, the front seat of your car, or any other place that has no Internet or phone, no wash to do, no refrigerator, no pictures in emergency need of reframing. Flannery O'Connor sat for two hours every day at the typewriter facing the back of her clothes dresser so she would have nothing to look at to distract her. (I guess if she'd let herself look at the front of the dresser she'd spend the day rearranging her socks or painting bunnies on it.)

Tell the writing you're serious about it by giving it a special place just for it. My ex-husband Jim and I moved to Petaluma for three years when the kids were small, and he fixed up a shed in the yard for me as a writing studio. Our next-door neighbor Ruby came in four hours a day to stay with our kids, Morgan and Patrick. I couldn't come out of my shed, I mean studio — the babies would see me — and there was nothing to do in there but write. That's how I wrote my first book, *History of Petaluma, a California River Town*. I was proud of that book. It wasn't *War and Peace*, but it took me a year and a half to write and it put something into the world that wasn't there before. I'm not sure I would have written it at all without that quiet studio in the backyard.

A TIME

You love writing, find it almost sexually seductive. It is something you do for yourself alone. Yet that exquisite pleasure, or torture, gets cancelled in favor of almost anything — a lunch out, a visit with a grandchild, even a TV show. You wouldn't cancel a doctor's appointment to take your daughter to school, but your writing hour, sure!

The calendar is your friend. Deborah Santana, who lives over the Golden Gate Bridge from me in San Rafael, wrote her writing times on the family calendar — "2-5 Deborah Dominican College Library" — so her husband Carlos would, ahem, get over his evil ways and take them seriously. Or maybe it was so that she would take them seriously. In any event, now she has a published memoir, *Space Between the Stars*.

You can also use the calendar to pick a starting date for the project you keep putting off. (Be ready with the specific writing exercises you'll begin with — or use this one: Grace Paley said, "It's possible to write about anything in the world, but the slightest story ought to contain the facts of blood and money in order to be interesting to adults.")

No email monitoring during your writing period! No poring over home-exchange sites — that darling bungalow in Provence — or thinking, "I must just email this to my husband …" Think if Thomas Jefferson had email. He wouldn't have gotten anything done! He'd be too busy clicking on links and instant messaging Sally What's-Her-Name.

Try not to skip. If you don't write on Monday you feel less like a writer on Tuesday. Professional writers write every day, so you should too. Act like a writer and you will be one.

Also, there's a huge bonus to daily writing: if you scribble notes for only two minutes after you drop the kids at school, or spend five minutes of your lunch hour out in the car writing on a yellow pad, you'll carry what you're working on around in your head the rest of the day. You'll be waiting in line at the Brookstone store to return your Ipod speakers and suddenly realize that if you start the story with the car crashing through the fence, it will all fall into place.

It allows you to dream. If you lock yourself into your Jetta at lunchtime every day and write, you can while away your regional sales meetings thinking about the book, planning what to wear to the publication party, making lists of whom to thank as you accept the National Book Award. These days, a blog makes a good daily exercise — especially if you have readers who will notice if you don't post. Many books have begun as daily blogs, like that one by a woman who cooked something different every day for a year, and another one by a woman who accompanied her husband to Bosnia, and wrote home to her email list (I'm including an email list as a kind of blog).

Another bonus: writing comes from writing. You find many of your ideas while you're writing about something else. Maurice Sendak was asked how he came up with his monsters in *Where the Wild Things Are*. He said, "Originally I didn't want them to be wild 'things'; I wanted them to be wild horses. In fact, the original title was *Where the Wild Horses Are*. The dilemma arose when it became obvious that I couldn't draw horses. So I had to think of something I could draw."

WHAT? YOU HAVE NO TIME TO WRITE?

I heard that the writer Rumer Godden wrote many of her books in five-minute sessions between all sorts of terrible things happening (cobras attacking her children in the highlands of Kashmir, that sort of thing). And you have to do *what*, again? Return phone calls? Pay bills? Repot the agapanthus? As Robyn Carr pointed out in a *Writer's Digest* article, "There are hardly any writers, outside of the federal penitentiary, who got started because they had time to kill."

Not having enough time to write is an advantage. In one episode of the 70s sitcom "Roseanne," the star told her husband Dan, "It's always been my dream to write children's books." Dan promptly cleared out the basement, putting in an old wooden desk, and plunking a typewriter, pencils, and a stack of blank paper on it. "Now you can write!" he beamed as he and the kids tiptoed away.

Next shot: Roseanne in the basement sitting in front of an untouched stack of blank paper with a panicked expression. It was as if the world said, "So, you're a writer, are you? Go ahead. Write." And then watched, sneering, arms folded. She had a place to write, a time to write. Freed from little anxieties, she was ready to be overwhelmed by much larger anxieties, such as having no ideas or talent.

The same thing can happen when people go on sabbatical to write, or set aside an entire expansive retirement for that task. *Wait! I was kidding! Guys, don't leave me here with this ream of paper! Guys …*

When the kids were small, I had a full-time job as managing editor of the local city magazine. I did manage to do my 500 words a day with my writing partner, Cynthia, but the only luxuriously long day I had to write was on Saturday, when my kids were with their dad. (I had them on Sundays.) There was no use trying to work with the kids home. They leaned over my desk doodling pictures on my outgoing mail, their hair sticking up. They flopped down in the chair next to my desk that I learned to call the "wishing chair," taking advantage of my being trapped there to ask for parties, trips, Mickey Mouse sheets, dual cassette recorders and 4-wheelers or to inform me that I had a lot of elbow skin and my desk was really dusty. (They both declared they wanted to be writers, because it's obviously work you do at home in a robe.)

I had only Saturdays, so I wrote all day, interrupted only by the occasional plop as the neighbor pitched our basketball back over the fence. It looked like a handicap, having only that one day, but, perversely, it worked: If I had had seven days a week to write, I would have been going out to lunch, cleaning out closets, or fiddling with my photo albums, all with the intention of writing tomorrow. I didn't have that option. (My friend Janis, who read a draft of this manuscript for me, interjected here: "This is so true. I was more productive when I had only the two hours of my son Alex's naptime to write. I never let myself get distracted. I never even let myself go pee.")

Don't even have Saturdays? Let something else go. Ayn Rand said she accepted no daytime or evening appointments for thirteen years while writing *Atlas Shrugged*. She probably had no friends by then, but still. All those books. She also said she regarded the blank sheet of paper in front of her as her employer. She had to fill it. "If you do not regard writing as a job," she said, "self-doubt will necessarily enter your mind, and you will be paralyzed."

SNEAK UP ON WRITING

Ok, you have a time and place for writing. Now what? Time to freak out! No, time to set a kitchen timer. Writing often feels like a duty — I'm supposed to be writing! A timer means you have to write only until the bell rings.

My student, Cecilia Worth, described what it's like for her to write in short timed bursts.

> I do not stop for a minimum of 15 minutes. What I have found is that it will be weird and superficial for a while, and suddenly, like breaking through a long cloudy airplane run and seeing the green field below, I consciously put off the voice that tells me to stop because I have to go to the store, to phone, to lay off because the topic is garbage. Sort of like I'm waving it off, while writing furiously, saying, wait, wait, I just have to finish this. This is certainly not a new exercise, but it works every time for me. I believe that doing it impresses my subconscious that writing is indeed a priority. Once I did this every day at the same time for three months, at the end of which my piece on a patient with HIV was published in the Sunday *New York Times* magazine.

Put the title of your work on a small banner across your computer, or on an index card propped up above the function keys. Or, instead of the title put down an inspirational quote, something uplifting, such as, "Do you really want another decade to pass before you write this?" Tell yourself five times a day that you will succeed as a writer, or get ten essays published before the year is out, or whatever your goal is.

Write a sketch of yourself as a successful writer. Here's an example of an imaginary book blurb by my student Kathleen Gilheany.

> **Kathleen Gilheany** is a *New York Times* best-selling author whose recent work has just been nominated for the Man Booker Award. *G is for Guillotine*, a paean to the alphabet detective genre, has been described by *The Guardian* as two parts Kingsley Amis, one part Bohumil Hrabal and a soupcon of Lillian Hellmann, all dished up over steamy political background; detective fiction turned delightfully on its side. It is the most delicious piece of writing served up on an unsuspecting genre-reading public since Truman Capote's *In Cold Blood*.
>
> Gilheany's first published work, a slim cookbook parody, *I Have Stick, I Have Fire*, a series of cooking escapades revolving around her mother's kitchen, was first published in series by the *Ladies Home Journal* in 2008.

LOWER YOUR STANDARDS

What not to worry about when you sit down to write:
Is it any good?
Is it too short or too long?
Why would anybody care about this?
What if somebody reads it?
What if nobody does?

What to worry about:
Did I write today?

Change the Goal

A few years back Pulitzer-Prize winning poet Suzan-Lori Parks ("Topdog/Underdog") changed her goal: from writing a good play, to writing a play a day for a year. The subject matter for the plays, most only a few pages long, ranged from deities to soldiers to what she saw out of her plane window. Afterward those plays were produced all over the country at the same time, but that's not the point. The point is she came up with a way to make herself produce new work every day. A poet named David Lehman did the same in challenging himself to write a poem a day. "Writing a poem every day for several years will diminish the preciosity of your writing," he said. "You find yourself willing to write about things that don't seem obviously poetical in the 'kiss-me-I'm-poetical' sense, as Kenneth Koch put it."

I also heard of an inventor who refused to let himself get up on Saturday morning until he'd thought up something new.

Forget trying to produce good writing. Think it stinks? Make it worse on purpose. Pretend no one will read it. Pretend it's notes for a piece, not the piece itself. Fake yourself out. Acknowledge that you can't write, have no ideas and no time. Remind yourself that you're not really writing yet — this is still the warm-up. Maybe just make a note or two about what you would write, if this were for real. Force your fingers to peck on without worrying about whether you're just whining on the page, or whether that last sentence is a train wreck, and whether "train wreck" is exactly a fresh expression.

Forget that artsy crap about writer's block. Did your father suffer from pie salesman's block? Steve Martin said, "Writer's block is a fancy term made up by whiners so they can have an excuse to drink alcohol." His trick is to find a wonderful sentence in a novel, and copy it down.

> Usually, that sentence will lead you to another sentence, and pretty soon your own ideas will start to flow. If they don't, copy down the next sentence in the novel. You can safely use up to three sentences of someone else's work — unless you're friends, then two. The odds of being found out are very slim, and even if you are there's no jail time.

Trust Yourself

Yes, this book talks a lot about techniques, but much writing is instinctive. You do it the way you use language without knowing an adjectival phrase from a hole in the ground (like the man in Moliere's comedy who discovered he'd been speaking prose all his life).

The poet William Stafford likes to write in the early morning, when he's not likely to be interrupted. He doesn't worry about what he's going to put down on paper.

> I get pen and paper, take a glance out the window, and wait. It is like fishing. But I do not wait very long, for there is always a nibble — and this is where receptivity comes in. To get started I will accept anything that occurs to me. Something always occurs, of course, to any of us. We can't keep from thinking. Maybe I have to settle for an immediate impression: it's cold, or hot, or dark, or bright, or in between! Or — well, the possibilities are endless. If I put down something, that thing will help the next thing come, and I'm off. If I let the process go on, things will occur to me that were not at all in my mind when I started. These things, odd and trivial as they may be, are somehow connected. And if I let them string out, surprising things will happen .... my writings become coherent; the successive elements that occur to me are clearly related. They lead by themselves to new connections.

Stafford has learned that almost any event or memory, recalled with detail and image, plumbed for what else was going on then, will lead you to something important.

It's vital to ignore all the questions of craft at the spill-it-all-out-on-the-page stage. Let yourself ramble, let it go where it wants. Follow the macramé hanging on the kitchen doorway to the person who gave it to you and then come back to you huddled on the couch and about to realize you're going to leave your husband. My friend Joan Frank, the essayist and novelist I mentioned much earlier, became a writer when she was 40. Until then she wrote huge, soul-scourging letters to friends while working as an editor, bookmaker, typesetter, and so on —whatever job left her brain free for writing. But the letter-writing seemed to take over.

Here's Joan:

> I kept copies of all the letters — had some vague exalted sense of the letters' significance, but not able to articulate it. Finally a big epiphany in the middle of a letter describing turning 40. Knew I had an essay in front of me. Thus, knew it was finally time to get to

the writing absolutely nothing left to fear: not mediocrity, not grisly failure. Hallelujah! Began with essays and took workshops leading to fiction. Now do both —with complex feelings about it.

Begin with what is charged for you, even if you don't know why. Go crazy. Make a mess. Get everything down as fully and as fast as you can. You must make the person you are talking to feel this thing in their guts, and the only way to do that is to tell if from your guts.

Sometimes you have to keep writing until you get tired of being nice. Write mean stuff. Write secret stuff, like how you never have a bowel movement while you're traveling.

At first just write a lot of pages. Don't feel as if you have to write the story in the order it happened. Or even that you have to fill a whole page. Fill a basket with stories — you can fit them together later.

Getting Stuck is Good

It can mean you're getting to the heart of things. That's scary, so you stop. I've noticed that overly fluent writers, those to whom words come fast, have trouble going deep in their writing: sometimes you need that block. If in the middle of your story you don't remember what happened next, or don't know what else to write, stop, walk around, and go back to the place you were writing about. Feel what it's like to be in that room, what you see around you, who is there with you and who isn't. Then start writing again.

Start Anywhere

Start with this phrase: "And another thing about ..."
If a memory surfaces — the sandy, sloping floors of summer rentals, a pipe on a window sill, two horses drowsing with their heads close together — put that down, especially if strong feelings come up as you start writing.

Notice what excites you in what you've written. Even if it's only a single phrase or sentence, start a new exercise with that as the beginning, just to see what happens.

You may want to polish each sentence before you go on to the next one. But how do you know what sentences you'll keep, when you haven't written the thing to the end yet? If you keep stopping to fix things, the unconsciously brilliant writerly you — Jackson Pollack throwing pailfuls of paint onto the floor — will get pushed aside by the fussy little critic sniffing, "No one will want to see paint splatters. Look, it's all over your shoes."

Write as fast as you can, and the work will be authentic. You might even do this in longhand, at a café, not at the computer. You won't have time to lie, or to pull back from revealing. Your best work can come to the surface, your intuitive grasp of patterns and structures, without you there to wreck it with your second-guessing of which words to use.

Get in touch with the fitful little unit that is you — you with your distinct memories and little knot of tics and compulsions and flights of giddiness, you with your habit of coming home at lunch to play the harp, you a street cop with a secret mania for origami. Only you lost your liver after eating mushrooms and had to lie down for a year and a half. Only you became a volunteer flying to Guam after tornadoes when you had never even had a meal alone in a restaurant before. Nobody can tell your stories; no one has your warped sense of humor, nobody drank vodka out behind the 7-11 with Debbie Hendricks the way you did.

You had your eyes done in Bangkok or you bought a new bed with each new boyfriend? Let's hear about it.

Know how Tom Wolfe got started? He was writing a story on a hot rod and custom car show in California for *Esquire* magazine when he found himself blocked. He knew how magazine pieces were written, and his wasn't coming out right no matter how many times he crumpled up the page and started over.

He gave up. He called his editor, Byron Dobell, and Dobell said, well, ok, just type up your notes and send them over.

So Wolfe started typing at about 8 pm in the form of a memo that began, "Dear Byron." He started with the first time he saw the custom cars. Freed of any need to plan the piece properly, he typed like a madman. All night. At 6:15 a.m. he took the 49-page memo over to *Esquire*.

At 4 p.m. Dobell called to say he was taking off the "Dear Byron" and running the rest in the magazine.

That became *The Kandy-Kolored Tangerine Flake Streamlined Baby*, a benchmark in journalism. Wolfe had found his voice by letting the writing flow out however it wanted to.

YOU SHOW ME YOURS; I'LL SHOW YOU MINE: GETTING SUPPORT FROM OTHER WRITERS

If you have the discipline to go off and just scribble in a mountain cabin somewhere, sending for groceries once a week and banging out pages in a fury until the cabin is knee-high in them, I applaud you. For everybody else, I would advise you to get support — classes, partners, groups.

When I don't have a writing partner or a group, I bog down, or go in circles, or endlessly rewrite. My writing partners have been like people with flashlights on a dark highway. They tell me which roads not to take, when to speed up, when to slow down. When I'm discouraged, they say, "It's fabulous, just keep going!"

Writing partners provide you with deadlines. They are objective — they see what's on the page, whereas you see what you thought you wrote. They ask good questions.

Below is a writing partner's comments on an emailed early section of my memoir, *Hold Me Close*.

> Wonderful, wonderful scene. I love the stuff about your relationship with your mother, and the way it ties in here. You might want to find a slightly more graceful way into the memories of your mother. I think Morgan's statement about you getting married in high school is a good start. Maybe she can ask you what your mother thought about that?
>
> Morgan was on bed, crying at my new coldness. "You're so mean! You never used to talk to me this way."
>
> "What do you expect?" I said helplessly. "After all the shit you pulled."
>
> "You did a lot of stuff, too." she sobbed. "You got married when you were still in high school! You did whatever you wanted to!" HOW DOES THAT MAKE YOU FEEL?

I went to sit in the kitchen. I looked at the white plate my mother had stolen from our wedding IS THIS YOUR WEDDING TO BILL, OR THE WEDDING MORGAN IS REFERRING TO? and then returned to us with pink roses and congratulations painted on it. NICE I shifted my gaze, and there on the opposite wall was the black and white photograph of my mother that I'd found and blew up, her standing at the sink with a cup of coffee in her hand, wearing a man's shirt with the sleeves rolled up and a denim skirt, exactly the way she always looked.

Morgan was still crying loudly, and suddenly I remembered one day when I was 16. I had called her at work. THIS GOT CONFUSING - I THOUGHT YOU CALLED MORGAN, STICK WITH YOUR MOTHER HERE As I waited for the busboy to get her, I could see her coming hurriedly to the phone, wiping her hands on the cloth tucked into her black belt, her notebook in one pocket of her black skirt, the other NOTEBOOK?

Already sagging with the quarters (that always lined the bottom of her big black purse) RIGHT NOW THEY'RE IN HER POCKET Even while picking up the phone near the dishwashing room, she'd be mentally juggling ten items, the Petrale sole ready for pickup, the table that had already asked twice for more coffee, the paper tablecloths fluttering on the tables on the grass and needing to be anchored with ashtrays. YOU MIGHT KNOW A LITTLE BIT TOO MUCH HERE — MAYBE YOU COULD SHOW US THIS WITH SOME OVERHEARD DIALOGUE OF YOUR MOTHER'S BEFORE SHE GETS ON THE PHONE

I pair my students off as writing partners, in and outside the class. Here's what a few of them had to say about that experience:

Elizabeth Crowe

I was at first a wee bit disgruntled with the writing partner I was assigned in class. Making a narrow-minded snap judgment across the room, I thought she looked like a kook. And I was right, but what I didn't know was how that would enrich the exchange. And the exercise of just tapping out 500 words bumped my writing into high gear. The act of just churning the thoughts out took a lot of the preciousness out of the process, also leaving little time for that critical, judgmental voice that resides in my head.

Patricia Holladay

Every Monday my writing partner and I exchanged reports on our writing accomplishments from the previous week, plus a projected report for the coming week. When I sagged on Wednesday, sometimes on Tuesday, the thought of my report propelled me forward to write at least the minimum I projected. I often exceeded that minimum once I began.

Karen Bird

My writing partner and I agreed to send each other an essay every weekday for two weeks, beginning the following Monday. We established no topical constraints, and vowed to use your model of positive and supportive feedback. I bought a yellow highlighter.

The first few days were exhilarating. The requirement of placing an essay in the mail each day was supremely motivating.

I admired the work my writing partner, Judy, sent me, and took pleasure in commenting on it and marking the passages that really spoke to me. However, when she returned the first essay I had written, I read it with amazement. I did not remember those sentences.

I had forgotten I had written about that topic. This happened with my second, then my third essay. I enjoyed the shock and surprise of reading my own work. Nine days of producing a complete essay each day was astonishing for me. Like the process of easing oneself into good physical shape with increasingly rigorous workouts, I now sense how regular daily writing practice may be essential to warm up my fingers, infuse my mind with new discipline and thought patterns, and establish a regimen of vigorous, sustained, serious writing.

Finding Writing Partners

I recommend my website, Matchwriters.Com, for finding like-minded writing buddies. Otherwise the best way I know of, outside of asking friends, or trying to get into a writing group, is to take a class and find your partners there. You want to find someone who is about your speed, so that one of you is not functioning as the teacher, the other as student. You will probably have several writing partners before you find the one for you. Things can go wrong for a lot of reasons — she'll pick at your grammar or give you blanket praise, or just not get you, or vice versa.

Also, if your writing club is to succeed, a writing partner must respond in the agreed-on time span (usually within a day). Otherwise, you are right back where you started— staggering into the kitchen in your robe and saying to yourself, "I will get some words down on paper today," and then two hours later deciding that you don't have time, but you will make it up by writing four hours tomorrow, and tomorrow brings a long boozy lunch with a college friend — and so it goes.

It's not easy to be a good writing partner. You see your partner's email with its attachment, but you don't open it because one of the books at the publishing house you work for has come in with the title page printed upside down and you have to call the printer in Singapore and argue him into paying for the mistake and rectifying it overnight. You got stuck behind a burst water main coming home, and then have to find your son's soccer cleats among the sodden belongings in the trunk of your car, and get water boiling for pasta, and....real life will always intrude. When the average American woman counts up the time she needs versus the time she has in a day, she comes up 21 minutes short. So we're busy.

But reading a partner's email takes only fifteen minutes, and if you do it, you get all the wonderful things a good partnership can give you.

If one of you says, "Oh, I don't have time right now, but go ahead and send me your stuff," it stops working. *It must be reciprocal.* That is the other value of the right writing partner: you're in it together. The partner is not just rubbernecking a passing accident. The partner is both paramedic and on the stretcher next to you at the same time.

Once you have a writing partner, you will either meet in person or, more commonly, exchange work on email on an agreed-on schedule. (I used to do it by regular mail, waiting eagerly for the post each day.) When you get your partner's emailed piece, just open the email and hit Reply. Now you can type in comments. Use all caps so it's easy for your partner to tell your comments from her prose. I use the word "NICE" in place of yellow highlighting.

You can also send the exercise as an attachment, if your computers are compatible. The advantage is that you can open the attachment in, say, Microsoft Word, which has a cool option under Tools called Track Changes. You turn it on and can make all sorts of suggestions without wiping out the original document.

Classes

Unless you get an instructor who seems to hate writing (yours in particular) and writing students (you in particular), almost any class you take is worth it if it makes you write. My students take my classes again and again, simply because when they're not in a class they stop writing.

What happens in a class? In response to assignments, you dig up stuff you'd put away as crap and find it wasn't so bad. Hearing what's said about another writer's piece makes you see a similar problem in yours — whereas it's hard to hear direct criticism of our own babies.

And you spend evenings with really smart people. At the first meeting of my classes the writers come in and settle on my motley collection of couches and chairs below the bay windows and white shutters in the last silence that their class will know. It's like seeing people who have no idea that in six months they will be cheerfully using each other's toothbrushes. They don't know, as they dart glances at one another or stand nervously in front of the tiny marble fireplace with its sputtering Duraflame log, that they will soon arrive and leave together; that, before they know it, friendships will spring up and three of them will be renting a house on Cape Cod so they can write together during the month of August.

....

THE CRAFTY WRITER
Workshops you pay for are the best — it's too easy to quit when you made no investment. I have a friend who wants to tell his story but has the misfortune to be very rich. I have no idea how to make him write.

....

GROUPS

When I read book reviews that take a writer to task for lengthy digressions or embarrassing personal sections or a snippy tone, I think, *Her writing group would have pointed that out, and she'd have fixed it. If she had one.*

A writing group is a small group of writers who meet on a regular schedule, usually at one another's houses, and read or listen to one another's work. The work can be emailed ahead if it's long, or read aloud on the spot. Some groups do writing exercises together, too.

Like a writing schedule, and partners, groups pull writing out of you whether you think you're in the mood or not. Your meeting is coming up Monday night, so you scribble something on your lunch hour.

When I was working on my memoir about my teenaged daughter, *Hold Me Close* (more on that book in the memoir chapter), two writer friends, Wendy Lichtman and Janis Newman, asked me to meet with them on Monday afternoons at Janis's Victorian on Liberty Street. Janis was working on a book about adopting her son from a Russian orphanage. Wendy was writing for magazines. I'd walk over to Janis' house with the dog, and Wendy would drive from Berkeley. The three of us would settle down with our tea and bottled water and our print-outs of what we'd emailed to each other over the weekend, and begin.

They asked questions. How did I react to finding an empty bottle of Bacardi rum in Morgan's desk? Did I feel guilty when I read Morgan's journal? When she became pregnant and the subject of getting an abortion came up, and Morgan said, "I would never do anything like that to my baby," did I feel accused, since she knew I'd had an abortion at 17?

We'd move on to Janis' latest pages from her book on adopting Alex. I'd point out that here was yet another scene set in a dismal Moscow restaurant; didn't they ever go anywhere else while waiting for the adoption to go through? I would exasperate Janis with my insistence on knowing exactly where everything was in relation to everything else. Wendy and I would tell her when she was being too tough on the adoption coordinator — the cat hair on the woman's skirt when she stood up, for example. And then we'd weep over the scenes at the orphanage, when wan, 16-month-old Alex took his first step into his American mom's waiting arms. Wendy would be working on a piece about getting her brother to stop smoking, or about the series of young people who have started their adult lives in her guest room. Janis' son Alex would come home with his dad, and the dog, Wagner, would quietly chew up the fallen pages of my piece. The phone would ring. But on we'd talk, into the afternoon, Monday after Monday, week after week. During those months, I wasn't writing a book (an undertaking so scary that many of my friends just refer to it as "the thing" or the "project") I was just writing three pages for Monday.

When I began teaching classes, I always encouraged them to go on without me as a writing group, since they were by then on intimate terms and had a shared vocabulary for critiquing work.

Here's an email from student Bernadette Glenn about one of them:

> Our class is still meeting twice a month. We meet as a "large" group with Clare and Diana who come into Berkeley from San Francisco. Sandy, Rodney, Valorie, Valerie and I meet twice a month at Sandy's house. Valerie had a piece accepted by *Parent* magazine for a grand sum of $750. We were all thrilled. Rodney had that very moving piece he read to the class about the death of his sister published in a Wisconsin paper. Clare had a wonderful piece in the *Examiner* about comparing New Yorkers to San Franciscans. I thought it was a really well-written. Sandy had the piece she did for our class (about not wanting to throw things out) accepted by a magazine and got a nice check for it, too. It's amazing how our little group has bonded. We're all writing and encouraging each other. But beyond that, there's very good work being done, being taken seriously and being published. I like it that we all look at the writing process as something vital to our lives and take it seriously, not just a hobby or for fun.

FEEDBACK: HOW TO GIVE IT

Be silent always when you doubt your sense;
And speak, tho' sure, with seeming diffidence:
Some positive, persisting fops we know,
Who, if once wrong, will needs be always so;
And make each day a Critic on the last.
"T is not enough, your counsel still be true;
Blunt truths more mischief than nice falsehoods so;
Men must be taught as if you taught them not,
And things unknown propos'd as things forgot.

—Alexander Pope

You may hesitate to critique another person's writing. Don't worry. It's a skill you build as you go, like any other. In the meantime, you're an attentive reader, have been all your life, and can help in many ways. You may not know how to fix something, but you know when something's wrong.

When Cynthia and I exchanged short essays in our writing club, we'd add little comments at the end. On a piece in which I said that if I held up a sign it would say, "Will Work For Praise," she scribbled, "I like the point you're making here, but it doesn't work very well for me on the page. You seem to switch abruptly from specific examples of how you need praise to generalizations about people."

On a piece about how women bond by whining to each other, she wrote, "This is SO true. But don't end with the part about your mother. Put her earlier and then say maybe she's an exception, or that maybe when you get old there's so much to complain about that there's no pointing in even starting. Come back to yourself at the very end." On a piece about trying to improve my writing habits through hypnosis, she wrote: "This is really tied together now, and the stories are fascinating. I don't love the ending, though, even though I highlighted it. It works okay, but I'd like a little of how you felt after the experience."

I loved it that her comments were so specific, and so often included ways to fix things.

Suggestions for Critique

Be encouraging. Don't comment on style, word choice, punctuation and other sentence-level matters in early drafts. You're to be congratulated for knowing a dangling modifier when you see one, but let your eye skip over it. There's plenty of time for that later. Your partner is trying on outfits — seeing if the red blazer will work all right with the long black skirt and the low heels — not going out the door to the interview. Polishing comes much later, when your partner knows which sentences she'll keep, and she IS (to keep the metaphor going) about to step out the door for the interview. Then you definitely want to let her know about the spinach in her teeth (for example, that she said "tenant" when she meant "tenet").

In the tender early stages writers need to know what they're doing right, not wrong. Say things like, "This is the part that interested me" or "This is what I want to hear more of."

Read for pleasure, making notes only when something — too long a digression, abstract language, lack of clarity — interrupts that pleasure. The Squaw Valley Community of Writers asks workshoppers to consider each piece as if it has already been accepted for publication — an approach that respects the writer's accomplishment before going on to offer suggestions to make it better. When I review manuscripts for memoir writers, I upload them on my electronic book reader, the Kindle, so that I can carry them around and read them like a real book, as if for pleasure. That way I am not looking for what's wrong — I'm hoping to just keep reading as I sit on the park bench, and not have to get out a pencil. It's an approach that assumes the book works.

Point out what works — in scene, or dialogue or images. Where were you especially moved? Be specific. "I loved your metaphors" is not as convincing as "I loved it when you compared the fat cat to a collapsed parachute." Avoid an authoritative tone, such as "This isn't working for me" (unless it's a toaster). "This might work better if?" or "It might read more effectively if?" are good gentle openers.

Also: Respond to the writing, not to the story being told. Don't commiserate, or give advice, or scold, or launch into your own story of being caught in a hurricane. A good way to keep the exchange "writerly," as I call it, is to refer to the protagonist of the piece as "the narrator," not as "you." Not: "Why do you think that about your mother?" but: "Why does the narrator think that about her mother?"

How's the pace? Tell her where your mind wandered, where you got bored. Where do you want the writer to pause, tell more? Where do you want him or her to speed up?

Ask for examples, and for ways to help the writer expand or deepen the piece. Ask *why* a lot. Why would Paula believe her mother? Why was the narrator sent to her aunt? What was she hoping would happen? Why does the mother start drinking?

Does the essay have an angle? If it doesn't, help the writer kick it around.

Is the tone working? If at any point the narrator irritates you or seems angry, let the writer know.

When does the conflict start? At what point do we become really interested? (It's usually the same paragraph.) Is the story chronological? Should it be? It's often more effective to jump into the middle of a story, and fill in the back-story once we're hooked.

Be gentle. Keep in mind that your writing partner used all the courage she has just to show her work to you: she doesn't have any left to defend it from attack. Be mindful of the gulf between your response and what she is hoping to hear. I blush to say I have not always been gentle myself. I returned a scene to my friend Janis with a comment that began, "I'm afraid this needs a lot of work." Full of myself, full of how I would write the book, I allowed myself to dwell on what wasn't working, not on what was. Janis said that when she read that first sentence she didn't dare read on.

Recognize when the piece works just as it is. Mark Childress, author of *Crazy in Alabama*, led a workshop in which the participants filled the air with ideas for the writer. He listened to it all and then said, "All this story lacks is a stamp." He told the writer to send it to *The New Yorker*, where it was published.

Feedback: How to Take It

> Honest criticism is hard to take, particularly from a relative, a friend, an acquaintance, or a stranger.
>
> —Franklin P. Jones

When I ask for criticism on a piece, criticism is the last thing I want. When I say, "Tell the truth," I mean, "Tell me in what ways this impressed and astonished you." My student Kristin Lund summed up a lot of our true feelings about feedback:

> I only wonder what you're really thinking if it is something truly original and pithy about my seminal work that you would like to share. For example, if you're really thinking, "This is the most poignant essay I've ever read on the agony of having a beloved ferret mistaken for a rat," think on. However, if you are really thinking, "Just kill me now. Don't make me sit here through any more of this crap dying of ennui," feel free to keep that to yourself. And just

because you use words like *ennui* doesn't make you any better that the rest of us. It just makes you boring in French.

It would be nice if all critiques were along the lines of, "This is perfect! I hate you! Send it out!" However, being a writer means learning to take comments, negative and positive, without crawling under a rock. As they say, no pain, no gain.

The advice you resist most may the advice you need most. My student Lynn Befera said:

> My best work and the most genuine language often comes a place of occasional joy, but mostly from pain and humiliation. The thing I can't and don't want to write about is absolutely the thing I must write about. It's important to hear thoughtful, constructive, honest criticism — it's the only way I can trust my writing partner, and it's the only way I can grow as a writer.

I was in despair when I got my editor at Broadway Books' first letter on my manuscript — she didn't understand me or my book at all! It took at least a year, by which time the book was out — to realize how insightful she was (I have quoted from that letter elsewhere in this book).

"I don't know, Dare," my mother said to me when I gave her some early pages of *The Granny Diaries*. She nodded her head doubtfully at the sheaf of typed papers on the coffee table. "The part about the names seems to just go on too long." I seethed, and picked up my pages huffily, but later I improved the section by editing down the part on names.

If you curl into a little ball when someone offers suggestions for revising your writing, then you probably can't be a writer. I know a talented would-be author of children's books who responds to critique as if he's been told he's a worthless person. His books are not published, and that's too bad, as he's a good writer.

You know a critique is good when the ball in the pinball machine goes in the slot. You think, *Yes*. It might zero in on something that was nagging you about the piece, and you find yourself slapping your forehead — "I knew I'd have to change that part!" Or it points out the strengths of the writing to you in specific ways, so you know what you're doing right. Your fragile little seed of excitement blooms rather than withers.

Caveats:
Never make decisions (such as tossing your piece, or sending it right off) based on one person's opinion.

Avoid readers who think their job is to find fault. It can do damage that goes beyond mere discouragement. It wrecks your forward momentum, forcing your attention back to what you've written instead of forward to what you want to do next on the piece.

Be clear about what you want from your readers. Maybe you just want to know if what they heard is what you said. Maybe you want detailed suggestions for revision, even if it means tearing the piece up and practically starting over. Maybe you just want praise at this stage.

Get responses EARLY, before you've poured six months into the piece and will be found stocking up on lethal Tylenol if a partner timidly asks you if you really need the scene where the aunt loses her umbrella. As we'll see in the next chapter, writing is revising — a process in which a good partner is invaluable.

Husbands, Wives, And Mothers as Readers of Your Work
Hmm.
My husband Bill was my unpaid column editor, reading first drafts and steering me away from my sophomoric attempts at satire. "Not your voice," he'd say, tugging it out of my hand. He's in publishing, which means he had some practice in telling life and writing apart. Generally, though, mates aren't the best choice of readers for you. It may be hard to get the straight scoop. Your husband doesn't want to lie next to a seething creature who's just been told the short story she spent the summer working on was "fine, dear" or "all over the place."

I heard that every time Virginia Woolf finished a novel, she'd take it to her husband Leonard to read, and he'd say the same thing every time: "Well, you've done it again, Virginia."

That's what you want to hear from your spouse.

CHAPTER EIGHT

REVISING THE ESSAY: THE FLOWERS OF AFTERTHOUGHT

Revising: The Process

Sentence Polishing

How Do You Know When You're Finished?

> Revision is one of the true pleasures of writing. I love the flowers of afterthought.
>
> — Bernard Malamud

When you read over what you've written, avoid the following two reactions:

1) This is wonderful, I must send this to the newspaper immediately!
2) This is such crap. I must destroy it.

Chances are it's neither. Most of the time, a piece works only after the writer struggles with it for a while — and by struggles, I mean finds a structure for it, puts in what's missing, takes out what we don't need.

In a way, most of this book is about revision, not writing. It's easy enough to bang out pages without a clear grasp of what makes an essay or a book work, but it's hard to revise that way. It's like fixing a car without knowing how the engine functions. You just make a lot of banging noises, and maybe break something.

You know how it is: you reread the piece you began with such enthusiasm. You are aghast. So much has crowded in that you would be hard-pressed to say what it's about anymore. What began as a moment on a train turned into the story of Uncle Desmond who always smelled of onions, and then somehow into a screed on how your whole family blames you for the sinking of the boat in Noyo harbor near Fort Bragg. It has become *My Life, The Mini-Series*.

So what do you do, throw it out?

Of course not. When I worked for a magazine, I'd watch the photographers drop off their work at the art department. From what you see of their work in a magazine, you'd think they shot brilliant image after brilliant image. But I watched them drop ten rolls of film on the desk, all taken of the same plate of steak. Many of them would be terrible — out of focus, badly lit, some merely all right. One would be just right.

It's almost not an exaggeration to say it's the same for writing. You have to expose a lot of film to get what you want.

THE DESIRE TO REVISE IS WHAT SEPARATES THE WRITER FROM THE JOURNAL-KEEPER

My dad, an old reprobate named Gene Daly, was a good example of a writer who never turned his prodigious talent into a set of skills. I know, because he wrote a million words, and sent them all to me to sort out for him. As old age neared, and no place waited at any family hearth for a man who'd left a wife and six young kids, he'd found a green-paneled 1953 bakery truck with grass growing up through its floorboards, got it running and wandered off to follow the blue lines on the California map. He was ecstatic in the Mohave Desert, writing on yellow pads by the light of the sun coming in what he called his "picture window" in the back of his truck. For want of anyone else to write to, he wrote to me, the one of his kids who had become a writer herself. I could hardly keep up with reading it all, acres of cramped handwriting, yellow sheets rolled together and smelling of tobacco.

Dad hoped I would shape his million-word journal into finished pieces and get him published. "I don't send you dolled-up, amended, stylish, severely-edited versions of what I scribble. Order is not my thing. I just send it. Your job to whip it into shape," he said.

My dad was a carpenter, and, as I told him, it was as if he sent me a pile of two by fours he'd sawed, a box of nails and some spools of wire and said: "I think these are pretty good. Would you mind whipping them into a house?"

He knew no one was going to publish his journal as it was. He once added hopefully, "I heard that Kafka's daughter pulled his writing out of chinks in the wall, smoothed them out."

Kafka, I wanted to retort, was dead by then, or he'd have done it himself. I pored over every line of my father's, hungry for messages from a dad I hardly knew. But no one was going to publish his journal as it was, the raw outpourings of an agile mind, but each thought as it came out, not a word or sentence blotted. He wrote that way because it was the only way he could get his thoughts down without crumpling each page in disgust as he'd done when he was young. (He should have held on longer, until the invention of blogs.)

Professional writers revise more, not less, than less experienced ones. As Thomas Mann said, "A writer is person for whom writing is more difficult than it is for other people." Even the best of them expect to do many, many drafts before they're satisfied with a piece. S. J. Perlman said for him 42 drafts were too many, 37 too few, but 39 were just right. (Then he grumbled that he was giving away his trade secrets.) Maurice Sendak has said he takes two years to finish one of his children's books, though each is no longer than 380 words.

You may not, ahem, enjoy revision. My friend and student Jackie Winspear said in class one night that rewrites reminded her of sewing class back in her English school. She'd hand in her apron, and the teacher would make her rip out all the stitches and say, "Try it again, Jackie."

I don't know how her aprons turned out, but I do know that the effort you put into rewrite is worth it. Dashing off a piece that works immediately produces one kind of confidence. But real confidence, the kind that becomes part of you, comes from picking out those bad stitches and putting in better ones, until you finish it.

I once got an assignment from *Departures* magazine for a 3,500-word essay on San Francisco. Another writer had been given the assignment first and had his piece rejected, so the pressure was on.

I started in June. I interviewed people and worked on the piece all summer, even taking it on vacation to Tahoe and working on it amid the bottles of suntan lotion, with my husband fidgeting in the background hinting that the trails got hot by noon. In September, I was done. I proudly gave it to Bill to read, then kind of hung around the kitchen. I scrubbed the counter and listened for little intakes of breath, watched for little involuntary smiles.

There weren't any. He scowled, blew his breath out. He knew how hard I've worked on it, he knew it was due in three weeks, and he knew he had to live in the same house with me, and still he turned up his hands and blurted, "Jesus, Sweetie, this is a mess. I don't even know what it's about."

That was a bad day. I saw myself calling the editor and saying, "I just can't do it, I'm sorry," and leaving him with a big hole in the magazine.

Then I tried one last thing. I called my friend Mary Roach. Now the famous author of *Stiff, Spook* and *Bonk*, she then made $90,000 a year writing funny articles about sumo wrestlers and holes in the ozone in Patagonia for national magazines such as *Vogue* and *Discovery*. Mary met me at Chevy's restaurant on Van Ness. She is skinny, a perfect ectomorph, with blonde hair, green eyes and a long face. While she read through the sheets I handed her, I shoved a spoon around an empty margarita glass.

Then she looked up. "But this is so good!" she exclaimed. "You have all these great quotes and this great stuff about the city being like an Italian hill town."

I brightened. She and I came up with a rough outline for the piece, and when I went home I went home and followed the outline, and turned what had been a mess into an essay I was kind of proud of. The editor put it on the cover.

The lasting payoff, though, was that the next time I tried to succeed at an article, I'd remember that terrible feeling of not having a clue how to write the piece, and how I had finished it after all. I'd think, *I felt this way before, that I'd worked and worked and the piece was crap, and then in the end I made it work.* That memory would become part of me. That's why you sometimes have to keep working on a piece until you nail it. So you will remember that you were able to do that. In my experience, there are just two kinds of writing: writing that works, and writing that doesn't work *yet*.

REVISING: THE PROCESS

Find ways to read a piece of writing as if you are not the one who wrote it. Let time go by if you can. Writing is like a piece of pie: let it cool before touching it with a knife. The Roman poet Horace is said to have waited eight years before deciding if a poem of his was any good. A day or two is good, too.

· ·

THE CRAFTY WRITER

In a hurry, and no one around but the dog? Here's a tip: Go to View if you're using Microsoft Word and read your piece on "reading layout." The piece is laid out on the screen like a book, and glitches stand out.

Even better, print it out. You can't see the whole thing on screen, and the medium is different — things you don't notice on the computer screen leap out at you. (All those repeated paragraphs, for example.) You can take your work to a cafe, along with other stuff you like to read, so that when you come upon your own writing it's almost as if it's someone else's. I uploaded parts of this book to copy shops and had it sent to me as a bound booklet that I carry in my backpack. I could work on it anywhere, and it cheered me up to pretend it's already a book.

Read it aloud. I am amazed — and so will you be — at how much the ear picks up that the eye doesn't. You won't have to search for awkward or boring parts — you'll *hear* them. Read it to someone else, or ask someone to read it to you. You might even want to read what you've written into a tape recorder. Listen for the emotion in your voice to find "hot spots" in your story; concentrate on those. You'll find the gaps between what you thought you wrote and what you actually wrote.

Notice when your attention wanes — perhaps at unnecessary explanations, too many names without accompanying identification or images, too many abstract statements, too little tension.

Down at the café, bring out your highlighter and mark the wonderful bits, even half sentences and single words. Jot notes — where the holes are, what scenes you maybe don't need — whatever. Cross out what's boring. You can't fix boring. Carolyn Chute told "Writers Ask":

> I write a lot of junk. On and on and on, all this junk. But every now
> and then this dramatic moment happens, so I lift that out and put
> that aside. And then I write all this junk: They're brushing their
> teeth, they're sitting there, they're looking around — you know.
> Then something will happen and I'll pull that out. Because those
> are the only strong things.

Do what she does. Cross out the junk, keep what's good. Write new stuff to
fill in the holes. Repeat.

THE CRAFTY WRITER

All your writing, whether it's outtakes from stories or abandoned drafts or stories that prove to be no more than anecdotes or the "darlings" we'll talk about
in a minute, becomes part of your inventory. Don't throw out anything! Your
best writing is mixed up with your worst. If you throw out the worst, you
risk throwing out the best. Get it all down and sort it out later. If you were a
miner, would you really expect to find an entire mountain of solid gold?

REVISING: THE WRITING
Give us the context

It's surprising how many writers will neglect to tell the poor reader where
we are, when it is, and who is talking to us, thus plunging us into a tale that
takes place nowhere in particular, at no time in particular, and happens to no
one in particular. You can give us this needed context in one sentence or two:
"We were in Venice, my friend Joan and I, girlfriends on a mission to find
culture and wine among the alleys and canals of the old city." Or: "I sat in
the back seat of our green Dodge Dart waiting for my mom. We were parked
outside our friends the Zasloff's house on a street lined with towering oaks."

Here's a good one from my student Shannon Falk: "When I was eight months
pregnant with our first child my husband was diagnosed with metastatic stage
four cancer — if the disease was rated in the same way as hurricanes it would
be a Category 5." Sentences like that are enough to tell us where we are and
what's going on, so we can relax as you get into the story.

Also, give chronology and distances. In a narrative, chronology holds the piece
together. People must know the *when* of it. If you're going to your mother's,

we need to know where you're coming from, where she lives, and the distance between. We need to know how events are related in time: "a few weeks later," or "the next Saturday," or "two months later." If you're writing something lengthy, you might even want to write out a timeline. You don't have to know exactly when something happened. You can say, "sometime later," occasionally. But even "sometime later" gives a nod to our need for chronology.

Get the Show On The Road: Beginnings

A piece about your divorce should probably not start with, "Once I had a bulldog named Clyde." Don't begin with the alarm clock going off or the drive to the party or the day you met the person you're writing about. If your piece is about not wanting to push your angry brother up a hill in his wheelchair, don't start in the hospital where you learned the extent of his injuries. An injured person became injured, a person on a hike always started out on a hike, a car on the side of the road was once on the road, a person getting a divorce once met her husband and married him.

Try starting where the trouble starts — at the bottom of the hill, your loathed brother smoking a forbidden cigar and cursing you for your weak arms — and flash back to the past as needed to fill us in.

If you start too far back you will be forced to summarize, skip over stuff, and generalize to catch up — little of which produces good writing or tension. You also risk boring us by giving us background information we don't yet care about and thus won't remember anyway. Chekhov knew this. His advice? "Tear your story in half and start in the middle."

(Also, by the way, don't introduce everybody at once, as in a crowded hospital room scene. Bring dotty Aunt Frances in where you need her, not before. Otherwise, we will be thumbing back through the pages, thinking, "Who is Aunt Frances again?")

After the exciting lead you can take us back to the beginning, if you need to, because we're hooked.

My student Lucas Peltonen begins in the middle of things in an essay called "The Hospitalization."

> The hospital orderly left me sitting in the wheelchair in the middle of the hallway in direct line of the blowing wind and snow. He trudged down the hall to the wide-open double doors that were allowing New York City's biggest snowstorm in 50 years to blow into the hallway. Tufts of snow were already forming along the walls. I was wearing nothing more than my underwear and a thin hospital gown with a gap running up the back.

Once we are sufficiently worried about a patient left in the teeth of a gale, Lucas can go back to the beginning of the trouble, "I attended a personal training seminar all day, but I had known from the moment I woke up that morning that I was in trouble…"

The shorter the piece, the earlier you bring in the conflict

Since I had only 700 words back in the days of my newspaper column, I often tried to present the problem in the first sentence:

> A month ago I turned off the TV, over Morgan and Patrick's ago-nized protests.

> I'm starting to resent being told to live in the moment.

> I had walked the streets of San Francisco for twenty-three years, and this was the first time I'd seen a gun.

> I went to Napa for the weekend with a man not my husband, while his wife was away.

A first paragraph can also include a surprise that makes us want to read on. Your reader has happened upon your piece, but he has other things on his mind as well: the "check engine" light" has come on in his car, his wife's life coach thinks he's a liability, and his job as bookkeeper at a construction firm is not that secure. You have to say something pretty startling to yank him out of his world and into yours, as my students do in these examples:

> The first time I saw my son, Alex, he was 11 months old. (Janis Newman)

> I just hung up the phone with my mother (in her sixties), who was visiting my mother-in-law (in her eighties). They were getting stoned. (Mary Patrick)

You want to know how to meet a man? I'll tell you how to meet
a man. Put an ad in your local paper for a 1977 Chevy Malibu
Classic. (Penny Wallace)

ENDINGS

You might look back at your first paragraph and grab an image or idea from
it, to give the reader the comforting feeling of having come full circle. Once
a travel editor complimented me on how in the first paragraph I had my boyfriend tying the little red sleeping bags that belonged to my kids to the top
of his Volvo, and in the final paragraph had the sleeping bags falling off the
car. I hadn't even noticed the sleeping bag thing, but of course I didn't tell the
editor that. (Later I discovered it's called a tieback ending.)

Cut

Ask yourself if a particular passage has a function in the piece. What were
you trying to achieve by putting it in, and what if anything would be lost if
you took it out?

Murder your darlings. That section on the trip to Paris — it's lyrical and fine,
isn't it? Everybody *loves* the Paris section. It may be the thing you started
with. But the reader doesn't need to hear about Paris to understand why your
marriage blew up. Any sentence, paragraph, scene or chapter, no matter how
powerful, which serves no story purpose is just so many wasted words.

Highlight it, right click to select "cut," and then back away from that laptop!
It's for your own good.

Practically every writer you can name has something to say about cutting out
such "darlings." Samuel Johnson advised, "When reading something you have
written, if you come across a passage that seems to you extraordinarily fine,
cut it out." The poet Ted Roethke said, "Any fool can take a bad line out of a
poem; it takes a real pro to throw out a good line."

Or move that darling down to the bottom of the page under "Notes." That
way it's nearby, where you can comfort yourself by visiting it anytime you
want to remind yourself what a fabulous writer you are. One writer cuts her
darlings out of her pieces with scissors and put them in a manila folder she

called her Goddess file. Whenever she needs a boost, she opens the file and admires those cuttings.

Whatever you do, don't just delete it. In fact I constantly save changes to a new file name, because I never know when I might want to go back and get something from an earlier version of a piece — or when I might accidentally delete something, and need to get it back. If you saved the new version under the old name, the old version is gone, like a fish in an Osterizer. Computers today have limitless room. Don't delete any drafts until the piece is in the magazine on the coffee table. (You might also email pieces to yourself, for safekeeping.)

Rearrange

Fiddle with the order of the paragraphs, taking out the dull anecdote about the aunt and putting in a better one about the uncle who liked to knit. Find a way to connect the story of the past to something in the present (or else it's just nostalgia). Not "The first snowstorm that I remember did not fall until I was nine" but "It's snowing today, so hard that it's as if a mattress burst above my window. The first time I saw snow like that I was nine."

Add

Keep going back to the well and adding new stuff, especially if you've cut the boring parts and left gaping holes. Go to the computer and think aloud on it. Start with this sentence: "What am I trying to do in this piece?" Race along for a page or two, see what else comes up.

Or add three lines under every existing line, to force yourself deeper. I have my students do this exercise, especially those who seem to be able to race through a complex story in three pages. For example, if you wrote, "I woke up. I got dressed," you'd have to add three more sentences in between "I woke up" and "I got dressed."

> I woke up. *Something had brought me up from the dream about a giant squid wearing sunglasses. I listened, but heard only the backfire of a car passing on the street. My muddy pants and shirt lay in a heap on the rug next to the bed.* I got dressed.

Abandon

If you work and work and don't seem to be getting anywhere, sometimes the piece you sat down to write will turn out to be the scaffolding — not worth keeping in itself, but what you needed to get somewhere else. I once wrote five or six drafts of a piece on a book I heard about called *Auntie Barbara's Tips for an Ordinary Life*. The piece never came together. But the word "frump" kept calling up memories, since my dad used to call my mother that. On the eighth or ninth draft, I found myself writing about my mother hanging out the wash.

> My mother used to wash our clothes in a wringer washer and then hang them on the lines, and as she pinned up each garment, she said, she thought about the child it belonged to. She never wanted a dryer, even after we could afford one, because it would steal this from her, this quiet contemplation.

That was the only line I liked in all those drafts. So I threw out everything else, and started again with that one line. I got a pretty nice column out of it, and then a book, called *Slowing Down in a Speeded-Up World*.

Sometimes it's worth admitting that something just can't get better — probably because it lacks essential elements, as we've been saying — and abandoning it. You might create a creative vacuum into which a waiting work will rush. It's like breaking up with a bad boyfriend before you can meet a good one. Believe me when I say an entire project into which you've poured years can be one big darling that needs murdering. Don't bring up the childhood memoir I've been alluding to here and there in this book or I will weep.

SENTENCE POLISHING

Only when you are pretty sure that the piece is roughly ready — the lead works, the tone is right, you've fiddled with pace, you like the ending as it is — can you allow yourself the pleasure of fiddling on the sentence level. What follows here is a list (in no particular order) of ways to improve sentences.

I assume that you have grammar and punctuation under control. If you don't, for Pete's sake have somebody who does look over your pieces before you send them out, or you'll look like an idiot.

Okay, one paragraph on punctuation. Do get it straight that in American English the quotation mark goes *outside* the period and the comma. Also use two hyphens to indicate a dash -- like that. When you type a space and one or two hyphens between text in Microsoft Word, the software automatically inserts an en dash (–). If you type two hyphens and do not include a space before the hyphens, then an em dash (—) is created. (You have to turn this feature on.)

Don't capitalize the names of the seasons. Or capitalize directions unless they mean regions: I went *east* until I arrived at the *East* Coast. If you live in the Bay Area, don't capitalize Bay unless you say its whole name: San Francisco Bay.

On to the more important matter: editing your sentences for clarity, crispness and originality.

Identify People on First Mention
Don't assume we know who "we" is.

"The door to the parlor was always locked. We went in there only around Christmas."

Who is "we"? We can guess it's you and your siblings, but that's what we're doing – guessing.

Show Where People Are
"When I returned this volume to my father, I said to him, 'Teach me architecture.' "

Where is the narrator? Where is his father?

Instead write:
"When I went into the study to return this volume to my father, I said to him, 'Teach me architecture.' "

Choose the Right Word
Did your boyfriend "leave," "flee," or "wander off"? There's a difference. Were you "examining" the price of beef-flavored jerky treats in Safeway, or were you "checking" them?

Choose a Tense—Past Or Present—and Keep It Consistent
With the sun falling before us, we were enveloped in a blanket of peace. (past)

Suddenly the wail of a car horn interrupts. (present)

Present tense adds immediacy, past tense a sense of depth. The past tense is best for most purposes, so use it unless you have a good reason not to.

Omit the Observing Filter

"I noticed that he wore two vests one on top of the other."

We know you're the one observing the scene. It's tighter to say: "He wore two vests, one on top of the other."

Avoid having your characters start or begin to do something, unless the rhythm of the sentence demands it

Instead of, "He starts to write," say, "He writes."

Death to Adverbs

Adverbs modify verbs: instead of "moved quickly," why not, "darted" or "ran"? "Extremely beautiful" is less powerful than "beautiful" — and for that matter "beautiful" tells us very little. English is a rich language. Why say "looked longingly" when you can say "gazed"? "Moved cautiously" when you can say "crept"?

Write with nouns and verbs, not adjectives and adverbs. (I almost said with lean, muscular nouns and verbs, but those are adjectives. Damn.)

My student Metece loved adverbs and adjectives. She wrote:

> Never one to pass up a *shining* opportunity for worry, I was *busily* fretting over the mountain of *unfinished* paperwork that loomed *accusingly* on my desk. I had just *begun* brooding over whether I'd gotten overcharged by that plumber who had *hastily* fixed my leaky toilet last Saturday, when it hit me: I felt good. After thirteen months of feeling *perpetually* exhausted, as if some *efficient* vampire was *systemically* draining my life blood, I *actually* felt healthy again.

Look at the passage. What does "busily" add to "fretting"? Isn't all paperwork unfinished? Isn't all "looming" accusing? All vampires can be assumed to be efficient unless an inept one comes along to say otherwise. The one word I would keep, or at least keep the meaning it wants to convey, is "hastily," as it's important to show the plumber did the job suspiciously fast.

When I said as much to Metece, my student from the above example, she laughed. "I still cling protectively to my adverbs," she said in a note, and enclosed a batch of red Christmas balls to hang from my tree, each with an adverb written in gold leaf. One of them, of course, said "protectively."

Other mushy words include: *almost, appears, eventually, practically, basically, finally somehow, sort of, really, usually, basically awfully, quite, ultimately, utterly, kind of, actually, definitely,* and *very.*

I would also steer clear of "Trust me," "trusty," "let's face it," and "Don't get me wrong."

Often you reach for an adverb when the real problem in the sentence is a flabby verb —with the chief culprit being the verb "there is." Why use that weak little auxiliary verb to say, "He was skiing down the hill" when you can say, "He skied down the hill?"

Scan your prose for slacker verbs. Instead of, "We were on Highway 10, going like quicksilver," you could write, "A quicksilver drive sucked us down Highway 101." Use interesting verbs, such as "pebbled under the skin" as opposed to "collected under the skin."

"There was a man standing on the corner" can be "A man stood on the corner." "There was a fire" can be "A fire broke out."

Never use the word "literally" at all. You will mean figuratively, like the cookbook author who said she *literally* cooked recipes in her head. You see it used wrong all the time — I just read a newspaper piece that quoted a broker saying, "People have literally picked up their house at the foundation and shook it upside down like a piggy bank." I have another in front of me, from San Francisco *Apartment Magazine*, which says that when people find out they might be able to buy a house, "You can literally see the light bulb come on over people's heads."

Also, "disinterested" does not mean "uninterested."

Put the Action of the Sentence in Chronological Order

Not "My ex-husband and I bought tickets to a B-52's concert shortly after we'd moved in together" but "Shortly after we'd moved in together, my ex-husband and I bought tickets to a B-52's concert."

"I may offer my seat to an elderly woman going home on the bus tonight" can be "Going home on the bus tonight, I may …"

Present Participle Nitpicking

Experiment with substituting this construction:
"Putting down her glass, she turned to face him."

With this one:
"As she put down her glass, she turned to face him."

Such constructions aren't wrong, but the pros rarely use them. You can rewrite them like this:
"The airport's over there, " he said, pointing out the window.

He pointed out the window. "The airport's over there."

"Well, that's that!" she said, putting the car in gear and pulling out onto the street.

She put the car in gear. "Well, that's that!" she said. She pulled out onto the street.

Beware of Body Parts Acting on Their Own

Not, "My eyes looked away" but "I looked away."

Not "My hands fiddled with the clasp of my purse" but "I fiddled with the clasp of my purse."

When quoting your own interior thoughts, use italics, not quotation marks. *Who doesn't know that?* she thought.

Also, go easy on interior monologue. Editors view it as a sign of weak writing, and large amounts of italics are not easy to read. While you're at it, limit rhetorical questions, too. *Why had I come here? What was I expecting to find?*

Avoid clichés

Work like a dog to get rid of clichés. They're like coins that have been handled too much. My friend Janet Fitch said she stared at a row of palm trees for an hour, trying to figure how what they were like. Mops? No, she'd heard that. She needed a fresh metaphor.

Never write anything you're used to seeing in print. "Chills ran up and down my spine." "The mother of all writing courses." "A heartbeat away from the presidency."

We all sink into a chair when we hear bad news, and feel the hair standing up on the backs of our necks when we're scared. You may have to write down ten familiar images until you hit on something new.

THE CRAFTY WRITER
Print out each paragraph on its own page for intensive review.

HOW DO YOU KNOW WHEN YOU'RE FINISHED?

> Thank heavens for deadlines. If they didn't exist, the process of revising and editing would go on forever.
>
> —student Maureen Leahy

How do you know when you're finished? When you catch yourself changing stuff and then changing it back. Or when you can't find anything in the piece to fix. You like the lead, the ending; the tone seems to work. The point you're making is clear but you're not hitting the reader over the head with it. The images are vivid and original. It's the right length.

You're finished. Back away. You don't want to be one of those people who begin dusting in the basement and are found in the attic twelve hours later polishing jam jars. (Or like the painter Pierre Bonnard, who would sneak into museums and rework his canvases.)

E.B. White had an agreement with his postmaster: once White had sent something off, the postmaster would not fish through the stacks of outgoing mail for it so White could make more changes. He was sending those pieces out for publication, of course, which is why we sweat and polish and rewrite: because the writing is not complete until it is in the hands of a reader.

How to deliver it into those hands is the subject of the next chapter.

CHAPTER NINE

WORDS FOR MONEY: PUBLISHING YOUR ESSAYS

Sending Work Out

Where to Publish

Hooks

Sweat the Small Stuff

Acceptances

Nothing beats a byline for a solid rush. I first felt that rush when my local paper, the *Marin Independent Journal* held a contest for the best comments on the Generation Gap. Inspired by the fact that they printed my sister Nora's effort in the paper, in the 18-to-21 age category, I cribbed notes in the library and scribbled something about how weird our parents were about money (won't even pick up prescriptions if they decide they cost too much) after growing up during the Depression. The paper printed it and gave me a prize of $125. It was the first money I made from writing. My name in that paper, not to mention my name on that check, was like what an addict must feel shooting up: How soon can I feel this again?

Of course, I did have to *send* my piece to the paper before it could accept it. The editors who publish essays, on the Web, or in newspapers or magazines, won't break into your living room and demand to be allowed to publish your work. You must find their address or their email, study the spelling of their name, attach your document or paste it in, and then press *send* (or stick a stamp on the envelope and put it in the outgoing mail, depending).

I know. It's like going out of your way to ask people to be mean to you. You write fifty drafts of the heart-stopping story of how you and your dad were reconciled at last in a bar at five in the morning. You put the last and finest draft in the mail — perhaps walking out to the mailbox on the corner so the mailman doesn't lose it among his fistful of red Netflix mailers. After all that you might get back, not a tearful acceptance ("Is it true that you will allow us to publish this beautiful work?") but a Xeroxed note saying. "This doesn't meet our needs at this time." If you get a response at all.

Why run into the street knowing the odds are good that you will be flattened by a truck? If you don't show your work to editors, they have no chance to not like it. Keep it in a drawer, or show it only to those special someones who can be depended on to exclaim over it. That way, you can warm yourself at the fire of your genius without anybody throwing water on it.

Or, if that sounds cowardly, mail a piece to the hardest magazine in the country to break into and then give up on being published when it's returned. My friend Tanner, a bank vice-president, did this. He worked hard on a piece about his boyhood in Mississippi and sent it to *The New Yorker*. When the magazine said no, he crumpled up the letter, put away his pen and went back to reading Civil War novels all weekend with his feet in the open oven for warmth.

It worked: he never again had to feel the pain of having his work rejected by an editor. Nor, incidentally, the joy of having it accepted.

Which it would have been, eventually. There's scarcely a publication in the country that does not include essays by freelancers, from *The New York Times* to the Op-Ed pages of sleepy town newspapers. NPR broadcasts essays. Online magazines such as *Salon.com* and *Slate* fill page after page with them. Humorist-essayist David Sedaris is a star.

SENDING WORK OUT

Of course it's scary. One student told me, "I'm not afraid of heights, or bears and rapists, but I'm scared to death of looking stupid, of having to give up my dreams, of having to realize that I can never be published in the *New York Times* Sunday magazine. I don't want any of those things to happen, but the fear of them happening seems to paralyze me. And yet, when I pick up Oprah's *O* Magazine, or I read an essay in *Real Simple*, or even *The New*

Yorker, I think, "I could have written that." That's the worst, isn't it? Seeing a piece that you could have written yourself in print?

Most of my students have been published. I have thick binders filled with their newspaper, magazine and Internet publications. Many of them are now professional writers. Here are some of their emails to me:

Evelyn Strauss, writing to share news of a sale of a piece on hypnosis to *Science* magazine:

> I forgot to say the most important thing, Adair — that it is so much FUN and so incredibly COOL to try to capture important moments in words. I just love that! I get such a RUSH when it's working, when I'm back to whatever moment it is and slowing it down so I can dig into it and capture it and translate it into words. And then it's so fabulous when I can tell it worked for the readers. That's more powerful than releasing that it's good. I don't give a rat's ass about good per se.

Kathleen Denny:

> We just broke out a bottle of champagne. This morning I got a UPS delivery of galleys for the August issue of *The Sun* magazine with my little contribution all set up so I can make corrections. So it looks like I'll be in that issue. And late this afternoon I got an email from the editor of *NurseWeek* saying that my article on the medical mission to Guatemala is in the south central edition. She'll send me copies. Check is on the way. This is lovely, just lovely.

Marsh Rose said of a piece about car repair:

> I sent it out and eight months later my phone rings at 7 a.m. A woman on the other end sounds as if she's hyperventilating and says she's an editor at *Cosmopolitan,* has my manuscript and wants to talk about it. I say, "Knock it off, Mom. It's too early." She convinces me who she is and says (I will never forget this), "We'll take it."

Holly Rose (no relation to Marsh Rose, above) had a piece accepted at *More Magazine,* and emailed me to say:

They love it, it's just what they wanted, and since they are editing it down to a running length of 2,000 words they are going to pay me ONLY $3,000.

THREE THOUSAND DOLLARS!!!!!!!! Excuse me, I have to go faint.

Christina Boufis emailed me to say,

> I attended your workshop at the writer's conference last weekend and wanted to follow up and let you know how you helped me land a piece in *O*, the Oprah Magazine. I'd taken your First Person Writing workshop in Corte Madera several years ago. You asked us to write five quirky (or odd) things about ourselves. I wrote a piece that I titled "My Big Fat Greek Hair" from that assignment. And one afternoon, in a moment of bravado and having had a large Peet's coffee, I called the articles editor at O Magazine. Her outgoing message said something like, "We do not work with freelancers. We do not take unsolicited pitches. Do not leave a message. Do not send a manuscript." Basically, go away. I left a message anyway giving her the title of my piece. She called back thirty seconds later and asked me to email it to her. While they didn't take that essay, they took another piece. So I wanted to thank you. It was a great assignment.

My student Jessa Vartanian, a 30-year-old high-tech writer living in San Jose, became one of several revolving columnists in the "Our So-Called Lives" section in Sunday living section of the *San Jose Mercury News*.

She made it happen. She put together samples and a cover letter and sent them in, but then heard nothing for three months. The editor finally called to say she was leaving the paper and was passing Jessa's stuff on to the features editor, named Holly.

"Two or three months later," Jessa said, "Holly called me out of the blue to say she wanted to run a piece. After that I kept sending her stuff. I figured you make a contact, you keep your face in front of them. I kept saying, by the way, I'd love to be a regular contributor. She called a month later, and then again, to run pieces, then called one day to say she wanted to take me on as a regular basis."

Jessa did it for two and half years, receiving $75 a column (she wrote mostly about dating). "It's the exposure that matters, not the money," she says. The satisfaction for her? "I open my guts and say what's going on in my life. I think everyone has the same basic thoughts but people don't say it out loud, so I think it's comforting when people can relate to the same experiences I've had. That's very satisfying."

These students found that if you write a good piece, and keep sending it out, sooner or later it will be published. There's a vast hungry maw out there that needs your work, legions of editors who are paid to read your submissions and put them in print. Few writers take gladly to this step in the process — selling — but once you start doing it and start getting pieces accepted it won't seem so daunting. You may never be thrilled at the idea of sending your work out to strangers for judgment. However, eventually you will establish a list of editors who like and look forward to your work, and you won't have to slap the bushes to see what flies up.

WHERE TO PUBLISH

Let's look at a quick overview of the markets for the personal essay. All of this information is now on-line — see the list of writer's resources at the back of this book. Or just write "submissions (name of publication")" into Google and see what pops up. (Although I should caution you that putting the word "essays" into a browser tends to give you a list of people who will do your college homework for you.) Keep in mind that the information below, like anything in print, may be out of date by the time you read it. Check the Net.

Local Newspapers

Newspapers are a good bet for first-person essays. They publish far more of them than they used to, and, unlike most magazines, they're generalists — they appeal to everybody and cover a wide range of subjects. These days you can find first-person essays on feature pages, on op-ed pages (for their location opposite the editorial page or opinion and editorial) and in many special sections. Start by sending pieces to local publications, not overlooking the free ones, the neighborhood shopping guides, anything. Neighborhood papers use essays, too, and often set them up nicely on a page by themselves. The *Noe Valley Voice* in San Francisco, for example, has a "Last Page" section that features essays by local freelancers.

Local publications want local pieces (and local writers, too). Stay alert for ways to tie what you have written to something happening near you. If developers are tearing down historic houses to build a mall and you once lived in one of them, bingo.

(Or send the piece to the region where it happened. One student's piece about a fellow worker killed in a volcano in Hawaii was published in the op-ed page of the *Honolulu Star.*)

Refer to the local place in the piece: "At Yoshi's the other night …" or "I was walking on one of the Mount Diablo trails …"

Internet
When you publish on the Internet the rules change. Depending on the site, you can write to any length, use swear words, email it in. Many of my students have published work in *Skirt! Magazine*, which appears both in print and online. One issue had about 16 personal essays, up to about 1,200 words: one on depression; one about spring, the season of being dragged to weddings by soon-to-be ex-girlfriends; one by a married woman who likes to sleep alone.

After the piece appears on the Web, you can print it out, and it will look like any other clip (or attach the url to your outgoing email so everyone can enjoy it). A *clip* is a copy of a piece that has appeared in print: writers who propose a piece to a magazine editor will often enclose clips to show the editor what their writing is like. Or, these days, often a writer might just direct an editor to urls where her work can be read.

Salon.com, which publishes smart and topical personal essays, offers advice for contributors that is typical of many on-line publications:

> We ask that you please send the text of your query or submission in plain text in the body of your e-mail, rather than as an attached file, as we may not be able to read the format of your file.
>
> If you wish to contribute, please spend some time familiarizing yourself with Salon's various sections and regular features. Please put the words "EDITORIAL SUBMISSIONS" in the subject line of the e-mail. You can find the editor's name on our Salon Staff page. And please tell us a little about yourself — your experience and background as a writer and qualifications for writing a particular

story. If you have clips you can send us via e-mail, or Web addresses of pages that contain your work, please send us a representative sampling (no more than three or four, please). Unless your pitch relates to breaking news, please send your submission during business hours.

We do our best to respond to all inquiries, but be aware that we are sometimes inundated. If you have not heard back from us after three weeks, please assume that we will not be able to use your idea or submission.

Magazines

Many, if not most, print magazines publish personal essays, usually at the back. I pick up issues in doctor's offices and go right to the back page, where I usually find a standing feature called "Last" Something. They are often light pieces, well-constructed and fun to read. A typical month: Steven Lewis writes in the "Last Word" of the *Ladies' Home Journal,* "The world can be divided into those who will let a telephone ring off the hook when they are even mildly indisposed and those who would cheerfully trample small children and flower beds rather than let it hit the third ring." Carrie St. Michel writes in *Good Housekeeping's* "Light Housekeeping" section about her eight-year-old son's obsession with moussing his hair. Constance Resemble writes in *The New York Times* travel section about how she wished she were a more intrepid traveler but she really liked seeing places from little trains.

The catch is that while newspapers are aimed at everybody, most magazines are narrowly targeted. Each magazine's demographics are different. *Ladies' Home Journal* readers are 38 to 42 years old. *More* targets women over 40. I sold a piece to them called "The Reluctant Grandma" and another on how in middle age we bristly daughters start to take it easy on our poor (but maddening) mothers. The *Redbook* reader is college-educated, married, and anywhere from late 20s to early 40s. *Cosmopolitan* is aimed at college students. I sold something like 24 pieces to its now-defunct "On My Mind" section (I called my husband Bill my boyfriend, which I hope is still part of his job description).

I know you blanched at that list of familiar supermarket titles — you don't read them, and so you can't imagine writing for them. Don't be fooled. Magazines are great outlets, and those simple little essays are not so simple. The writer knew the magazine, what it had published before, who the readers were, and what the editors were looking for. The best way to tell the audience (demographic) for a magazine is to look at the ads. Advertisers don't throw their money around — they know exactly who buys the magazine. If you look in a magazine and don't see advertisements for diapers, send your piece on hiring that under-caffeinated princess for your two-year-old's party elsewhere.

Just to give you some examples so you see how many places there are to sell work to:

Redbook runs first-person essays about dramatic or pivotal moments in a woman's life. *McCall's* likes essays on things that are always present in your life but you never hear about — like a piece on the flags people fly outside their houses. "My Turn" in *Newsweek* publishes an essay a week. One of the best (and probably hardest to get into) outlets is the "Lives" column in *The New York Times* Sunday magazine. They are looking for provocative and fresh viewpoints. The maximum length is 900 words and payment is $1,000. They also publish the "Modern Love" feature in that paper's Sunday style section. *Fine Gardening* has a regular feature, "Last Word," that runs a personal essay usually in a gently humorous vein; a recent one was about people who label their plants.

The Bark, which covers canine culture, uses "at least a couple of essays in each issue," according to editor Susan Tasaki. Past examples include a woman who researched the language of dogs after she noticed her own puppy "laughing" and a woman who sees dogs in a new light through the eyes of her children. They're looking for 1,200 to 1,500 words.

Brain, Child is a literary magazine, dedicated, it says, "to the meatier issues of motherhood." In a recent piece, a white mother discussed fixing the hair of her adopted African-American baby.

Plenty magazine looks for witty personal essays of about 750 words exploring a humorous or moving experience in the realm of "going green." Past essays include a mother who gave up her gas-guzzling car to become a pedestrian and a woman who owns an eco-friendly home in the mountains. *The Sun* runs a number of literary essays, some of them pretty long. Past examples include a story about a woman in a relationship with an abusive drug addict and a story of a Fulbright scholar who comes to terms with her prosthetic leg while living with a troubled host family in South Korea. *The Sun* pays from $300 to $750 for essays.

It's smart to check out corporate magazines, too. There are thousands of these custom magazines, such as *Safeway Select*. They lack the glory of *Vanity Fair*, admittedly, but they pay well and are much easier to get into — everybody's too busy mailing pieces to *Harper's* to notice that the Neiman Marcus magazine runs nice little essays.

The airline magazines love little insider destination pieces. (Just make sure your city is on their route.) I did pieces on San Francisco's microclimates and the sea lions that live at Pier 39 for American Airlines' *American Way* magazine. One of my students sold it a piece about Jelly's, a salsa place on the San Francisco waterfront that is so cool that people take cabs there directly from the airport.

Creative Non-Fiction has themed issues. They feature the best new creative nonfiction writers and are open to personal essays. Guidelines and upcoming themes are posted on their website. They pay $10 per printed page.

Backpacker features a regular "Backcountry" section that runs 1,200 word personal essays about lessons learned backpacking. Payment is $.60 to $1.00 per word.

Bereavement: A Magazine of Hope and Healing is dedicated to helping people through grief. This publication is looking for personal experience pieces of 2,000 words or less. It doesn't pay, but offers writers international exposure.

Cup of Comfort, the bestselling anthology series, features creative nonfiction stories and narrative essays about experiences and relationships that comfort, inspire, and enrich.

Field and Stream has a regular "Finally" department that runs an essay of 700 to 800 words every month. Send submissions to them at Field and Stream, 2 Park Avenue, NY, NY 10016.

Fourth Genre is a literary magazine centered on creative/literary nonfiction. They welcome personal essays.

Hope Magazine, Humanity Making a Difference pays $50 to $2,000 for personal essays about how people have successfully coped with challenges.

Literal Latte is a New York City-based literary magazine that considers personal essays of up to 6,000 words. The editors of this lively, high-quality literary magazine publish at least one previously unpublished author each month and claim to find 90 percent of their material in the slush pile. ("Slush pile" means the pieces that are not commissioned, but come in unsolicited.

Literary Mama: Reading for the Maternally Inclined is an online litmag that publishes several short creative nonfiction pieces rooted in the experience of motherhood every month.

OnEarth Magazine publishes personal essays on nature or the environment.

Reminisce seeks short personal essays that have a nostalgic quality.

The Threepenny Review, a San Francisco based literary tabloid, pays $200 for personal experience essays from 1,500 to 4,000 words. They do not accept electronic submissions, but guidelines are available on their Web site.

Tin House pays $50 to $500 for unsolicited articles and more for assigned articles. The personal experience essays that they print cover a number of topics.

Travelers' Tales considers personal, nonfiction stories for publication. They pay $.10 per word. Issues are themed. Upcoming themes are posted on their guidelines page.

Smithsonian Magazine prints essays on the "Last Page" that range from 550 to 700 words and usually have a humorous tone. The editors warn, however, that they want personal narrative, not jokes. Payment ranges from $1,000 to $1,500.

Radio
Many of my students have read their short (two minute) essays (300 to 375 words) on topics on local interest over the radio on Perspective on KQED, our local NPR station. (http://www.kqed.org/radio/perspectives/submissions.html)

NPR's *This I Believe* seeks personal essays. Be sure to read the essay-writing tips on their site.

HOOKS: WHY THEM? WHY THIS TOPIC? WHY YOU? WHY NOW?

Whether it's a local paper, a national monthly magazine or an Internet site, you want to offer the publication a reason to publish your piece in this particular publication at this particular time. These are called hooks. ("Hook," confusingly enough, is also used as a term meaning to hook the reader into reading a piece). My student Rita Hargrave sent this note to the *St. Louis Post-Dispatch* in November of 2008 and got an acceptance by return email.

> The toughest domestic challenge for President-elect Obama and First Lady Michelle when they step into the White House won't be housebreaking the First Puppy or choosing a china pattern. The real battleground will be what to do with Malia and Sasha's fuzzy locks. Press or Perm. Afro-puffs or pageboy. The age-old struggle between African American mothers and daughters. I hope the enclosed essay, "The Trouble with My Hair," will interest the readers of your newspaper.

Topical

Relate your piece to something that is happening in the news. If you once dated Prince Charles, and he's coming to town, that's an angle for a piece on princes, on dating, or on your sorry relationship history. If you used a Wilson tennis racquet to become junior league tennis champion when you were 12, and Wilson is going out of business, there's an angle for a nostalgic piece. If the news is full of Olympic ice-skaters, hit editors with your piece on taking up ice-skating at the age of 41.

Seasonal

My student Margee Robinson, who lives in San Francisco, sold a piece on earthquake preparedness to the *San Francisco Chronicle* Home and Garden section, sending it in just before the 100th anniversary of the quake in San Francisco, so it was both topical and local.

Seasonal topics are almost as good as topical ones. Valentine's Day is a good bet for your piece on, say, matchmaking, or your third-grade love, the one who bought you a stupid bottle of cologne encased in a stupid pink plastic swan.

If you're writing about a family dinner, why not make it Thanksgiving? Publish your piece about your mother's breast cancer in October, which is

Breast Cancer Awareness Month. My student Pat Milton published "Stalking the Winter Coat" in the *San Francisco Chronicle* in April. That's late for winter coats, but she fixed that by putting in that she bought the coat in an end-of-season sale. You can get calendars that list all sorts of events, well-known and as obscure as National Salmon Fishermen's Week. If you have a piece about volunteering in school, send it out in time for it to appear in late August, when school starts up. (Magazines plan six months ahead of time, so keep that in mind). My student Karen put her father in a piece about spare change and it was accepted by the *San Francisco Chronicle* for Father's Day. She wrote about turkey leftovers in a piece about becoming her mother and published it on Thanksgiving.

Magazines and special sections of newspaper have editorial calendars that list special theme issues ahead of time. *The New York Times* magazine, for example, sets aside certain weeks for subjects such as Men & Health, cars, giving, travel, home design, style and entertaining, fashion and special topics such as motherhood, television, spending, sports and technology.

The Mechanics of Submission

Always try to find out how editors prefer to receive submissions. Be aware of what they've already run.

Let's get the discussion of rights out of the way. A copyright is legal ownership of a written work. You need do nothing: you own the copyright automatically the minute you produce the work. (In 1978 the law was changed to say you own it for your lifetime plus 70 years). Don't put a big "C" for copyright on your pages — it'll just scream amateur.

Magazines buy various rights, but most often they ask for First Rights — the right to publish your piece first, for a specified time. Be careful about giving away All Rights — it means they own it forever.

Newspapers buy one-time rights in their own area. This means you can sell the same piece at the same time to other papers outside their publishing area. You can send it to the *Seattle Times*, the *Boston Globe*, and the *Miami Herald*, but not to, say, the *San Francisco Chronicle* and the *San Jose Mercury*, an hour south, which compete.

Tips on Submitting

1. If you're submitting something to a publication that runs 800-word essays, don't send them a 1,000-word piece with the idea that they will either alter their format to accommodate your wonderful piece or will themselves cut it down to 800 words. They hate that. Make sure it doesn't resemble something they just ran. Their publication is their baby, and they like to think you read it carefully.

2. Send only one piece at a time.

3. You can email or fax if the piece is "time-bound" — it's about Father's Day and has to be run in June or not at all. Find out whether they prefer mailed or emailed submissions, and give it to them the way they want it. (Forget those rush delivery services — you should see the piles of unopened FedEx packages marked "URGENT! Open immediately!" tossed to the back of cubicles along with the promo toys and the press releases. Save your money.) Emailing submissions is more and more the accepted practice, and indeed many publications have switched to an on-line submission process. It IS the way to go for Internet publications. (When you email, put the section you're submitting to in the subject line: "Real Lives.") Once you and an editor are in contact, you will be using email and phone.

4. Can you submit the same piece to different publications at the same time? It's not a problem to do that with newspapers, generally, but magazines might not look at your piece if they know you're sending it to others at the same time (multiple submissions). So it's your decision whether to up your chances by doing that, and whether to let the editor know. My only hint is to say that you get caught only when you have multiple acceptances, which may be a problem you wish to have.

5. Keep a sheet of paper listing your submissions by date, article, and publication. Makes it a lot easier when you want to call and say, "I sent you a piece on such-and-such a date."

6. A *query* is a proposal to write a piece. Professional magazine writers query a piece, that is, describe the article to the publication and get a contract to write it, tailoring it carefully for the publication. Humor and first-person pieces are rarely sold with queries, because so much of an essay's appeal lies in

charm rather than content. The editor has to read the whole thing to know if he wants it. Imagine even E.B. White selling what became a famous essay this way: "Here is 3,000-words on my pig. Would you like to buy it?" Or an unknown Joan Didion pitching a piece on headaches, "I get migraines a lot, and I have written an essay about this experience. Would you like to read it?"

7. Do include a cover note, however. This can be a few lines or half a page. Give the editor a brief description of your piece and how it relates to the publication's needs. List any relevant publishing credits you have. (If you haven't been published before, don't bring the subject of clips up.) Try to spark their interest. Editors sometimes know from a one-line description in the cover letter whether they're going to want the piece or not. An editor said when he read the line, "Enclosed, please find my essay about how I fell in love with the nurse while getting a colonoscopy," he just knew, before he even read it, that he had to buy that piece. On the other hand, "Enclosed, please find my piece about life and love and redemption" can have the opposite effect.

Put their name and information on the left side of the page, yours on the right, higher up. Just a half page or so — introduce yourself, maybe give a career highlight or two, a brief summary of the piece and why you think they'll go for it. If you know a writer or pretty much anybody who works at the publication, ask them if you can say something like, "I'm writing at the suggestion of so-and-so." If the editor has asked to see the piece, of course get that essential piece of information up front.

Here's a cover note my student Nancy Devine emailed to the *San Francisco Chronicle,* which subsequently accepted her essay.

> I'm a longtime *Chronicle* reader sending an essay for First Person entitled "Reeling in the Daze." Laurie Kretchmar, a writer, editor, and former editor of Working Woman, asked me to send you this essay. She said she liked how I described the way time expanded or contracted for me as a mother. I am a health writer who also loves writing essays. I have written for NurseWeek, HealthWeek, Eternelle, WebRN, and several Stanford University Newsletters, among other publications.

SWEAT THE SMALL STUFF

Double-space your piece, leaving wide margins. If you're emailing, many editors prefer that you just copy your submission into the email itself, to spare them the risk and bother of clicking on an attachment (which may have viruses). Put your name and information high on the left on the first page, and include just your last name and page number as header on subsequent pages. Proofread carefully to see if you any words out. (Ha).

If the look of the thing matters to the person who's going to buy your manuscript, it matters to you. I'm not the most meticulous person in the world myself, but I see the logic: how will your editor know you can do the hard thing — making an essay compelling, lively, and meaningful — if you can't do the easy thing, and catch those typos, blank pages, and coffee stains? Errors make the person you're trying to impress think more about the holes in your education than about what you're saying. And beware of relying on spell-check — it can't tell the difference between *scared* and *scarred*, *roles* and *rolls*, *bear* and *bare*.

Find the name of the editor in charge of the section, get her title right, spell her name right. (When I was an editor at *San Francisco Focus* magazine I once got a letter addressed to "Adair Lard." As my sister used to say, I resemble that remark.) Go to the publication's Web site and look up the section editor's name and title. If the email addresses of the editors aren't listed go to the advertising/sales section to see how the company's email addresses are formatted — editors' names will be formatted the same way.

Send a Postcard with Your Submission

If you are sending only the manuscript and you don't want it back, just enclose a stamped, self- addressed postcard with your return address on the front. On the back type this, adding boxes to check off:

> NAME OF ARTICLE:
> "I can use this, will advise when."   ☐
> "I may be able to use this, will hold."   ☐
> "I can't use this."   ☐
> COMMENTS:
> NAME AND NEWSPAPER:

How Long Do I Wait to Hear Back?

Give the publication some time before following up with an email, something along the lines of:

> I sent you a piece on such and such and just wanted to check
> to see if you've had a chance to look it over. I have some other
> publications in mind that it would be well-suited for, but your great
> magazine is the publication that I think suits it best, so I wanted
> you to have first crack at it. I hope to hear from you soon.

If you've sent in your piece and heard nothing back can you call them? Yes, but wait as long as possible. Freelance submissions are submissions nobody asked to see. The editor needs them, but first she has to hustle upstairs and find out why the four spreads she was promised for Saturday were cut to two, and edit the piece on 50s drive-ins that just came in, and wade through her email. Also, your piece is buried under her lunch and the ton of magazines and mail and cardboard flats of plants that have also been sent in unsolicited: you might call after or before hours, so she can get your message and hunt the piece down before she calls you back.

Rejections

Not to be a broken record, but again, change the goal. You can't decide you're going to be published. You have no control over what the editors out there do. But you can follow F. Scott Fitzgerald's example and decide to paper the room in rejection slips before you get discouraged. Rejection slips prove you're a working writer. (Plus they're useful to show the IRS when you deduct the expenses of your freelance business, including a home office, travel, and lunches, so make copies or photograph your wall.)

A rejection with a handwritten note on it that says, "We can't use this, but try us again," is VERY good. They write such messages only to writers they want to encourage. They know you'll be so excited at their interest that you'll back a van up to their back door and dump in everything you've ever written. My student Carol Lena got this for a short story she sent out, for example.

> Dear Carol Lena Figueiredo:
> Thank you for sending us "Physics of Love." Unfortunately this
> particular work was not a right fit for Puerto del Sol, but I was

very impressed by your writing. There is much to admire in your selection of detail, development of character, and clean, confident prose. This piece may benefit from greater attention to scene in its early pages; scenes in the present action, rather than back story, might help develop tension and reader engagement early. Please remember that this is the opinion of only one reader. Thank you for trying us, and we look forward to reading more.

Rejection notes, either nice ones like this or terse "Sorry, we can't use this," are part of the writing process. Most magazines publish less than 2 percent of what floods into their white plastic U.S. Mail boxes every morning. Take what you can use of what they tell you and drop-kick the rest. If your work has energy, and you can spell, it is virtually guaranteed that you will be published sooner or later. Be persistent. My student Kathleen Denny emailed me to say that the *San Francisco Chronicle* had published a piece she'd done a couple of years before about the work-summer vacation tension, from the vantage point of an airline mechanic. "A couple years ago, no one was interested, but this editor loved it. Persistence pays off!"

Kim Ratclif emailed me to say: "I wrote a piece in your class and sent it to Garden Design's "Dirt" section — never heard a peep out of them ... until two and a half years later. New editor finds it at the bottom of his slush pile, likes it, has me update it, and it runs three years later!"

ACCEPTANCES

Be professionally friendly with editors. Thank them for running your piece, the featured-space layout, the stunning artwork, the light touch with editing. If they take the time for a personal rejection, thank them for that, too — it took extra effort on their part and it might help them remember you the next time you submit something. Be, uh, submissive.

Money

Pay no attention at first to whether you are paid or how much — that all comes later. Big-city newspapers tend to pay only $75 to $150 for freelance essays, while national magazines pay well — I received $5,000 for a 2,000-word piece on being a grandma from *More Magazine*.

Editing

> There is no passion in the world is equal to the passion to alter someone else's manuscript
>
> — H. G. Wells

How much you let editors mess with your writing is likely to depend on where you are in your writing career and how personal the piece is. I myself let magazines do whatever they like — I even let *More* Magazine run an essay that made it sound as if I didn't like my grandkids. (When it came out I answered emails from indignant grannies accusing me of being hardhearted, and could hardly type my replies because I was holding two-year-old Maggie and four-year-old Ryan in my lap.)

It's fairly common for a new writer to be so distressed at what "they" did to the piece that she huffily asks to have the byline removed. Resist this, unless the piece is so personal and close to your heart that you can't allow it to go into print with the changes. Editors work hard, most of them improve a piece, and it just doesn't pay to complain. Go on to the next piece.

Most Important

As you go forward, I urge you to celebrate intermediate triumphs. Laminate your first published piece into placemats for the family breakfast table. Just nail that piece after 20 drafts? Look around to make sure you're alone, bring your elbow sharply back to your side — Yes! — then walk sedately out of the room. When you nail a difficult paragraph, lock yourself in the conference room, put your feet up, and reward yourself by reading poetry for an hour (one of my favorites is Archibald MacLeish's "Not Marble Nor the Gilded Monuments.")

Test your progress not against the outside validation of being published but against what you have learned about good writing. Am I using more images? Am I more focused? Are my themes deeper, better developed? Am I forming writerly habits?

In the next chapter, we move on from essays to the full-length memoir. If you're interested in getting a memoir published, you might start by sending some excerpts out to magazines. Those excerpts will impress your future editor, and they're good training. It's easier to learn how to construct a story in

5 pages than in 200. Then you can go to an agent or editor and say, "Here's a piece that was published in *The New York Times*. I'm working on a memoir about it." As one editor admitted, "We're all looking for validation." Sue Shapiro told mediabistro.com that a couple of pieces she published about smoking gave momentum to her book, *Lighting Up*. Also editors sometimes troll through magazines looking for writers to approach about doing a book.

CHAPTER TEN

WRITING THE MEMOIR

Will Your Idea Work?
Throw Your Book on the Floor
All I Want is a Room Somewhere
The Arc

Much what we've been saying about the essay applies equally to the memoir, which we take up now. You may be wondering if you'd like to write one, or perhaps you've have already embarked on one, or you're simply curious about this popular new genre. Book-length personal narratives and reflections have always existed, but suddenly in the 1980s, with Mary Karr's *The Liars' Club* and Frank McCourt's *Angela's Ashes,* everybody was writing and publishing and reading them. It's easier to publish a memoir these days than a novel. You don't have to be famous first anymore — you can be famous afterward. The lives of the obscure have been found to be as compelling as those of the celebrated; it turns out that we may have all been more interested, all along, in the little man behind the curtain than in the Great and Terrible Oz.

My own memoir is *Hold Me Close, Let Me Go,* published by Random House. I wrote it for a reason many people do: something hard happened in my life. At 13 my daughter Morgan started doing her imitation of a cyclone, while I played the trailer park. She began sneaking out of the house at night, smoking, drinking. As she got older, things got much, much worse. In a scene at the beginning of my book, in fact, I am throwing my pregnant teenage daughter out of the house.

I wrote it because I read lots of advice books on how to raise teens, but I couldn't find a book that echoed back how it felt to be trying everything the books suggested — reflective listening, grounding, dividing issues into

Her Problems and My Problems — and still failing. I wanted to hear from another mother who had had to tell her daughter she couldn't live home any more. I needed a book about the mother, not about the teenager.

So I blithely sat down to write one. I had no idea that writing a memoir was anything more than just writing down what happened. Type, type, type. It was as if I decided to build a house and just started nailing together boards. And I was already writing a 700-word column twice a week — wasn't a memoir just, well, longer?

In my usual generous way, I made all the mistakes, so you don't have to. (Or you may not have to make as many, anyway.) Before I go on to that, let's have some definitions.

What a Memoir Is

Forgive me if I'm being overly obvious, but a memoir is, of course, a book. That means it's at least 50,000 words long. A memoir (not pronounced mem-wah, please!) is the book-length story of how you desperately wanted something, how you went about getting it, and what you found out about yourself along the way. It's about one particular event, relationship or theme, and usually covers a shorter time period than do memoirs, with an "s," which are more loosely organized collections of stories and anecdotes going back through the author's entire life, not just one period of it. (Those tend to be written by celebrities, and devoured at poolside). In *It's Not About the Bike,* for example, Lance Armstrong wrote about his battle with cancer, not about his whole life.

A biography, in contrast to either a memoir or memoirs, is the complete story of a life. You don't get one of those unless you're famous.

Do You Have a Memoir in You?

You may already have something in mind to write about. You were shot by your husband's lover. You started your own outlaw radio station. You lost all your money in the stock market and found yourself starting over at 60. You renounced the life of a wealthy socialite to become a nun. A carelessly parked van careened downhill and plucked the husband from your side, or a blood vessel burst in your brain when you reached for the soap in the shower.

If you don't yet have an idea for a memoir, this chapter may help. Or consider this: My friend Tristine Rainer, author of the excellent book on structuring memoir called *Your Life as Story,* says that when her students are stuck for a memoir subject, she asks them: "What do people always ask you?" In her case, they always asked her about her friendship with Anais Nin, and she's writing her own memoir about that.

Imagine yourself at a college reunion, talking to an old friend whom you have not seen in years. After you get past the usual small talk, she asks you to tell her what you really have been up to and how your life has changed — or how you have changed your life — since school. What one or two stories could you tell her that would most represent your life?

Or your best friend is struggling through a difficult time in his life and doesn't believe that he'll ever be able to succeed in anything. What story of yours would you tell to convince him that he should not give up hope and that one day, with enough effort, he will move past his current difficulties and succeed?

WILL YOUR IDEA WORK?

Let's assume you have an idea for a memoir. Is your idea going to pan out, be worth the sacrifices and the learning curve it will take to write it? A memoir means at least a year of typing and retyping and printing out and eating Cheerios out of the box and skipping parties. Take it from me and the boxes of sodden drafts of the unpublished childhood memoir (the working title is *Lagunitas)* in my basement: it's a good idea to think your story through before you commit a huge chunk of time to it.

1. Is It Over?

What you are writing about must be over before you start the book. If you are still battling cancer, or going through a divorce, or in the cult, or the marriage, or the middle of the move to India, you may not be ready to put the experience into perspective for us.

Certainly it's going to be hard to come up with an ending. I am working with a young woman on her memoir about bulimia and I have a suspicion that her ordeal is not yet over.

This was one of the mistakes I made. I wrote the first draft when my little hell child was still a dyed-head, baggy-jeaned seventeen. There I was, already tapping industriously away at my Dell in one room while she wason the phone arranging to meet her druggie boyfriend in another.

Was I ready to reflect on and offer perspective on my experience? Hardly. I hadn't even got my sense of humor back. When I complained to Morgan's dad that when she forgot her keys she tore a hole in the fence and broke into my house, he said, "But look how badly she wanted to come home." Only years later did I see that was funny.

I needed those years to have a stab at perspective. A friend looked at some pages of the first draft for me and said it read like "a report from the trenches."

I let more time go by, and tried again. This time I had achieved some distance. My friend read the new pages, and, now not bothering to conceal her dismay at the first draft, wrote:

> The draft you sent me last round concentrated on the mess of life with Morgan and I felt mired in it. This one is more reflective and concentrates primarily on you and your process, which I find more interesting. It still reflects all your feelings of deep confusion and betrayal, but because you seem to have developed more detachment, I can follow the events as part of a story rather than as an ongoing assault.

D'Arcy Fallon, author of a memoir about the period she spent as a young woman on a Marin County commune, said in her note to the reader:

> I needed a lot of distance to write *So Late, So Soon*. It percolated inside me for nearly three decades before I could love the person I had once been and begin to see my brethren with appreciation, humor, and compassion. By the time I started writing, I wasn't angry but oddly … curious about us all, as if my life at the Lighthouse Ranch had happened to someone else.

Journal

Even if you're not ready to write actual pages, *do take notes!* They will be invaluable later. It's like taking a home video — that boring footage of everyone chatting at the table will be riveting in ten years. Write the notes in images, in literary style, not in journalese. "Felt terrible again today this Thursday" won't do much good when you sit down to write the article or the book.

I began taking notes when Morgan was 13. Here's a sample entry that was useful when it came time to write the book:

> Saw the actual report card yesterday. 4 Ws. Morgan had friends over, new clothes from The Gap, dark red lipstick on, and I was so mad I could hardly be in the same room with her. They bought hugely oversized jeans and shirts, like clown clothing. She did her homework with a pink marker, three or four words to each piece of binder paper. At around 3 a boy came over, with a name something like Balloon, and they drifted out together.

Louise Desalvo told *Poets & Writers* magazine that she realized that the kind of journal writing she was doing — just describing events or dumping her feelings onto the page — wasn't helping her. "Yes, I was writing about my feelings, but I wasn't linking them to the circumstances of my life." She bought a book by James W. Pennebaker called *Opening Up: The Healing Power of Confiding in Others,* about the kind of writing that can help you deal with painful life experiences. She began doing them, and those autobiographical sketches turned into her memoir *Vertigo.* "The idea is not to just write about the event, or about the emotion, but both," says Desalvo. Desalvo's own book is called *Writing as a Way of Healing.*

2. Are You a Victim or a Hero?

Even if your story has an end point, there are other pitfalls. If something awful happened to you that you could not have avoided, that carried you along in the river like a piece of driftwood, the book may not work. Illness could fall into this category, the perfidy of husbands, the shock of being fired, betrayed, cheated, etc. A good memoir is not so much about the painful blow that life unfairly dealt you, as it is about what happened next. Even if you were raped, the story is not about what happened to you, but about what you did afterward.

Thus we return to the subject of change. Like an essay, a memoir shows how human beings change under pressure, not about the bad things that can happen to people. If you marry a doctor who turns out to be a crook, that's not change. It's bad luck. If you marry a doctor who turns out to be a crook, and you knew all along something was wrong — those unexplained phone calls, a repossessed Porsche — then you have a story to tell. It will be about what you found out about yourself, not about him, the night of his arrest.

Ask yourself, why would someone want to read this book? Ask yourself: why would *I* want to read it? Don't confuse an obsession (with a boyfriend, say) with a compelling subject. It can be an elaborate form of brooding.

I find myself telling writers a lot that what you want to write is not always what the readers want to read.

In a good memoir, you are like the main character in a movie. You not only have a problem, but you try a lot of different things to solve your problem, have setbacks, make mistakes, and push on. The memoir writers I've worked with include a man who was dumped by his wife and went on a diet that transformed his life; a woman who solved her financial and relationship problems by becoming an over-40 call girl, a woman who fled the state with her child to escape his abusive father; a man who reacted to greed and excess in real estate development by virtually inventing green building in America. Those are stories with action — stories in which the narrator's own efforts affect the outcome. These stories have satisfying endings. Not all real stories do. One student is working on a memoir about a love affair she had with a married man when she was very young. Her appealing story of a naïve young secretary dazzled by her married boss works well until she becomes a home-wrecker, seeing him in secret. And then the man dies when the author is 26, which is what happens in life — sometimes things just stop, rather than end.

When your story is compelling but lacks a satisfying ending, you might want to consider fiction. Seriously — that's the answer when real life doesn't deliver the right literary elements. I've been thinking about writing about the two years my mother spent in home hospice before she died, and all the family drama of that period, but an ailing parent is not an action plot: I had no control over events, and thus could only react to them. If I write about it, I may have to do it as fiction.

What's important is that the book be one or the other: fiction or non-fiction. If you publish it as the latter, don't forget you made a lot of stuff up, like

James Frey, who wrote *A Million Little Pieces* as a novel, then published it as a memoir, without explaining that along the way he had taken some liberties — the three months he said he spent in prison that turned out to be a few hours in an Ohio police station, for example.

Like an essay, a memoir should end with some sense of how the tale changed the teller. It can show how someone who is pinned down by life finds a way to move forward, or how someone comes to terms with his or her grief. My writing partner, Janis Newman, wanted to become a mother, and adopted a Russian boy. She ends her memoir, *The Russian Word for Snow,* with: "I looked back into his eyes, and at that moment I knew that I would forever put myself between him and all the dangers of the world — a vicious dog, a speeding car, a bullet from a gun. I had become a mother." Other endings might include how a father who had refused to see the evil in his son comes to terms with his own poor judgment, or an employee sees that she, not her jerk of a boss, is the one who is keeping her trapped in her job — and quits. The cult member recognizes that his group IS a cult — and leaves.

In my case I learned that when I was feeling most like a failure — grounding Morgan only to watch her go out a window, taking her to drug counseling only to have her quit — I was doing my job as a mother, because she saw how how hard I was trying, and that was a strong message in itself.

3. Is There a Market for It?
The very popularity of memoir means you have to work harder to make yours different from what's already out there. There are lots of memoirs now on various subjects: illness (Lori Gottlieb's *Stick Figure: A Diary of My Former Self*), and on drinking (Caroline Knapp's *Drinking: A Love Story*). There are lots of memoirs set in mental wards, such as Susanna Kaysen's *Girl, Interrupted.*

One of my students, working on a book about her stroke, found a dozen or more memoirs already out on the subject. That doesn't mean she can't do hers — it just means she has to find a new angle — or premise, as it's called when you're talking about a book.

I've been working for about 150 years on a memoir of my childhood — yet another tale of a father with itchy feet, another liturgy of suffering by yet another writer who read a lot as a child. Talk about memoirs that have already been done! Books on bad childhoods include the titles that helped launch the memoir craze, such as Tobias Wolff's *This Boy's Life,* Jeannette Walls's *The Glass Castle,* Mary Karr's *The Liars' Club* and Frank McCourt's *Angela's Ashes.* Way worse fathers! To get mine published, it will have to cover new ground, or I will have to write the hell out of it, or, probably, both.

YOUR IDEA WORKS: WHAT NEXT?

Let's say you have decided on a story, and it has the essential elements: it's resolved, you had an active role to play, it changed you, it has enough unique elements to stand out in the bookstore. Time to get cracking, I'd say.

Non-Conventional Dramatic Structure

It is possible to write a memoir without a conventional dramatic structure, one that offers more meditative and impressionistic examinations of self, rather than in the conventional form of a story (which we'll look at next, at length). It's an elastic form, after all. You can move back and forth in time, as in Philip Roth's *Portnoy's Complaint* (billed as a novel, I know, but a memoir all the same, like almost all his stuff). You can write remembered fragments that gain a coherence of their own. Such memoirs serve theme rather than event. Sven Birkerts, in *The Art of Time in Memoir,* describes memoir as a circular genre: "each is in its own way an account of detection, a realized effort to assemble the puzzle of what happened in the light of subsequent realization." The writer — and the reader — fills in strategic blanks with surmises and imaginings, in a book that can seem almost like collage. The result can be more lyric — more poetic — than novelistic. *Safekeeping* by Abigail Thomas is, as my student Kris said in a report she sent to the class, "Not so much memoir as a stained glass window of scenes of a grown-up woman who has learned to rejoice in being herself. Reading it, we feel the crazy beauty of life."

The risk with collage is that while it looks temptingly simple — much as an abstract expressionist painting might to a first-time viewer — it requires an intuitive calibration of effects to attain the sense of unity that would otherwise be supplied by story. You must repeat images, colors, patterns — something to recognize and track. The less headlong narrative there is, the better the writing has to be.

Another approach is to link autobiographical essays together to form a story, as in the wonderful *The Boys of My Youth* by Jo Ann Beard. It's billed as a collection of stories, but the recurring character is named Jo Ann and the family members are the same from essay to essay. Is it a memoir or a collection of discrete essays? Hard to say.

Another example is *Family Bible,* by Melissa J. Delbridge, a collection of personal essays about growing up in Tuscaloosa. Some classic memoirs, such as Mary McCarthy's *Memoirs of a Catholic Girlhood,* have hardly any scenes at all: they're more like long, lively essays. Sarah Manguso, author of *The Two Kinds of Decay,* about her autoimmune disorder, decided she would go easy on herself in her effort to write about the experience of being sick: she'd just write some pieces, and not even in order. "I just wrote until I couldn't think of any more vignettes. I wrote a thousand words a day for thirty days, and I had the book."

Conventional Dramatic Structure

In the rest of this chapter, we'll look at the structure that is most popular, and reader-friendly: telling a story. Here're some ideas for getting started.

Discovery Draft

> Don't think. Write. We think before we write a story, and afterward, but during the writing we listen.
>
> — Madeleine L'Engle, author of *A Wrinkle in Time*

At first you may want to just write the story out, if you can. Go forward, not back, even if you realize that you had only two children on page three and seem to have only one on page eight. It's satisfying to get at least a picture of the general shape of the thing as it moves from beginning to end. You can even try to write the whole story through in one short time period, using Red Bull or cappuccino or whatever drugs are handy.

You'll make discoveries while writing. Mary Karr, author of *The Liars' Club,* said in *The New York Times* that she'd written a goodbye scene "to show how my hard-drinking, cowboy daddy had bailed out on me when I hit puberty." When she researched that memory, though, "the facts told a different story: my daddy had continued to pick me up on time and make me breakfast, to invite me on hunting and fishing trips. I was the one who said no. I left him for Mexico and California with a posse of drug dealers, and then for college."

"This," said Karr, "was far sadder than the cartoonish self-portrait I'd started out with."

TRY THIS:
Cluster ideas for your book. First described by Gabriele Rico in *Writing the Natural Way,* clustering allows you to jot down ideas and make rapid connections between them. Write down whatever you're working on in the center of a page, "scene at the lake," or "falling down the stairs," draw a circle around it, and then free-associate. Use this technique to generate new ideas rapidly. It works because you can range all over the place, making fast monkey-mind connections — the way we think.

Caveat

I said above that you might try to just blurt the whole book out fast, but I'm not sure that's the best approach for a memoir. It might be better for fiction, where your unconscious is feeding you ideas as you need them. When you're working on something as long as a book, you will never have neatly divided writing stages: here I will just write and write, next I will think about the structure of the book. You are always going to be doing both. Even as you do the vital bursts of writing — making discoveries that will become part of the book — you want to step back now and then, and think about what goes in and what doesn't. Many writers find it useful not only to write events down on cards, as we'll talk about in a minute, but to string some sort of clothesline up above their writing space, to keep a visual record of ideas for the overall structure of the book.

Write Down the Dates

Write down the important events of the book, and then the approximate dates on which they took place (day, month, year — guess or just pick a date if you can't be sure). Keep a list of the birthdates of the people in your book so you know their age at any point.

With *Hold Me Close,* I knew my chronology would take Morgan from 13 to 17. She was born in 1978, so my period was 1991 to 1996. With the second memoir I've been working on, about my father and my childhood, I started with the most reliable date I had: my sister Robin's birthday, May 9, 1963. She was conceived (simple subtraction tells me) the August before, in 1962, when my father came back from Mexico and he and my mother made a futile last stab at the marriage.

Knowing the dates tells you a lot — what was going on at the time in the world, how old everybody was, what was going on in the news, what song might be playing on the radio, the weather, etc. You can easily look any date up on the web. I looked up Jan 3, 1962, for example, to see what day of the week my tenth birthday was on, and whether I was back in school by then or not. I discovered that my father was turning 40 at the end of the summer of 1961 — a good fact to know if I am trying to figure out why he became so restless around that time.

I looked up what my mother would have heard on the radio in 1959, what a 1940 Plymouth looked like, and got a map of Pearl Harbor. I Googled "the year 1961" so I could have my sister taping c-shaped curls to her cheeks with cellophane tape for the bouffant look made popular by Jackie Kennedy.

Historical perspective is part of it, too. To write a memoir about my childhood, I had to learn to think of my parents not just as people in the exciting lifetime role of being my parents, but as people living in a certain time. That would allow me to write comments that provided context, like explaining why my parents had so many kids so fast: "After the war the whole country was obsessed with making babies, with hearth and home."

You can also use historical background to widen the lens, so the narrative does not seem tightly focused on your states of feeling. If you're writing about losing faith in your religion, tell us about the world of those who believe in it. Create a world for us. I know I like to be plunged into a world I don't know. To set a story on a ship, you must have some knowledge of ships. If you write about becoming a painter, learn a lot about painting — maybe watch as a painting is created, from first brush stroke to final sale to a gallery. Do some background reading if necessary. I collected a lot of books on the era (early sixties) that my childhood memoir is set in. I read *The Hot House, Life Inside Leavenworth Prison* for the two years my dad spent in that storied federal slammer. My grandmother was a WAC, so I got *Not All Soldiers Wore Pants*. *Homeward Bound: American Families in the Cold War Era* gave me the perspective I needed on my parents' marriage, as did (to an astonishing degree) *Blue-Collar Marriage.*

Interviews

Interviews for a memoir? Good question. Why would you have to interview other people, to write an account of the way you remember things? In a memoir, it's not what happened to you that's significant, after all, but what you *think* happened to you. It's what you remember, and why you remember things that way. Your memories and your myths about yourself are, after all, who you are. I have a vivid memory of the day my father stapled my licorice whips so they hung down from the kitchen ceiling, and everybody was laughing and jumping to get them. He wanted to teach me not to hoard. Did it happen? I'll never know. No one else has any memory of it. Is it important anyway? It probably is.

Most memoir writers know the *emotional truth* (how it felt to you) is more important to the story you've telling more than the *literal truth* (what day it was, exactly what Dad said, whether or not it was really raining that day). What *happens* is fact. Truth is *how we react to what happens.* You are after all not just remembering: you are updating the past, sifting through it, even giving us several ways to view one event.

The literal truth can't be reproduced anyway. It would take thousands of sentences to describe taking a sip of coffee, and even then you would have to leave something out, like the weight of the coffee cup in your hand, or the particular way you use your thumb to counterbalance it. To write anything down, anything at all, is to select from among possibilities, to choose the blue shirt and leave the red shirt forever at the back of the closet. All writing is selection and omission, and thus all writing is fiction. Or, at the very least, any memoir is one person's impression of what happened.

That said, family interviews can add interesting material to your book. Your memory is not only wildly inaccurate, but there may events you don't remember at all, or weren't present at, that figure in your story. When I met him for dinner at an Italian restaurant in San Rafael, near the lumber company he manages, my brother Shannon turned out to have a crazy photographic memory. I had talked to older siblings and left him for last, as he is two years younger than I am. To my astonishment, he remembered everything about that childhood 42 years ago. "I can step out the front door of our old house," he said over his steaming lasagna, "and see it all, just like in a movie."

My brother told me a lot, including the saddest story I ever heard, about how when the shouting started between our parents, he'd go out and knock on neighbors' doors, one after the other, and get himself invited in. It was all the sadder for the expressionless way he told it, cutting his pasta and forking it in. I will use that story, relating it as something my brother remembers, and I'll use other anecdotes from him: when my father got angry at his friend Johnny Herrell (who seems to have been sleeping with my mother), my father loaded the little cannon he'd made in his metal shop on the pack of his pickup, loaded it with gunpowder, backed it up to the Forest Knolls Lodge, where Johnny was inside wrapped around a Budweiser, and shot it off. I would advise you, if you can arrange it, to have a brother with a photographic memory.

I interviewed my mother, too. She didn't much like talking about the old days, so I cleverly made a special appointment for the purpose. She couldn't not talk when I had driven 20 miles across the Golden Gate Bridge to her mobile home park in San Rafael just for the interview. When we went outside at the rickety plastic table on her patio, I made a great show of setting out the tape recorder. My mother told me a lot of things I didn't know, including that she secretly bought a plot of land, and then sprung it on Dad with the idea that he would build a house on it. (I asked my mother about Johnny Herrell, too, since you ask, but her answer will have to wait for the book.)

....

THE CRAFTY WRITER
Make an appointment to interview a relative. Block out a specific amount of time — two hours say — and maybe have your interview subject gather some items to talk about, such as photos.

....

TRY THIS:
Ask someone you trust to tell your story, either verbally or in writing. Perhaps some aunt or uncle or cousin would love to send you their recollections. This exercise can be amazingly illuminating for both you and the other participant. (Try not to bristle as your sweet old aunt remembers you as a spoiled layabout.)

Organizing Your Material

As you work on your book, you'll accumulate a lot of material. Keeping it sorted out can be a challenge. You might drop your materials into baskets, one for each chapter, or event. Or keep a different-colored folder for each event (i.e., "Mom's Wedding"). I also love the cardboard open file system they sell at places like Office Depot — so much easier than those hanging files in a drawer, the ones that are always slipping off their tracks.

Search

Want to find something you wrote that has disappeared into the bowels of your computer? To find the place where you wrote about, say, your rottweiler, Mary, go to the START menu on the computer task bar and find the little icon of a magnifying glass followed by the word "SEARCH." Open that, and you can search not only for the name of any file in your computer ("Mary") just by typing in a keyword, but you can also search for any word in any file ("Rottweiler"). Just try to remember a unique phrase in that file.

Paste Special

For years I couldn't figure out how to get rid of all the crazy fonts that popped up in a document, thanks to my habit of cutting and pasting sections from old files. I know how to use the PAINT tool, but that merely cloaks the old formatting — it's still there, and will reappear when you move stuff. Would I have to type stuff in all over again, just to permanently change the formatting? In this hi-tech day and age? No! I highlight the section with the crazy font, cut it, and then paste it back in using PASTE SPECIAL (under EDIT, in Microsoft Word) and choosing UNFORMATTED. Whoee! I can also highlight the section and click on EDIT, then CLEAR, then FORMATS.

The Office Clipboard

It's under EDIT in Microsoft Word. Open it and you can cut or copy up to 24 items of any length in a sort of holding tank beside your document. This means that when you cut a paragraph to move it, you can park it in the clipboard temporarily. Very, very handy.

Protecting Your Work

Maxine Hong Kingston lost an entire book in the Berkeley fire. The easiest way to prevent that now is to regularly email your files to yourself — they'll be safe in cyberspace even if your whole state burns down.

THROW YOUR BOOK ON THE FLOOR

Okay, back to the writing. Begin by writing only the pivotal moments; the ones you know will be in any version of the book no matter what. The day you discovered the bastard in bed with your best friend. The day you decided to go to California. The moment your son didn't come home from school. (You sometimes don't always know which events deserve more real estate and which deserve less until you write them out, of course).

Cards

It's helpful to see the book visually. Jot a brief description of each event in the story on a piece of paper or index card, then lay the cards out on the floor in the order you think they go in. Tell your family not to walk on your cards, or, if you're married to my husband, not to put them into a neat pile.

Problems will arise as you study your cards, which is the whole point. Better to find and solve them at this stage, when they are still jottings on itty-bitty cards and not hundreds of pages of polished manuscript that you have to toss to make the story work. As you pace up and down your row of cards, challenge each event's right to be there. At the same time, ask what's missing.

Status Quo

The first card might contain your status quo scene: the one that shows you in the midst of your ordinary life before the trouble starts. Nearly every movie begins with such a scene: the marriage before it ends, the child before she gets sick, the young spoiled German woman before she falls in love with the Jew hidden behind the stairs. My student, Steve Curtis, a charter boat captain, was served with divorce papers as his boat was leaving the dock in Sausalito, in full view of the passengers. In his status quo scene, just before the process server arrives, we see the ordinary problems of trying to please the tourists on board, a married man going about his work day.

A status quo scene might show you fretting about a meeting just before the stroke in the shower that leaves you unable even to figure out how to call 911. The status quo scene must contain its own conflict so it will hold the reader's attention, but that conflict needn't be huge: if you're meeting your husband for Friday dinner (at which he'll disclose his illness, or his affair, or your mutual bankruptcy), you can be worried they'll run out of the smoked halibut you've been looking forward to all week.

The Initiating Incident

Next card is the initiating incident: the event that forces you into the struggle of the book. My student Linda Curtis had a clear initiating incident in her memoir in progress about having to leave her religion (and her entire world) behind when her belief in Jehovah's Witnesses collapsed.

Before the trouble started, she was an unquestioning Jehovah's Witness. That's her status quo. Then, on a ordinary Saturday morning, she was out knocking on doors, maybe peeved that her partner across the street was not doing as much as she should (status quo conflict).

She knocked on a door. A man in a faded college sweatshirt with a pair of shears in his hand opened. It was her boss from work, a man she admired and respected. He was as surprised as she was — his star employee stood next to his porch swing with a copy of *The Watchtower* in her hand. He'd known she was a Jehovah's Witness, but it had always been background information. Surprised and embarrassed, Linda had no choice but to go ahead with her spiel. She opened her mouth and out came the usual words, "The very existence of the intricately designed wonders in the universe surrounding us argues that an intelligent and powerful Creator produced it all … "

For the first time in Linda's life as an unquestioning Jehovah's witness, the words sounded hollow. Her trouble begins. Her struggle in the book is to conquer these new doubts that will tear her from her religion, her husband, her mother and father, and all she knows.

Your own initiating incident (called the *complication* in the short story) may be the day you stumbled on a walk across the college campus, and realized that your desire for independence is being threatened by the worsening effects of your cerebral palsy. It might be the morning your mother referred to bananas as "those long yellow things," or the day you realized your thinning child was not going to stop her obsessive dieting on her own.

These initiating incidents are *always* dramatized.

For another of my students, Frank, the trouble did not being the day his estranged girlfriend, Diane, announced she was pregnant with his child. He figured that was her deal. He had never stood in a drugstore aisle puzzling over the numbers on the Huggies boxes, and was not planning to. It was only out of a sense of duty that he showed up at the birth room at the hospital. He stood in back while everyone bustled around with monitors and beeping machines and chips of ice. No one in the birth room seemed to know why he was there, including him. "Like me, everybody understood that my part in this was over." Then he saw his newborn daughter with her wet dark hair and tiny face, still a bit mooshed from her ride through the tunnel, and just like that his shriveled bachelor's heart opened like a rose blooming in fast motion on the Discovery Channel.

The desire that will drive the book arrives like a jolt to his heart: no way is he not going to be part of his child's life, not going to ransack shoe stores for the perfect jellie sandals, and not hear her say "Daddy," and mean him.

Why is that trouble? Because when he arrives at his ex-girlfriend's condo with a teddy bear under his arm, she is distant and distracted. The nanny has been instructed to stay during his visit. And so begins a man's struggle to be part of his daughter's life — and his ex-girlfriend's determination that he will not.

In many stories there will be no one definitive initiating incident. If you have no single incident that begins the trouble, you can sometimes use a prologue to create suspense. I did this in my book with a two-page prologue that consisted of a scene of my sixteen-year-old daughter, Morgan packing. It included the lines, "She was not running away. I was throwing her out." (Looking back, I realize now I might have chosen as the initiating incident the night my daughter got in a car with two teenagers from a different school on a Friday night, and I realized she was making choices that could kill her, and I could do nothing to stop her. If I were writing the book again, I might start with her getting into that car.)

ALL I WANT IS A ROOM SOMEWHERE

In thinking about a memoir ask the same questions you asked yourself in the narrative essay:

What do you want?

What are your motives for wanting this?

How do we learn what you want? Dialogue? Actions? Interior thinking?

What or who stands in the way of your achieving it?

What actions does that desire set in motion? That is, what do you *do* to get what you want?

What happens in the end? (Keep in mind that we learn about ourselves from what we *don't* get, as well as from what we do get).

The answers to these questions should give you a starter list of events for the book:

Arrival in Hong Kong
Meeting Jason
Jason disappears
Mom arrives unexpectedly

Once you have the event that starts the trouble, you should be able to say what the main character — you — wants. This desire drives the book. Think of the Yellow Brick Road gang in *The Wizard of Oz:* Dorothy wants to go home. The cowardly lion wants courage. The scarecrow wants a brain. The tin man wants a heart.

Playwright John Guare said, "I learned about playwriting from the jackets of show albums. I noticed that the first or second song in any musical was the 'want' song — "All I Want is a Room Somewhere."

In the Stanislavski acting method, every character in a drama has a central desire or objective — a motivation — that drives him through each scene and through the story. That's why actors rehearsing a play stand around saying, "What's my motivation?" What did you want, in your story? You should be able to state it in a sentence:

I wanted my family to choose me over their religion.
I wanted to be a good father.
I wanted to love my husband.
I wanted to be a pastor, though I was already 52.
I wanted to be the best damned stroke victim on the planet.

The more specific you are about what you want, the more involved the reader
will be in your efforts to get it. A vague desire, such as "I wanted to be happy"
or "I wanted to be loved" will, by being broad enough to include almost
everything that happened to you, set you and your reader adrift. Likewise, try
not to use "I wanted to fit in" as your desire. *Everybody* wanted to fit in.

In her book on writing memoir called *Your Life as Story,* my friend Tristine
Rainer called it the desire line. It helps you focus your memoir. Your story
may be about how you became a high achiever despite the chaotic family you
grew up in, *and* about your fear of getting Alzheimer's like your mother, *and*
about how you discovered the power of sex. It's about your marriage, and how
you became a Muslim, and how you never felt at home anywhere, and about
the alienation of your children. The desire line makes you choose one as the
story you mean to tell, and let the others come in as minor chords.

Not Sure What Your Desire Line Is?

Try writing a synopsis, narrating the events of your story in prose. "This is
a story about a woman who falls passionately in love with a man and then
sacrifices her talents and her professional ambitions so that he can become
successful. Over time, she bitter and resentful while he becomes absorbed in
his own career. The more successful he becomes the less he needs her and the
needier she becomes (and so on)."

TRY THIS:
Write it as a fairy tale.

EXAMPLE:
Once upon a time there was a little girl whose father could not see her at all.
She tried to make him see her, but he couldn't. The picture he was looking at
was crowded with other kids, and guns, and dogs, and books, and he heard
only the sound of the faraway train, though there were no trains in their

valley. And then he went away. When she grew up, he came back. He had found only trouble and loneliness. Everybody else had gone away from him. He was glad to see her. He needed a friend now. He still didn't want to be anybody's father. Just thinking about it made him feel like a failure, and he had felt like a failure for a long time already. (And so on)

If you look at that example, you can already see that the story is going off the rails: it seems to be about him, not about the little girl. In your fairy tale, make sure the main character is given a series of actions to do. If you can't come up with them, the story may be flawed.

TRY THIS:
Write a one-page fantasy in which you get whatever it is you want in the story you're telling.

EXAMPLE:
In a memoir of being a rebellious teen, the desire line might be: "I wanted to destroy myself. My mother stopped me. My love of music stopped me. I realized I wanted a productive life." In the one-page fantasy of this, the writer might imagine his own funeral.

You can outline a memoir in simplified form, as we did in the essay chapter:

THE DESIRE LINE: I wanted X.

ACTIONS: To get it, I did X.

OBSTACLES: X stopped me

(repeat action/obstacle many times)

RESOLUTION: I got it and I realized (theme) X

Or I didn't get it and I realized X

I stopped wanting it because I realized X

When I was writing the first drafts of *Hold Me Close,* I thought my desire line was "I wanted my daughter to be safe."

But that was about her. In a memoir, the subject is you. I had to keep searching until I got the right desire line, which was "I wanted to be a good mother." Following is an outline of some of the things (in bold) that I did to achieve my desire:

I tried to be strict
I sent her away
I let her boyfriend sleep over
I sent her to a drug program
I said I would not support her and her baby
I threw her out
I let her come home
I took her side

In a scene in which the teachers are alarmed at Morgan's behavior, I show this beat:

> The biology teacher was there, too. He tapped a pencil against the knee of his gray slacks. "Morgan is predictable," he said to the dean. "I can predict she will be late, she will be unprepared, she will disrupt the class, she will try to cheat." I wanted to throttle the old bat. This is my child, you horse-faced, dried-up, old bags.

Obstacles

Obstacles are both external and internal: other people, adverse events, and most of all, ourselves — illusion, wanting the wrong thing, passions, insecurities, vanity, and pride. If the book is to be interesting, it should be about how you got in your way, how you screwed up. If you tell me you drank all during your husband's rehab, I'm interested.

What need, or desire, or blindness made you believe your fiancé's promises? Why did you go along with what the evidence of your senses screamed was wrong? What are your vulnerabilities? Your ego? Your romanticism? Your addiction to excitement? Your sense of entitlement? Your avidity for money? Your fear? What are you afraid of, and how is that an obstacle to getting what you want? Show us how your own actions and wrong thinking made everything worse. If you tell me you made no mistakes during your tenure as vice president of the country during the Iraq war, I lose interest.

In *Hold Me Close* I start out preening myself on what a natural mother I was. I pitied those parents whose kids were slipping out into the streets. Obviously I was a much better parent than they were, and had a better kid. In time we

see me screaming at her to do her homework, enraged because she was standing in my house and not doing what I wanted her to do. We see me giving in
when I should have held firm. "I was Morgan's mom, wanting to be firm, but
I was also Morgan, wanting desperately to go to that party."

We see that my family and my own history contradicted what I was telling
her. "Morgan knew no one in my family has died of smoking, and my family's been on fire for years. When we go across the bridge to visit my mother
in the county, we enter a friendly club, people who go through each other's
purses looking for smokes, bum matches, and argue about who stole whose
Merit Ultra Lights."

The mistakes you make as you struggle are part of what goes into your arc,
which we'll talk about next. Those cards on the floor? They follow your arc,
event by event, beat by beat.

THE ARC

When I lead the memoir workshop at the Squaw Valley community of writers
one year, and explained how to draw the arc of a memoir, one woman took
me aside. "No one ever mentioned the idea of drawing an arc to me before,"
she said worriedly.

That would be like a housing contractor going to trade school for years
without anybody mentioning the idea of blueprints to him. The arc is the
emotional journey you take in the book, from start to finish: the "plot" of
the memoir. I mentioned earlier that you want to both write from the heart
as you proceed on the book, and now and then draw back, as you would on
a road to take note of your surroundings. That drawing back to get the big
picture includes working out the arc.

Working out the arc (of course you refine it as you go) assures you you're on
the right path: everybody's got a story of burning down the page with the fire
of inspiration for 100 compelling pages and then hitting a wall.

The arc will show you the best place to begin. I started the story too far back
in my own memoir. I wrote a hundred pages on Morgan's eighth grade. The
people who read those pages yawned at my tales of a kid slamming doors,

talking back, skipping school, and not speaking to me. "What's the big deal?" they said. "Every teenager is like this." I had to throw out months' worth of writing and start when the much bigger trouble started. An arc would have shown me that I was spending my emotional capital on little stuff — showing fury and fear and loss of confidence when my kid refused to study for a Spanish test. What would I have left to show when she was arrested?

The reason it's called an arc and not a straight line is that it represents an emotional *build*. Things must always get worse.

Writing partners help, as always. In one note my friend Janis said:

> I'm starting to get a sense of you losing confidence in yourself as a mother, and I think it's important to make sure you stick with that. You should have spikes of confidence — but after each one, have an action that drops you down even farther. This book is about hanging in there — especially when you have no idea if you're doing the right thing — so we need to see you completely floundering, but not giving up.

The arc tells you what to put in and what to leave out, and how and where each scene fits in, and thus how to forge ahead with intention and focus. One of my hired editors, Judith Dunham, told me, with a flash of irritation (I was deciding what order to put the elements of this book in): "In my experience, an author who is having a hard time never ultimately succeeds without starting with some sort of outline."

Drawing an arc helps you avoid the trap of putting in a lot of stuff just because it happened. Doing that leaves you with an episodic plot, one in which the climatic scene of the mother leaving the house with a suitcase might get no more space than a long scene at a party with a boyfriend in which nothing much happens. The reader gets dragged through the acrimonious lawsuits, the coffee wagon you set up in the parking lot of your brother's power tools company, the trip to Montreal in the middle of it that didn't change anything.

Once you know the desire line, you are ready to write the arc, outlining the inner changes you undergo as you progress toward your goal. When you write out your cards, ideally, the cards are not merely descriptions of the events that happen in the book. They are descriptions of *the events combined with what emotions you were feeling at that point.* Each emotion that's acted on to move the story forward is a beat (thus events are also called beats). The event is always keyed to the emotion. Thus you would not pick up one of those cards on the floor to read, "And then I went back to my wife," but "and then with renewed determination to save the marriage for the sake of the kids, I moved back in with my wife."

Example of Working Out An Arc
A San Francisco district attorney worked with me on a memoir about the year he spent in Kosovo as an international prosecutor. I've capitalized the emotional beats.

(BEAT) Phil was a BORED AND FRUSTRATED public defender in San Francisco wearily PREPARING for yet another in a long line of red-on-blue Mexican gang crime cases. HE WAS GOOD AT WHAT HE DID, AND THERE WAS SOME PRIDE IN THAT, BUT HE WAS OFTEN VISITED BY A SENSE OF FUTILITY — there were a hundred DAs in San Francisco, and cases would still get prosecuted if he were not around.

(BEAT) He got a chance to be a prosecutor in Kosovo.

(BEAT) There was an opening for an international prosecutor in Kosovo. (His initiating incident)

(BEAT) EXCITEMENT. He wants to go. Maybe he drives past his stop thinking about it.

(BEAT) NEXT DAY, HE THINKS, THIS IS CRAZY, HE CAN'T GO HALFWAY ACROSS THE WORLD. HE JUST GOT MARRIED, HE CAN'T WALK OUT ON HIS LIFE.

(BEAT) But he CAN'T STOP HIMSELF from doing research into the job. And it won't do any harm to fill out the application.

(BEAT) SURPRISE, they say yes! ELATED, he tells his boss.

(BEAT) DISAPPOINTMENT. Boss says you can't go or you're fired. Here's a big turning point: he now has to choose between the adventure job and his whole career. We see what he will lose if he quits his San Francisco job.

(BEAT) Then a decision: "SCREW IT, I WANT TO GO ANYWAY." (I am doing the complexity of his story a disservice here, as I am to all the stories I sketch in few words — I'm just trying to show how the combination of emotion plus event is what goes in the arc.)

(BEAT) When he arrives in Pristina, the capital of war-torn Kosovo, which is being administered by the United Nations so the Serbs and Muslims won't return to killing one another, Phil is FILLED WITH ELATION AT HIS NEW SENSE OF PURPOSE, until

(BEAT) he discovers to his DISMAY that he will be the only international prosecutor in a region of roughly eight hundred thousand people. An impossible job is made harder by his unfamiliarity with the judicial system he has to use — one in which you can't even cross-examine witnesses. There is no functioning police force or judiciary. The place bristles with guns.

(BEAT) HE REALIZES IT'S GOING TO BE HARD TO MAKE A DIFFERENCE, HERE, TOO. At his first trial cops were shot at and victims were too terrified to testify. Other prosecutors have been killed.

(BEAT) NOT ONLY WILL HE NOT BE ABLE TO PUT WAR CRIMINALS BEHIND BARS, BUT HE'LL BE LUCKY TO GET OUT ALIVE HIMSELF.

(BEAT) Tempted to catch the next plane out, he thinks of his dad's heroics in World War II AND IS FILLED WITH NEW RESOLVE. His father didn't quit.

(BEAT) Phil will stay, but now is JUST GOING THROUGH THE MOTIONS, waiting out his time.

(BEAT) Then one day a man comes into the office with a story that renews Phil's sense of purpose.

And so forth.

Chart The Emotions, Then Choose Scenes To Show Them

For the first beat, for example, Phil must begin by showing how bored and useless he felt in his present job. How will he depict that? Maybe a memo goes around, and there are a hundred names on it, reminding him that he is one of many people who can do this job. Maybe he remembers a time when he was sick or gone and it made no difference. Maybe we get not a scene, but a montage — him appearing in the same courtrooms, in front of the same judges, and against the same defense attorneys year after year. You can jot notes for events before writing them out.

Hire an Editor

Consider hiring a professional to help you think the book through. I know many successfully published writers who credit their breakthroughs with hiring one of the many talented editors (sometimes called book doctors) that the economy and the consolidation of publishing has washed out of New York publishing houses. Many of them advertise their services in the back pages of *Poets & Writers* magazine.

I've hired several people to read the manuscript of the book in your hands at various times, in addition to strong-arming my husband and friends into it. Judith, the editor I mentioned above, pronounced the draft she read as "not a manuscript but a compilation of ideas, anecdotes, and quotations from yourself and other authors." Her comments went on for pages. I flushed as I read them. I cursed Judith and her ancestors and the horse she rode in on. I sent her notes to friends saying, "Can you *believe* this?" They loyally assured me that Judith was a Nazi, and said not to pay attention to her.

And then I calmed down. And read Judith's comments carefully, rewrote, and make the book much better.

Then I made it worse again, restoring darlings, moving things around. Tell me you haven't done this yourself.

I finally asked my sister, Robin Cruz, to read it, and she turned out to be the perfect reader, willing to ask the dumb questions and tell me when I was being "lofty" (her word). She not only let me know which chapters were slow, but how to fix them. She was lavishingly admiring of what she liked, which helped me accept what she didn't.

An editor helps you see the skeleton of the story. An autobiographical writer can find it hard to stand back from what she lived through. An editor, like a writing partner, sees only what is in front of him: what works, what doesn't, what's missing, what you said before, etc. An editor is trained at proposing solutions and at reading manuscripts analytically.

As the novelist Michael Crichton said:

> You generally start out with some overall idea that you can see fairly clearly, as if you were standing on a dock and looking at a ship on the ocean. At first you can see the entire ship, but then as you begin work you're in the boiler room and you can't see the ship anymore … What you really want in an editor is someone who's still on the dock, who can say, "Hi, I'm looking at your ship, and it's missing a bow, the front mast is crooked, and it looks to me as if your propellers are going to have to be fixed."

According to the Brenner Information Group, it takes, on average, 475 hours to write a fiction book, and 725 hours to write a nonfiction book. A good writing coach can save you a whole draft of a book in a couple of hours, just by going over your plot with you. If someone saves you a draft, she saves you 725 hours.

You can hire people to read essays as well. Working with a paid editor helps long before you actually meet with him or her. I had a consultation with a woman who said she's spent all weekend getting ready for the meeting — and thought about her book so much that she'd made a lot of progress in the three days since she'd emailed me.

BACK TO THE CARDS: CUT, REARRANGE, ADD

Building an arc asks you to include not what was important or meaningful to you, *but what is important or meaningful to the story.* You must stand back from the tangle of emotions, motives, repetitions, and complexities of something you lived through with the cold dispassionate eye of an editor: what do you include?

What should you cut? In this respect writing memoir is harder than writing fiction. At least with fiction you know what to put in and what to leave out. If there's a car crash in a tulle fog, it's there because you need it. You made it up. In a memoir the car crash may have nothing to do with the story, but it was such an explosive event that it may take several drafts to see that you don't need it.

If during your story of attending your mother in her last illness, you had a bout with bone cancer or met a new man, are those events part of the story? How do you know? Everything felt intense. What events will you minimize, accentuate? Whose truth are you serving when you do?

Cut

Ah, remember murdering your darlings back in the chapter on revision? It *really* applies here, in a memoir, where so much crowds in — your whole life, everything that was going on at the time. We need the scene in the shower when your right arm went limp, but do we need the ambulance trip? It was a joyous time when you brought your Chinese orphan home and the whole neighborhood came over to meet her, but did anything change? If not, mention the party in narration and go on. I had a scene in my memoir in progress of my dad carrying goat feed home on the bumper of his car after the store owner said it would fall off (it did). I loved that scene, but eventually had to admit it was not essential to the story.

When my friend Chimere was working on a memoir, she told me:

> I naturally thought I needed to put in every awkward pre-lesbian love scene. They were some of my most candid and precious moments. I thought, "They will love it, it's real, sexy kinda, and develops my character." But really, after the first one or two I should have said, "I continued to choose women who turned out to be straight for the next six years before I wised up."

She learned to avoid emotionally repetitive scenes — scenes that give us a different example of something we already know. You dramatize something once, and put similar events in summary: "This became a pattern over the next year."

ARRANGE
Back Story/Flashbacks

Don't shove all the stuff you think the reader needs to know into the beginning. Remember what Holden Caulfield said in *Catcher in the Rye:*

> If you really want to hear about it, the first thing you'll probably want to know is where I was born, and what my lonely childhood was like, and how my parents were occupied and all before they had me, and all the David Copperfield kind of crap, but I don't feel like going into it, if you want to know the truth.

If you are sick, we already know you were once well. If married, once single. If you have a boyfriend, we know you met somewhere.

You got your tubes tied when you were sixteen, but in a memoir the reader doesn't need to know it until the scene where you meet Bill Gates and he wants kids. Flashbacks must add to the emotional complexity of what's going on in the present. Keep them out until they make an important connection to what is happening in the present.

Use of flashbacks also depends on your story. If you're writing about a stroke that came unexpectedly, you don't need events leading up to it (except to show the status quo). If you're writing about being a bad father, however, flashbacks of your parents may be important.

A good general rule: don't pull the reader out of the narrative to tell him what happened in the past unless it's for a good reason.

I loved the way my student Eva sneaked this flashback into her memoir about her anorexic child:

> Louis looked up at me, a half-smile crossing his lips. An outsider might think he was fighting back a grin but I knew better. Louis wasn't laughing. He felt helpless, the same way he had felt helpless when I walked into the bar that afternoon where he sat hunched over a glass of scotch, after he told me he'd been sober for a year. The same half-smile had crossed his lips in that

moment, when, four months pregnant with Colette, I picked up the glass, poured the scotch over his head and walked out. I had gone home alone. Louis stayed away for a time after that, one night, two nights. How long had it been? And I had cried all the while, letting loose my sobs, pounding the floor, cursing him for his weakness and deception, cursing myself for my foolish gullibility.

Add

Your cards may reveal that events crucial to the book aren't yet there at all. Sometimes those will be the ones you couldn't face writing: My friend Mikel, who was born in Limerick, the son of a factory owner, wrote a rollicking tale of getting drunk across the face of Ireland as a young man. He gave us lots of pub scenes and lots of scenes with girls, but what we want, though it may be painful for him to write, is the scene in which he turns up on his wife's doorstep and takes fifty pounds from her.

FANTASY

Scenes don't have to have happened to belong in the book. Fantasies belong in autobiographical works as much as real events do — they show us what you're feeling, what you want, what you're afraid of. In *A Heartbreaking Work of Staggering Genius* Dave Eggers shows how helpless he feels during his mother's illness by fantasizing a wild plan to get her out of the hospital:

> We'll get her out in a few days. Beth and I have vowed to get her out, have planned to break her out, even if the doctors say no; we will hide her under a gurney, will pose as doctors, will wear sunglasses and go quickly and will take her to the car, and I will lift her and Toph will provide some distraction if necessary, something, a little dance or something; and then we'll jump in the car and beg one, will bring her home, triumphant ...

I used fantasy briefly in *Hold Me Close* when I needed to show why I was determined to make Morgan do her homework.

> I shook out Morgan's clown-sized overalls and folded them into a square. I saw her, 40 years old, in a stained white blouse, hair lank across her forehead, carrying five plates through a swinging metal door in a restaurant because no one had made her do her home-work in high school. I hadn't plucked the image out of thin air: my

mother had been forced to go to work as a waitress after my father left. She came in tired, pasta stains on her white blouse, and left slabs of leftover teacake and bags of French bread on the counter.

WHAT ABOUT THE *I, I, I*?

A memoir must be written in first person, but you may feel uncomfortable if every sentence begins with "I," as if you imagine yourself the Sun King around which the world revolves. One solution is to remove some of those "I's" when you can. Instead of saying, "I felt chilly," you can say, "The temperature had dropped."

So those are some thoughts on the memoir. You'll notice that I often referred to the "events" in your book. Which of those events will go in scene and which in narration? Some memoirs, such as *Angela's Ashes,* are almost all scene; others, such as Vladimir Nabokov's *Speak, Memory* are almost all narration. The more you want your book to be fast-paced, like a good novel, the more scenes it will have. Writing a scene is not something you're born knowing how to do (though watching a lot of movies and plays helps), and you will dozens of them in a typical memoir. So, onward.

CHAPTER ELEVEN

MAKING THE SCENE

Narration

Do You Resist Writing Scenes?

Bringing Your Mom to Life

Dialogue

In this chapter we'll devote some time to finding out exactly what scene and narration are — a subject that leads us naturally to dialogue, and to the characters, the people in your book who will be moving through those scenes and speaking that dialogue.

NARRATION (ALSO CALLED SUMMARY)

This is the writing in between scenes, in which you pull the camera back, cover ground quickly, or reflect and offer perspective. If the scenes are the pearls, narration is the string.

Here's an example of narrative from my student Chris Lunas:

> It wasn't as if I slowly drifted away from liking the good boys. I made a conscious decision one day while I was taking a shower. Before that day, I loved smart, straight "A" kind of boys. In seventh grade, I fell in love with Jay Alves, the best player on the basketball team, the only team sport played at Cunha Junior High. Jay was already close to six foot, and skinny with very white skin, knobby knees and freckles. He wore his black hair parted on the side and slicked down. After he found out I liked him, Jay would make a point of turning around and giving me that twinkly smile right in the middle of Language Arts, and he didn't care who was looking.

Narration not only allows you to describe, but speeds us through time, and offers a chance for the narrator to reflect (as we'll see in the next chapter). A student wrote, "Every week I heard you tell me directly or indirectly that my story couldn't drag on and on. I kept resisting that advice because I believed that the fact of its dragging on was part of the story. Now I realize that a lot of ground can be covered in summary that works."

I had to learn that myself. When I was working on *Hold Me Close*, I was so happy to have learned how to write scenes that I used too little narration, with the result that my first editor at Random House, Harriet Bell, said in a letter: "You take far too long to get the gist of the story. While some of the escapades, lies, and details are important, it would move things along if you summarized the daily grind of living with Morgan. The retelling of everything Morgan did makes it difficult to separate the annoying stuff from her really heinous actions." I learned to use narrative to move faster, as I do in the excerpt below:

> The second half of Morgan's freshman school year and the first half of her sophomore year passed in a haze of arguments, stalemates, and outbursts. I remember watching a movie with Bill, and going upstairs to throw Morgan and her friends out of Jim's flat when Jim was out. I found Holly and Morgan hiding in the downstairs shower, giggling, stoned, and shushing each other.

TRY THIS:
Write two pages of back-story about your parents. What happens before the events you book portrays? Use voice and detail. One student did this exercise and emailed me to say, "The summary assignment has me reeling with new information about my parents, some very weird correspondence regarding their early life with me, etc. So I think it's a valuable tool in providing a story with the kind of authentic detail that makes for interesting reading."

Going from Narration to Scene
You can move out of narration into scene by saying something like, "And then one day ... " Here's a scene from my student Beth Touchette in which she starts with narration, then moves into scene (in italic):

> My mother first told me of my paternal grandfather's mental illness. My mother worked as a nurse, and knew a bit about medical

procedures. Six months after she met my father in Denver, he took her back to Lake Ontario, in central New York, where his family was having a clambake. *My mother couldn't help noticing the rough stitches in her future father-in-law Pierre's neck. As my father's five brothers and sister, mother, and assorted cousins sat down around the red gingham tablecloth, my mother announced, "Gosh, Pierre, those doctors really botched your tachometry." Everybody was silent, because the stitches weren't from an emergency breath-opening procedure.* My grandfather had attempted to slit his own throat six months earlier, and my father hadn't told my mother about it.

You might also find yourself going from continuous action (what always happens) in narration to scene:

"Most mornings I got out of bed and went straight to my writing desk where I'd stored a thermos of coffee the night before."

Then: "One day I found my husband sobbing in my chair."

What is a Scene?

A scene is an event that takes place in real time. Something significant happens in it, something that has not happened before in the story and will not be happening again. A scene can be of any length, from a few lines to twenty pages, though in general, the more important the scene, the more space it should take up. It's usually one in a sequence of distinct events that leads, like steps in a staircase, from the beginning through the middle to the end of your story; each scene brings the story to a new place in the narrative. In a memoir, you might have fifty scenes, interspersed with narration.

WHEN DO YOU NEED ONE?

When we have to be right there with you, in the room, and won't settle for merely being told what happened. Each time something happens that produces a change in you, you drop into scene to show it.

You need a scene at turning points:
When you realize that you can't face one more day at the job you've held for years.
When you get the diagnosis.
When you realize your daughter is deaf.

A scene has a little arc of its own: from hope to despair, or from frustration to having a plan. Your overriding desire in the book may be to become a mother, say, but there's also a series of smaller desires that push you along in each scene — to talk your husband into it, to force him into bed when the thermometer says it's a good time, and so on. The hot spot in the scene is the moment of change. You are working up to asking your husband for a divorce when he suddenly asks you for one.

Sometimes your hot spot is subtle, shown largely in action (someone not answering a question, leaving a room). Other times it will be stated outright. In his memoir, *This Boy's Life*, Tobias Wolff remembers driving with his new stepfather. He sets the scene:

> We drove farther into the mountains. It was late afternoon. Pale cold light. The river flashed green through the trees beside the road, then turned gray as pewter when the sun dropped. The mountains darkened. Night came on.

The stepfather leaves the young Wolff alone in the car, and the narrator thinks, "I didn't want to get in more trouble. I wanted everything to go right."

That's a change, that last sentence. The kid is, at least for the moment, through rebelling against the stepdad.

Scene over.

DO YOU RESIST WRITING SCENES?

Scenes require a certain kind of writing energy. It's easier to just continue to set down your thoughts, or to park yourself on a bench and think back. Even when you get a scene in motion — "Mary strode into the bar and spotted her husband with his ex-wife" — you'll be tempted to swing back into narration or back story or talk. "What a rat. After I had put him through dental school. My mother was right ..." and so on. It's just more comfortable than staying in the room, and easier than doing the step-by-step imaginative labor of dramatizing a scene.

A student, Marsh Rose, kept sending me scenes in which two characters sat over coffee and told each other things Marsh wanted us to know. I made her

get in her aged sports car and drive down from Cotati to San Francisco to
spend a day at my kitchen writing a scene. Every now and then, I'd cruise in
from another room to peer over her shoulder and say, "No, you're just talking,
or giving us back story. Stay there in jail while you try to get Marilyn to come
in for her therapy appointment." Marsh did. She had to fight her penchant
for going from funny line to funny line. At the end of the day, Marsh had
a scene. Six months later, a book. If you can write a scene, you can write 50
scenes. If you can write 50 scenes, you can write a book.

Do Your Commenting Between Scenes

Notice, in this rough draft by a student, how much is commentary (in caps),
and not scene at all.

> *I thought the worst part of my first medical checkup in a couple
> of years was going to be Dr. Jones's index finger reaching up my
> butt looking for nuggets or polyps or something else. It's not an
> abnormal fear of a gloved hand that has kept me away, rather the
> good doctor's guidance that an annual physical wasn't necessary
> for a man of my age.* But, as I sit, waiting, in the corner of a small
> examining room, wearing this Bounty paper towel, *it's hard to argue
> that "not every year" equates to one every five years. Is there even
> a word for that?* Joel Jones, a seasoned, stooped man with a kind,
> professorial manner, greets me warmly. *The first time I saw him
> was back in January, 6 months before, when my back seized up
> during an early morning run. He'd told me to gobble down Advil like
> they were MMs. On my own, I pushed up into downward facing dog
> at the yoga studio, pulled down weights on the lat press machine,
> and allowed myself to be manipulated (albeit at the chiropractor's
> office).*

Imagine if you were watching a movie and they froze the frame and starting talking to you like that. (Actually, in the Woody Allen movie, "Vicky
Christine Barcelona," there's an off-screen narrator. Irritating.)

You can — must! — have reactions in a scene, but keep them short and per-
tinent to what's happening. Notice how my student Eva Williams does this in
a scene from her memoir in progress, in which the ex-husband and the narrator try to coax an anorexic daughter to eat. I've put the narrator's thoughts
in italic.

"Colette, you've got to eat," Louis said. His voice was firm. *I could see the simple If embroidered on the cuff peeking out from the sleeve of his suit jacket. Louis Filatreau. It was one of his custom shirts, the ones he had specially tailored to fit his long body. He hadn't always worn custom shirts.*

I waved him off, forcing a smile. *I knew he felt bad, even responsible, in his mother-hen kind of way. I knew he genuinely wanted to help, but in this moment I couldn't think of a single thing he could do, except go away.* He had a sandwich on a plate in his hand; his lunch — tuna mixed with plain yogurt instead of mayonnaise, on a toasted whole-wheat bagel. *It was the lunch he ate most days.* I watched him disappear into our bedroom. *Maybe if I left them alone, Louis could get through to Colette. Maybe he could do what I had not been able to do: make her eat, make her laugh; make her forget whatever it was that had thrown her into this annihilative abstinence.* "I'll go change," I said then. "I'm not going back to the office today anyway."

Notice that Eva avoids commentary that takes us out of scene. She doesn't write sentences such as: "I remembered six years ago when she was in the Brownies," or "They've always been close, the two of them."

TRY THIS:

Let's practice writing a short scene. Who's in this scene? You, for sure. What do you want? What's keeping you from getting it? What's at stake? Write 10 images of people, 10 quotes, five images of time and place. Jot down images. John Steinbeck said, "Just take a period. Then try to remember it so clearly that you can see things — what colors and how warm or cold and how you got there. Then try to remember people. Then just tell what happened. It is important to tell what people looked like, how they walked, what they wore, what they ate."

Locate us in time and space. How old were you? What was happening in the world at that time?

I know that in my childhood memoir I have to have the scene where I ran after my dad as he was leaving for good. Much of what I remember — sometimes all that I remember — are feelings, and large events, and sometime small details. I have to put in — find out, or make up — what I don't remember, so that I don't end up writing: "I was around eleven, I think. I don't remember the weather, or why I woke up, or what my father said to me, or …"

I can start with period details: It is May 1962. My sister, Nora, 14, was taping c-shaped curls to her cheeks with cellophane tape. Women wore stirrup pants with stitched-in creases that tended to bag at the knees. The Four Seasons sang, "Big Girls Don't Cry" on the radio, and several convicts had escaped from Alcatraz and were on the loose.

There are only two people in this scene, my father and me. He is almost 42, and I am 11. He wants to leave without having to think about what he's doing. I want, not for him to stay — no one by then wanted that — but a sign and acknowledgment of what had been between us. I wanted it to matter to him that I too would be left behind, along with all the others.

I have to get something down. Once I do that, I can start rewriting, trying to make it work. However, as someone said, you can't rewrite a blank page. Therefore, I get something down, anything.

> A noise wakes me up. A chain. The radio in the kitchen is sputtering something about John Glenn, orbiting the earth. I see him in his spacesuit going round and round in an endless blue arc. His silver suit is catching the rays of the sun 40 volts down to the dark. I snap the dog's leash off the chain. Dad always took his dog to work with him. "No," Dad says, "Let him be, Dare." And then I know. The knowledge moves through me like a wave, right down to my feet. It's not him. I will miss. But myself. The way I was before this happened.

Those rough notes give me something to start with. And, amazingly, as soon as I write something, anything, down, it begins to be real, even for me. It's as if it happened exactly as I say.

MAKING NOTES FOR A SCENE
What is the event in your scene? Does something clearly happen?
What do you want in the scene?

What's keeping you from getting it?

Where's the best place to set the scene? In the scene grounded in time and place?

How do you respond to what happens?

Is your response all interior, or is there action?

What's the mood of the scene?

What changes in the scene, and how does that move the story forward?

How does this scene connect with the one behind and the one ahead?

Is the event important enough to be a scene, or could you just summarize it and leave it at that?

What's the purpose of the scene? This could include conveying information, a confrontation, a decision, a revelation, turning point, capitulation, resolution. Can you summarize this purpose in a sentence?

Is it clear where the scene begins and ends?

Do blocks of flashback or commentary or description break up the flow?

Can you enter the scene at a later point?

Check: for every action, is there a response?

TRY THIS:
Find an emotional sentence in a piece and expand it into a short scene. (Make it a loaded sentence, like this one: "The first time my mother had asked me if I was a lesbian, I was not ready to talk about it.")

....

THE CRAFTY WRITER
You don't always have to give us transitions between scenes. Just hit the space bar a couple of times, and jump into the next one. At the end of the scene, try for a dramatic curtain line — "Yes, I slept with her!"— that will push us into the next page. (It's a good idea to have one at the end of chapters, too).

....

BRINGING YOUR MOM TO LIFE: CHARACTERIZATION

In a scene, the action unfolds right in front of us — we hear your characters, see their gestures, smell their cigar smoke. That means scenes provide a good way to sneak in description and characterization — why say your sister is greedy when you can show her taking more than her share of cookies?

When your mother appears in your memoir, she is not your mother, but a character. So are you, for that matter. You can't just transfer Mom from your childhood kitchen to the pages of your book. The real Mom is too complex, too reasonable, and too contradictory to be a vivid character without an assist from you. Also, you know her, and it's easy to forget we don't. When you say, "My mother was home," give us images so we know whether to picture an Argentine matron polishing her hall mirror or a Louisiana nurse's aide passed out in front of Judge Judy with an empty bottle of Gilbey's in her hand.

Use fantasy to show what your mother is NOT like:

> For a brief moment, I fantasized my mother as June Cleaver or Samantha Stevens, even. She would greet me at the door with a smile and lower herself to her knees to meet me eye to eye. She would hold the prize behind her back until she had my full attention and then, with great fanfare, and proffered hand, reveal the source of her excitement.

Find the details that say a lot about who somebody is. "My mother had a habit of cutting up a good likeness and superimposing it, gluing it, on another not quite as flattering." You might mention that your mother polishes her nails only once for a wedding, then takes the polish off. (I seem to be picking on moms in this chapter.)

Description can reveal character, as in this passage written by my student Robert Doane about his father's study:

> There were special drapes that my mother hated, printed with over-scaled succulent foliage in dramatic tones on an ivory background. These went floor to ceiling and overwhelmed the room, making it seem like a set design. He had worked in Hollywood. When I was about eight he explained to me that he had mixed the hue for the walls himself, because he suspected the painter (an artist himself) was secretly color-blind. The drapes reminded me of the end papers of his books, which were miraculously marbled in an elegant riot of many rich colors that simultaneously imitated nature and commented on it.

Here's a fanciful image from a wonderful essay called "On Memory: Eel or Crystal?" by Inga Clendinnen in which a girl is assembled like a robot:

> In childhood my sister was an assemblage of parts: the stockings I washed, the silver dancing shoes I stroked to brightness, the light brown hair with golden glints I shampooed and rollered on Saturday mornings, the armfuls of net and tulle engulfing the kitchen table on Saturday afternoons. Together we concocted the radiant being who swept out of the house on Saturday nights to captivate local society at the Geelong Palais de Dance.

Don't forget to sketch yourself. One student wrote, "When I'm home and not expecting company, I usually wear a T-shirt and shorts. Sometimes just the T-shirt. When I am expecting company, I am likely to add my pearl earrings and the shorts for sure." Instead of saying, "I was working all the time," give us images of you hunched over a desk eating Peking Duck out of a carton.

Show people in action

My student Liz Roberts described a roommate like this:

> I knew immediately that Chuck, for one, would be right at home, because as soon as he arrived he kicked off his shoes and dropped his wet jacket on the floor. He accepted my offer of orange juice with alacrity and later padded into the kitchen in fuzzy turquoise socks to help himself and Sandra to more, plus a shot of my tequila.

Show groups

Here's my student Rita's depiction of her dating competition for the young male doctors at her medical school:

> The town was crawling with legions of sultry, enticing black women clutching Coach handbags and parading around DuPont Circle in Ferragamo shoes and jangling gold bracelets. Vanilla-colored women with full breasts, rounded hips and straight raven black hair, smelling like musk and cherry blossoms. Slender, nutmeg-colored women running their red lacquered nails through layers of streaked blond curls like Hollywood starlets. This elegantly coiffed brigade prowled the dingy green halls of medical school hunting for

a brother with a starched white lab coat and a stethoscope dangling from his neck. Even scrawny guys with bifocals, skinny legs and high water pants strutted around as arrogant as palace peacocks, plucking and discarding women like soggy Kleenex tissues, confident that another honey was coming around the corner.

Try thinking about your characters the way a fiction writer does. Make lists: (1) what you know about the character, (2) how you know it (if you've described the person in as being neat, you might write "aligns the pot handles on the stove.")

TRY THIS:
Write a detailed, specific list of five "loves," "hates," and "always" for each of two major characters, and in each case say WHY. Then add to this a third list: what each character wants, and why.

Once you have the trick of thinking of your relatives as characters on the page, you have a shot of coming up with paragraphs like this one from Mary McCarthy's *Memoirs of a Catholic Girlhood*; it combines narration with reflection, character, and humor, and is typical of the wonderful tone of that book:

A distinction must be made between my uncle's capricious brutality and my aunt's punishments and repressions, which seem to have been dictated to her by her conscience. My aunt was not a bad woman; she was only a believer in method. Since it was the family theory that we had been spoiled, she undertook energetically to remedy this by quasi-scientific means. Everything we did proceeded according to schedule and in line with an over-all plan. She was very strong, naturally, on toilet-training, and everything in our life was directed toward the after-breakfast session on the "the throne." Our whole diet — not to speak of the morning orange juice with castor oil in it that was brought to us on the slightest pretext of "paleness" — was centered around this lever.]

Mary McCarthy's choice of words captures the essence of who she is — brilliant, observant, sardonic, and wise — while bringing home to us the horrors that passed as childrearing in her family.

Here's a paragraph from a student paper that captures a family at dinner:

Once during a meal Pop raised his eyes from the paper and pointed across the table to some cheese he wanted to put on his bread. My oldest brother, then nineteen years old, said to my father, "It has a name." The rest of us trembled inwardly with fear. You just did not dare to make a remark like that to Pop. Phew, such luck. Raising his right eyebrow a bit, Pop said, "Kaas," cheese in Dutch, without a please. My brother passed the cheese to Pop without a word, but I saw the twitch of a little smile at the corner of his lips. The rest of us let out a held breath and the older kids and Mom pretended to talk again, unperturbed.

Speaking of characters who double as your relatives, *Turning Memories into Memoirs* has some interesting things to say about myths and archetypes. Skimming it, I can see that my mother, like so many Irish mothers, falls into the "martyr" archetype: those who need to be rewarded for their sacrifices, and who use them to evade personal growth. My father falls into the "orphan" type: "Because they feel detached from roots, family, etc, 'orphan' artists are free to tell the truth as they see it."

Then we have "the prince-left-at-the-pauper's-door," one of the better descriptions of my sister Nora. (If Nora could have worn a paper bag over her head her entire childhood, she would have.) "These people are imbued with a sense of their innate worth. They may happen to be poor at the moment, but they are really princes or princesses and have a right to special status in life. These people may look disdainfully on the other 'paupers' among whom they live."

. . . .

THE CRAFTY WRITER

List the characters in your books and add a sentence saying how each contributes to the progression of your story along your thematic line — i.e., "Nora is the child in the family who never had any illusions, but saw things as they were, in a hard light." If they aren't part of the core struggle of the book, out they go. Of course in a memoir it's hard to toss characters out wholesale — I'd certainly like to cut my siblings down to a more manageable three or four, as opposed to seven. But I notice that in *The Color of Water* author James McBride lets his numerous siblings come and go in a kind of shadowy way, and doesn't have to develop all twelve of them.

. . . .

DIALOGUE

Let's talk about dialogue. Dialogue is very readable, makes writing move fast, and is the fastest way to reveal character. There are two main kinds, *direct* and *indirect*:

INDIRECT DIALOGUE: "John said he'd back the car out."
DIRECT DIALOGUE: "I'll back the car out," John said.

You can combine them: "They argued about who was going to back the car out (they were both a little drunk), then John said, 'I'll back it out.' "

Dialogue Tags

Even in a heated exchange between two speakers, keep putting in dialogue tags that tell us where they are and what they're doing, so they don't become disembodied voices. Keep dialogue short and punchy. We're not allowed to say much before we're interrupted by others or by something else going on.

Cut out the extra words people use that clutters their speech ("Well" and "You know"). You don't need people to *whine, whimper, sneer, growl,* and — ugh! — *enthuse* or *quip*. It's fine to keep repeating, "he said," "she said" because the eye skips right over it. Dialogue must include conflict — we won't put up with two old friends chatting, like this:

"Hey, glad you could make it. Coffee?"
"Yes, that would be nice."

Subtext

Dialogue gets interesting when there's subtext: what characters are saying between the lines. Here's an example of dialogue with subtext in a scene by my student Wendy Baker:

> I'm lying on the couch in the morning in a ratty nightgown, doing what I've been doing for six months — staying home, not doing anything. I'm watching TV with the sound on low. My mother is down the hall in her bedroom getting ready for work. She heads for the bathroom with her mug of instant coffee, spoon still in it, to do her hair. She calls, "There's ham in there. I might make some soup out of it when I get home."

I say nothing.

"Your brother won't be home until after the game."

Still no response from me. Mom comes in the hall and stands at the end of the couch putting a last pin in her French twist. "I want you to help me today and cut up that ham. It's just a piece of ham. I want you to slice it up."

"No," I say after a silence. I rush to my room and slam the door behind me.

She shouts, "It's just a god damned piece of ham!"

The exchange seems to be about a mundane chore the mother wants the daughter to do, but the subtext is the daughter's depression, and the mother's worry.

Scene and narration are elements you find in fiction, but there's another crucial element, unique to memoir, as we'll see in the next chapter.

CHAPTER TWELVE

WHEN TO TELL, NOT SHOW: REFLECTIVE VOICE

Ask Why
No Shrinks

> Consciousness, not experience, is the galvanizing core of a personal story.
>
> Patricia Hampl

In a memoir the author both tells the story and interprets it. In an essay this is called perspective. In a memoir, it's called reflective voice. It's the voice in the book that comments.

In *A Slant of Sun*, Beth Kephart uses reflective voice to describe how she feels about having an autistic son:

> It seems to me that my inability to enter my son's world is a personal failure, a crisis. I do not mention it to the few friends who call. I hide it from my family, and I decline to talk about such things with my husband, who somehow always understands where Jeremy's [toy] cars are going and why; knows, just by observing, which car is the odd car out and free for moving. I can't talk to my husband because he is the better parent, and so in the dark at night, I lie awake and wonder, worry about the instincts I am lacking, and conclude — horrified — that love alone may not be enough.

"I lie awake and wonder, worry about the instincts I am lacking, and conclude — horrified — that love alone may not be enough." That's reflective voice: it is the voice in the book that makes sense of things. The reflective voice employs phrases such as:

If this hadn't happened then I would never have done this ...
It's the first time I really ...
Before then I had felt ...
Later I imagined ...
Then I thought ...
Now I realize ...
Sometime I may decide ...
I didn't know what my mother was thinking then, but I think I do now ...

Why Do We Need It?

It's not enough to tell us that you did 100 jigsaw puzzles in a row after your sister died. We want to know *why* you did. That way your story is about human nature — about us, not you. We assume you are telling us your story because you now have some insight into it: insight into why you and others behaved as you did, into why things happened as they did.

In a memoir, you are two people. First, you are the harried, clueless, sweaty person living through the events as they unfold on the page, with no perspective, no idea of what's going to happen, and perhaps no idea why you behave as you do. For example, the *you then*, in the story, may think of her son as just a little eccentric. But *you now* is also the author, looking back, and knows that you were missing the signs of autism.

Reflective voice tells us why you think you missed those signs: "I didn't want it to be true, so I told myself lots of kids sing jingles from commercials."

The reflective voice, is, by the way, how you can get an adult voice in a book about your childhood. If you use the voice of the adult narrator looking back, you can get both the immediacy of the kid's view and the adult perspective. *To Kill a Mockingbird*, for example, has an adult narrator looking back. (It's a novel, I know, but an autobiographical one.) The difference can be as simple as this:

Kid voice: "Mommy always."

Adult author: "My mother always."

Readers grow tetchy when the author fails to offer insight into what people did. "You're telling me this because?" we want to ask. In an earlier chapter I mentioned my Limerick friend Mikel, who wrote a memoir about his drunken Irish childhood. His vivid scenes of a job on a fishing trawler and high-rise construction jobs brought out an interesting theme: the forgiving world of fellow men, where the worst family bungling can be washed away with a pint. As I read his pages, I knew what happened, knew what choices he made. But I didn't know *why* he made them. Like, why *fishing*? What in him seized on this particular fantasy? Why does he decide at one point to go to Australia? On his first day of school at five years old he went up a tree rather than into the classroom like the other boys. I wanted to know why. What is this contrary act an early indication of?

The young protagonist in Mikel's story is drunk and numb much of the time. But the author is the experienced, wised-up Mikel, recalling these adventures from his Victorian house in San Francisco's Haight-Ashbury neighborhood, telling us about his younger self's antics because he has some insight into them.

Vivian Gornick in *The Situation and the Story* says, "Good writing has two characteristics. It's alive on the page and the reader is persuaded that the writer is on a voyage of discovery." She says that J. R. Ackerley in *My Father and Myself* "is a wholly engaging man, not because he sets out to be fashionably honest but because the reader feels him actively working to strip down the anxiety till he can get to something hard and true beneath the smooth surface of sentimental self regard."

Gornick believes that every memoir is about a flash of insight—hers was that she could not leave her mother because she had become her mother. This insight organizes the writing. She says that the successful memoirist may not know any more than the rest of us, but they know who they are at the moment of writing.

John Beckman, an editor in Sonoma that I paid to read the manuscript of *Hold Me Close*, found an early draft of mine:

> Jagged, composed of too many jump cuts, rather than a memoir
> that flowed and grew in understanding over time. In a way, too
> much show, and not enough tell. If we had more of your thoughts
> on your work, Bill, family, the nature of the times, and how all of

that fits emotionally into the crisis, there would be more perspective. We need to make you more sympathetic to the reader, and the
best way for you to do this is to step back from the narrative and
comment on why you did what you did.

Grateful for such criticism, in later drafts I tried to get better at reflective
voice. Trying, for example to account for why I kept my new husband around
when the tension between him and Morgan drove her into the streets, I said:

> I wanted to be a good mom, wanted it desperately, even, but
> their childhood coincided with the prime of my life, my career, my
> romances, all the pleasures and distractions of an urban life. I was
> their mom, and this was their childhood. But at the same time, I
> was a woman who had just found the man she wanted to spend the
> rest of her life with. I was mid-span in my own life, and this was it:
> my chance at lasting love.

Editors and reviewers take memoirists to task for the absence of reflective
voice. In *The New York Times*, Elisa Dixler, reviewing *Expecting to Fly* by
Martha Todd Dudman, said: "Her focus on the details leaves the big questions unanswered. Why did Martha stop taking drugs? Why was she so angry
at her kind, supportive parents? Was her rebellion sparked by the atmosphere
of the 60s, or was it more personal? Was it safer to take those chances in the
60's than it is now? And how, really, does she feel about her experience?"
A good agent will ask similar questions long before the book is out and being
reviewed. A friend told me her agent handed back the first six chapters she
was given and told her she wasn't going deep enough. All the pages were all
marked with "Why?" and "What really happened?"

ASK WHY

As E.M. Forster famously pointed out, there's a difference between saying,
"The king died, and then the queen died," and " The king died, and the
queen died of grief." Instead of, "When I was eight, my mother sent me to
live with my aunts in Rhode Island," we want, "My mother sent me to Rhode
Island because ..." because why? She's met someone who didn't want kids
around? She couldn't afford to keep you? If you don't know the answers, you
can offer a guess. One student speculated on why her mother behaved as she
did this way: "Now I realize my mother's fears were so profound, and so deep,

driven into her bones from the days she fled Russian revolutionaries in her mother's arms at age two, from Poland. Her first years must have been spent in terror."

You have to know why you are drawn to the patient who thought she was going to have puppies. Why that memory is so strong a part of you? You have to keep going deeper, until you realize that you were struggling with coming out as a lesbian in your fundamentalist family, and that you felt kinship to the patient as an outcast. And in making them for us, of course, you make those connections for yourself.

The best way to get in reflective voice is to keep asking questions and try to answer them: Why did your parents leave Oklahoma? Why did your mother want you to be Chinese, while your father wanted you to be Chinese-American? Why did your mother take a job as a carhop? Why did your grandfather run off? Why did you marry a jerk? Why did your parents not notice all the food you stole from the fridge in the worst stages of your bulimia? Why did you think you could sleep with someone you cared about and not get attached?

As we saw in the essay, questions can actually drive the book, so that the search for answers becomes part of the suspense. Who set that fire? Whose baby was it? Why did the family move to Idaho? Why didn't your mother leave, or stay? The events of the story shed light on the question that is troubling you — was my father a good man? Am I a good mother? Will I survive my illness? Why do I keep picking the wrong men? Lynn Freed said in *Reading, Writing, and Leaving Home*, that the writer has to defictionalize her life, "to disentangle it from the myths and fictions that we all create in order to control what we cannot alter. And then to work down, down, down, to the morally anaerobic heart of the matter within."

Use reflective voice to account for your own actions. My student Erika Johnson reflected on why she got married so fast:

> Even at thirty-three I was old enough to have experienced the consequences of sliding into romantic relationships for no real reason except that the opportunity presented itself, and specifically the opportunity to care for another person. As finicky, even obsessive, as I could be in terms of my environment — the structured way in

which I went about my life — I knew I was surprisingly sloppy in the manner in which I made decisions.

NO SHRINKS

Shun all descriptions of the characters' spiritual state. You must try to have that state emerge from their actions.

— Anton Chekhov

Of course the insights in a memoir can echo the realizations of psychotherapy. But beware: imagine Flaubert writing about the childhood trauma that made Madame Bovary unfaithful to her husband, or Anna Karenina, not hit by the train after all, pouring her heart out to her shrink. Or Romeo and Juliet discussing their relationship before each rushes off to a shrink to find out why they keep falling for unattainable objects. The point of the book should not be to show how the events of the book affected you psychologically. Psychological explanations rob your characters of free will. If your book is about the injury done to you in childhood, well, then the damage is done. Story over. If I tell you my father's mother died when he was five, and he was kicked from pillar to post, you will think you have the why of his story already — everything he does afterward will be seen in the light of that injury — and thus seen to be inevitable. If he had no choices, there is no story.

The writer Marilynne Robinson (*Home* and *Gilead*) says that the therapeutic narrative is part of the "mean little myth" of our time: "One is born and in passage through childhood suffers from grave harm. The work of one's life is to discover and name the harm one has suffered."

While you're at it, avoid scenes in which you talk to a shrink. Unless you're Tony Soprano (and even he got away with it only because he was a mob boss). In her memoir of her relationship with her mother, *Fierce Attachments*, Vivian Gornick mentioned therapy exactly once, and that well into the second half of the book, where she consolidated what was probably many sessions into a short summary of questions posed and her own startled responses.

Tip: If you need to relay the insights gained in a session with a therapist, you might instead shift those conversations to a sister or a friend.

And, please, no shrink jargon! Your mother did not suffer from financial abuse, she was robbed. No *control freak*, *denial*, *validated*, or *passive aggressive*. No *closure* or *boundaries*.

THE CRAFTY WRITER

If you think your book is getting too psychological, too process-y, in a particular part, think: could I film this? If you have pages and pages that contain nothing you could point a camera at, worry.

And no dreams! You have a vivid dream life, and your dreams have often given you a deeper understanding of who you are. But they are not inherently dramatic — they didn't really happen, after all — and they are too personal. Use them only if essential.

CHAPTER THIRTEEN

PUBLISHING YOUR MEMOIR

Find an Agent

The Proposal

Promoting Your Book

Self-Publishing

Nothing in me wants to sell a book. I want to stay home and write, and blush and nod when someone pleads to be allowed to publish my unworthy pages. Nor do I want to help publicize it. Privately I hate the new deal that says every writer who taps out a book must, the moment the printed version of it arrives in stores, transform herself from an introvert with spiders in her hair to a master of witty repartee.

I'm living in a dream world, of course. Today whether you choose traditional publishing, or, as we'll talk about in a minute, self-publishing on the Internet, you must think about how you personally will help your book reach an audience long before the book hits the stores.

But first you write the book and find an agent.

STEP ONE: WRITE THE BOOK OR AT LEAST TWO CHAPTERS OF IT

Almost all nonfiction books are sold with proposals. You don't have to write the whole book first, as you must with a novel, but can sell it on the basis of a couple of polished chapters and a detailed outline. If you feel you must write your book if it is ever published or not, finish it first. Then dip your toe in the waters of the publishing world. If you want to write it only if you are sure you can get it published, then write those couple of chapters and then find an agent.

STEP TWO: FIND AN AGENT

The days of sending a book straight to a publisher are gone, unless you are targeting a university press or a small press. (I do sell small point-of-sale books to Chronicle Books, but my husband Bill is the cookbook editor there, so I am a sort of faculty wife.) So you will need an agent. An agent is someone who agrees to represent your book in all dealings with a publisher. He or she decides which editors at which publishing houses would be interested in it, and sends it — or your proposal — to them with a cover letter explaining why they should buy your book before competitors discover it. When the book is accepted, the agent gets you a good contract and tracks the book thereafter, helping sell foreign rights or paperback rights, trouble-shooting, and turning the editor upside-down until your check falls out of his pockets. The agent usually gets 15 percent of your royalties.

My agent, Fred Hill, got *Hold Me Close* into a New York auction (that's when several publishing houses bid on the same day) and Random House (actually its subdivision Broadway Books), the winner (and the only bidder, but never mind), gave me an advance of $110,000 for it (which I promptly put into about-to-crash tech stocks, while a writer friend put his advance into a Tuscan villa that he still has, but never mind that either).

A good way to find an agent, besides asking around, is to go to a large bookstore and leaf through books that are like yours. Note which agents are thanked in the acknowledgments, then contact them. (Dave Eggers has said he sought out David Sedaris's agent, for example.) Literaryagents.com is a good place to find names, too. You might pony up for Publishers Lunch, a insider newsletter that tells which agents are doing the hot deals. Find it at publishersmarketplace.com.

Take your time on this: you don't want to spend years writing a book, and then five minutes on the question of who is going to shepherd it into the world for you. Avoid agents who charge a reading fee, by the way. They aren't supposed to do that.

Contacts

If you can drop a name, do it. Contacts are as useful in publishing as they are in any other business. It's easier to sell work to agents or editors you know personally. My student Susan Parker, who wrote a memoir called *Tumbling After* about taking care of her quadriplegic husband, says of the thirteen houses her first agent sent it to, only the editor at Norton that Susan met at a workshop, showed interest. (It was ultimately sold to Crown).

A lot of the agents and editors live in New York, of course, and you may not want to move there on the off-chance of smacking into one of them while jogging. But writing workshops and conferences are held all over the country, and they offer a chance to meet agents, editors and famous authors face to face. There's a list of them in every issue of *Poets & Writers* magazine. (Even if you know the editor personally, though, you should still get an agent to represent you.) If editors or agents offer workshops near you, sign up for them.

The Query Letter

Once you have the names of agents you want to approach, what's the next step? You don't send them the book. You don't even send them the entire book proposal (I know we haven't talked about book proposals yet, but believe me, we will.) You send them a one-page sheet of paper called a *query*, in which you try to convince them you are a hot writer with a hot project. You do want to have your book proposal ready to go, so you can send it to them if they ask to see it.

One page is short — no more than 300 words — but you'll sweat over it more than any other page you write. An agent is not going to sign up the writer of a boring query letter.

Or an unprofessional one. Start with a simple header at the top of the page giving your name, address, telephone number, and email address. Make it double-spaced, on plain white paper, with 12-type in a black font (Times New Roman is good). If you're emailing, put, "Query: (title of book)" in the subject line. If snail-mailing, include a self-addressed stamped envelope for replies. Use block paragraphs — no indentations. Don't begin "Dear Sir." Big turnoff. Know who the agent is. "I am writing to you because you represented *I Was a Teenaged Professor* and I think my book is similar."

Then give us a single sentence that says what's in the book. "This is *Godfather I* meets *Girl, Interrupted*." The query letter is not, "This is about the experiences I had in Africa in the 1970s." Sue Shapiro said she pitched *Five Men Who Broke My Heart* by saying in the query, "Here's a memoir for anyone who's ever wondered what happened to their first love, or second, or third, or fourth, or fifth." The agent knows there are no truly fresh ideas, only fresh spins on old ones. Tell him your spin.

Pretend you're on a talk show and have like two lines to get your book across. (I was on book tour in Louisville, Kentucky with Morgan, heading sleepily to some predawn farm TV program, when our guide said, "Think sound bites! You won't have much time!") The agent has a lot to do, and wants to put your letter in the "No Thanks" pile and go on to the next. Your job is to get him to pick up his Blackberry instead.

In the letter, stick to the manuscript — no need to talk about how you will market the book, and for god's sake don't mention other books you have waiting in the pipeline after he's looked at this one.

The next paragraph gives the agent your credentials. Say something about your background, why you wrote the book. Do you have an MFA? Are you an experienced published writer? Appeared in literary magazines? (I've heard that moves you to the top of the pile).

If you've never been published before, no reason to bring that up. You do have an advantage in having no sales figure track record: you have never failed. Your book could be the next *Eat, Pray, Love.* Experienced authors with fifteen titles out (books that did all right but did not "break out," as they say) change their names so they can burst on the scene with all the freshness of a pretty girl at her first dance. Jason Roberts (*A Gentleman in the Distance*) worked for nine months on his proposal, then he sent it to the agent of Dava Sobel (*Longitude*). On her advice, he omitted all mention of his previous computer books. "It was as if I had never written anything," Roberts said.

Keep the tone of the letter quiet and assured. Don't sell the book. That's the agent's job. Don't give her the hype; just the facts (the persuasive facts of course). Let her discover you.

Write the query out long and then punch it down to one page. Hone it. Make it exciting and interesting, and concise. End by saying, "I would love to send you my proposal."

What not to say:

I'm an unpublished writer.

I don't know if this will interest you.

I had a bad experience with another publisher.

(As my dad says, don't supply the rocks that are to be thrown at you.)

Snail Mail or E-Mail?

Some agents prefer queries to come in the regular mail with a self-addressed, stamped audience. Check their websites for how they like to writers to approach them. Yes, you can send the query to several at once, but it's considered fair to let them know you're doing it.

Be patient. They're busy.

Don't be discouraged that you don't land an agent on your first or second round of inquiries; it can take time. Rejection is not a comment on your book.

Interested agents will respond by asking you to send your book proposal (again, not the whole book). If they like the proposal, they might ask to read the whole book, if it's done. Once an agent accepts you (and, by the way, check the agent out — you are now his employer, after all) he may or may not ask you to sign a contract. Some agents will ask you to redo the proposal or make editing suggestions on the book, some won't.

Then they send it out to publishing houses, and get you a contract. Now you have a new person in your life: your editor. The editor may want further revisions. (Be advised—they say that new authors are the most demanding and the most resistant to revision. Be cool. Don't demand to know the marketing plan right away, don't refer to the treatment other authors get, and don't turn the book in late.)

STEP THREE: THE PROPOSAL

(This is really part of Step Two). A proposal is like a business plan. It's meant to convince an agent, and after him the editors he will send it to, that your book will sell. In brief, a proposal outlines what you're going to do in the book, how it's different from everything else out there, why you're the best person to write it, and who will buy it.

Title

This is the very first thing an editor looks at when reviewing a proposal. Your agent can help with this. My agent hated *Naked, Drunk and Writing* as a title for this book, but I like it. (He preferred *With A Hot Heart and a Cold Eye*.) Other titles I had for a while included *Turning Your Worst Moments into Money*, *The Luminosity of the Particular*, and *Dance Lessons*.

A good title grabs attention and yet says clearly what the book is about. This might be something you and your agent can brainstorm on together, unless of course your agent doesn't have the sense to admire a great title like *Naked, Drunk and Writing*. You use the subtitle in a memoir to say exactly what the book is about.

I had a hard time choosing a title for my memoir about my daughter. A friend, Mark Sloan, suggested I call it *Chicken Soup For What's Left Of Your Soul After Your Teenager Has Ripped Your Heart Out Of Your Chest And Stomped On It With Her Platform Sneakers*. I also liked *How I'm Doing? Call 1-800-Let's-See-You-Do-It*.

I found the real title when I heard that the story of raising a child is "Pick me up, hold me close, put me down, let me go." That seemed longish, and my friend Donna Levin helped me shorten it. (It came out in Japan, and a Tokyo friend said the title translates as:"How to Appreciate a Very Bad Daughter.") Titles and covers are marketing devices, and thus the publisher's call. My friend Janis Newman wanted to call her novel about Mary Todd Lincoln *The Madhouse Summer of Mary Todd Lincoln*, which I thought was a fabulous title, but the publisher wanted titles like *Asylum* and they finally compromised on *Mary*. I wanted to call my book on being a grandmother *Know When to Hold 'Em: Playing Your Cards Right as a New Grandmother*, but the sales and marketing folks at Chronicle Books didn't go for it, and they're the ones who have to get it into the bookstores. It's called *The Granny Diaries*, to coast off the success of *The Nanny Diaries*.

Overview

The overview tells what your book is about in one or two pages. If who you are and the work you do is a selling point, these go into the overview. Include the timeliness of the topic: is it something that's in the news a lot lately? One of my students is writing about losing all her money in the stock market and starting over at 72.

Author Bio

Don't be modest. Who are you? What makes you an expert on this subject? Most importantly, what gives you a platform? A platform is a way to reach the audience. Do you give workshops? Presentations? Have a website that gets lots of hits? Have you been featured in national magazines, on TV or radio? Most of us will not have impressive answers, but neither did many now-famous authors when they started out.

Marketing

The author bio and marketing seem to be the same category these days. Say who will want this book. Come up with numbers if you can: if your book will appeal to those who adopt Chinese orphans, tell them how many such families there are. Publishers aren't impressed when you airily claim your book appeals to everyone. They want to know what shelf the bookstore will put it on. (And which talk shows will be interested).

By the way, don't waste a lot of time talking about what you could do or what the publisher can do. Mention instead what *you are already doing*. Everyone can make their book a bestseller if they get on Oprah, but don't even bother mentioning this unless you've been on Oprah before, or the two of you play tennis on Sundays.

Competition

Are there other books on the market similar to yours? Show how your book stands out from them. Imagine your book on that shelf in the bookstore, with other books on bulimia. How is yours different? Name the top three or so competitive books and be specific about how yours is way different and way better. Maybe your memoir on breast cancer specifically focuses on women of color, or how it affects one's kids. (By the way, *read* those other books.)

TOC and Chapter Summaries

Include a nicely formatted Table of Contents and chapter summaries — chapter-by-chapter breakdowns of the entire book. This is the editor's first real look at the way you write, so work on them and make them fun to read — i.e., don't start each one with "Chapter One will include. . . ." Put your voice into it and make them read as if they were the chapters themselves. Chapter summaries can be anywhere from one paragraph to five pages long each.

Sample Chapters

The proposal will include two to three sample chapters or two sample chapters and an introduction. The grammar, punctuation, and style should be perfect. This is annoying to me, because you haven't written the whole book yet, and you know I stress not polishing anything until the whole piece of writing is at least roughly in place. You would think an editor could overloook a few tyops or **STRANGE** fonts...

Sorry. On second thought, it's not a bad idea to hire a copy editor. When choosing which sample chapters to write don't just automatically go to the first. What chapters are your strongest and most intriguing?

Agents are wily. Susan Parker, author of *Tumbling After*, told me her first agent dropped her after the editors who'd seen it complained that the book was "too dark, not enough about Ralph, not enough reflection." Though the book was done, her new agent, Amy Rennert, sent out just 50 pages — the least dark, the most reflective, and the most about her husband Ralph, paralyzed in a biking accident. It sold.

Publicity

Supply your agent with newspaper and magazine clips, tapes of radio and TV performances, copies of articles you've written or been interviewed for. It's better to send too much rather than too little. Your agent can weed through it and decide what's useful.

What Else?

Make sure your proposal has page numbers.

Are you cute? Do you have an author photo? It can't hurt to include it.

Sample news pieces: Did *Newsweek* do a cover story on the topic you're writing about? Include a copy.

It's not a bad idea to include blurbs in the proposal. A blurb is a short sales pitch or comment on a book that's used on the jacket or in marketing materials. Get your famous friend to give you a blurb you can use right in the pitch letter. (I asked Annie Lamott for the blurb on the cover of this book.) Blurbs from the famous work best, of course, but exuberant testimonials even from unknowns can work, too. Sometimes busy people will say yes if you offer to write the blurb for them: "I need something like this …"

PROMOTING YOUR BOOK

A *New Yorker* cartoon by Roz Chast shows a writer on the phone: "Mud-wrestle in my underwear on national TV while holding up a copy of my new book?" he's saying. "NO PROBLEMO!"

Your publisher may or may not send you on a book tour. Mine sent Morgan and me to five or six cities. That was nice, even if we did not exactly sell out stadiums. I remember that when we arrived in Fort Wayne, a city with brown grass in front of porches, Joyce, our media escort, told us our appearance at a downtown bookstore had been moved to an upstairs room at the university on the edge of town, as part of a new experiment.

"Let's give people a few minutes," said David, an employee of the bookstore, as Morgan and I took in the rows of empty chairs. A boy named Todd who said he was from the local paper slouched in his seat. A woman with a six-year-old came in. "Any advice for this age?" she asked. Morgan and I delivered our talk to her, the only one not being paid to be there.

"Tell me what a book tour is for again?" Morgan yawned on our way back to the Hilton in Joyce's Jeep.

"At least that woman with the little girl came," I said.

"She works for the bookstore," Morgan said. She had her head back on the seat, her eyes closed.

But the next night, in Louisville, I was relieved to see twelve or so people waiting for us at the Hawley-Cooke bookstore. A woman in the second row, around my age, held a tissue to her nose the whole time Morgan and I were speaking. Her husband, in overalls and a baseball hat, sat stolidly next to her. As Morgan and I talked, my eyes kept going to her. "It can be so hard," I said. I described the day I had to tell Morgan she couldn't live at home anymore, and saw tears slide down the woman's face. "I wrote the book for you," I told her silently.

Unless you are nationally famous (in which case your fame does it for you) these days you are expected to do more and more of the promotion for your book, from hiring publicists to setting up and paying for tours. Authors have turned out to be ingenious at this. Laurie Wagner, author of *Living Happily Ever After*, said that an aunt threw huge book parties for her in Los Angeles. "At the first event I sold 160 books to family and friends. The next event I sold 120. And the events generate word of mouth."

When San Francisco's Kirk Read got his coming-of-age memoir, *How I Learned to Snap*, published by Hill Street Press, an independent house in Athens, Georgia, he understood that publishing it was all they could afford to do. "I told them, just send me 200 books and I'll sell them," Read told me. He drove to 100 tour dates in 40 cities, everything from book group meetings to huge university lectures. He made purple T-shirts and buttons depicting a hand snapping and gave them out at each stop. He promoted his hardback so vigorously that Penguin bought the paperback.

Do-it-yourself promotion pays off, if not in huge sales then at least in keeping a good book in print long enough to find its readers. This is important in a day when bookstores give a book about three weeks on the shelf before they return it to the publisher. Linda Watanabe McFerrin of San Francisco, author of the story collection *The Hand of Buddha*, traveled to 25 states on an Amtrak pass for a month to promote it. She taught workshops and stayed with friends. Constance Hale (*Sin and Syntax: How to Craft Wickedly Effective Prose*) conducts writing and grammar workshops. "My publisher did next to nothing," she told me, "but each time I teach a class there's a little notice in some catalog or mailer about my book."

My friend Mark Childress, author of *One, Mississippi*, told me that early in his career he drove across the country and tried to go in and shake hands with every bookstore owner in his path. Charles Frazier wrote to bookstores across the south saying they might be interested in his novel, *Cold Mountain*. When he isn't setting up readings at bookstores, author James Holliday speaks at Rotary clubs, always making sure they have his books there for sale afterward. He even spoke to the American Glaucoma Society. "There are conventions and conferences in town all the time, and they need some alternative to their subjects," he told me.

One of the great overlooked bookselling circuits in the United States are the local chapters of Hadassah or Jewish women's groups. They're terrific at building word of mouth and sales.

And you can make yourself available to book clubs, a gratifying transaction on both sides, because the book club is delighted to have a real live author to talk to, and the author is delighted to speak to readers. I'm meeting with a grandmother's group soon, and they will all have acquired and read the book first. I hope.

SELF-PUBLISHING

As long as you're doing the promoting, why not publish it yourself, too, and keep all the profits?

There is something of a boom in do-it-yourself publishing. It's amazingly easy: you upload your file and photos to Internet print-on-demand companies such as Blurb, IUniverse, Xlibris, Lulu (the one I use) and Amazon's CreateSpace, and a week later there's your book, looking as if it came off a bookstore shelf. Many of the books published this way are meant for family and friends, but others find a much wider audience. You can also have it privately printed at outfits such as bookprintingrevolution.com.

From the beginning I wanted to self-publish the book you're reading. I'd get my copies and open a little stand downtown somewhere, like the lemonade stand I made as a kid out of plywood and two sawhorses, and sell my book to passersby. Or at least sell it from my website and directly to my students.

With self-publishing, you do everything: write the book, get it printed, sell it. I have friends who have done it, or have done it through the sort of halfway measure called custom publishing, where you pay some of the freight and the publisher pays part. It's a way to get published in an era when publishers are taking only the big bets.

The main problem is distribution. *Publisher's Weekly* skips self-published books, libraries won't buy them, newspaper reviewers throw them in the mail bins on the floor, and bookstores are reluctant to schedule book signings if you are unknown and, to them, unpublished. On the other hand many now cheerfully take books on consignment.

I worked with David Gottfried, author of *Greed to Green* who decided to self-publish, and succeeded in getting the organization he founded, the U.S. Green Building Council, to underwrite the costs and sell it at conventions. Like many self-published authors, David found it difficult to get the book into bookstores, but through his own connections and website had within four months sold the first printing of 5,000 copies — a respectable result. A printer in Berkeley supplied the copyediting and hired an illustrator to do the cover. He even got Paul Hawken to write a glowing foreword.

A number of self-published books are subsequently picked up by mainstream publishers. Lisa Genova, a Harvard PhD, wrote a novel about a woman with early-onset Alzheimer's disease. Turned down by the agents and editors she approached, she printed the book herself, and sold them out of the trunk of her car. Word spread; the book was picked up by a publisher, and *Still Alice* became a *New York Times* bestseller.

A self-published book that doesn't find a huge market can still be useful to its author. My student Lee Pryor's self-published *The Savvy Entrepreneur* got him an adjunct professor job at Tulane University and other perks that made it well worth it. He also put it on Amazon and sold hundreds of copies that way.

Ideas for Promoting Your Book

If you have a good topic for radio talk shows, you might buy a listing in Radio-TV Interview Report (www.rtir.com), which goes to radio producers across the country. Also consider the PR Leads.com Expert Resource Network for speakers, authors, and other experts (www.prleads.com), which forwards requests from journalists looking for spokespeople on different topics, an excellent way of generating publicity for your book.

The American Booksellers Association (ABA) has a directory (www.bookweb.org) of over two thousand independent bookstores, organized by city. Or try www.newpages.com. You can write a friendly letter describing your book and including any reviews, asking them to consider carrying it in their store.

BLOGS CAN HELP YOU SELL A MEMOIR

Bloggers such as Mimi Smartypants, Pamela Ribon, Wendy McClure and Jessica "Washingtonienne" Cutler have turned their blogs into book deals. Colby Buzzell, an American soldier, wrote a blog about his experiences as a machine-gunner in Iraq that became a book, *My War: Killing Time in Iraq*. Julie Powell wrote a cooking blog, the Julie/Julia Project, that became *Julie & Julia,* a bestseller. A Baghdad blogger named Salam Pax turned his online war diary from Iraq into a collection called *Salam Pax: The Clandestine Diary of an Ordinary Iraqi*. Ana Marie Cox, editor of wonkette.com, sold her first novel, *Dog Days*, to Riverhead Books (with a $275,000 advance) on the strength of her blog audience.

Margit Ingman had a hard time convincing publishers that her book on postpartum depression could sell. Then she asked readers of her blog to say why a book like that would interest them, and inserted their comments into the proposal. That convinced editors she already had an audience, and she sold her book, *Inconsolable*, to Seal Press.

CHAPTER FOURTEEN

WRITING IS GOOD FOR YOU

There is a vitality, a life force,
an energy, a quickening that is translated
through you into action.
And because there is only one you in all time, this expression
is unique.
And if you block it, it will never exist through any other medium,
the world will not have it.
It is not your business to determine how good it is,
nor how valuable,
nor how it compares with other expressions.
It is your business to keep it yours
clearly and directly,
to keep the channel open.

— Martha Graham

Writing a book, or an essay, or anything else that allows you to reflect on your life, has benefits that go far beyond being published.

I've been making my living as a writer in one way or the other for decades now. I've published some books, a lot of magazine articles. I've written a lot, including drafts of whole books, that has not yet been published and perhaps never will be. After the *San Francisco Chronicle* was sold to the Hearst Corporation and I left the paper where I'd been a columnist for over a decade, I stepped up my teaching, and switched to books. Being published is nice, but a lot of what writing offers has nothing to do with that. The true benefit is what it does to the inside of your head. It wakes you up. Cynthia Ozick said writing "mimics that low electric hum, which sometimes rises to resemble actual speech that all human beings carry inside their heads — a vibration, garrulous if somewhat indistinct, that never leaves us while we are awake. It is the hum of perpetual noticing."

Becoming a writer allowed me to experience my life more fully, the way a travel writer tries to travel with all his senses alert, taking notes, asking what that arch is called, holding up a tape recorder to capture the sounds of a Mumbai traffic intersection. You have to taste the eyeball soup, identify the scent of a perfumed street, ask to see not the usual moldy sights but the tour guide's house. You're like a photographer who takes his camera with him everywhere. Because you have that camera, you see not just the houses, but the light on them. That's not a bad thing, noticing the light.

And it can make you feel a hell of a lot better. Recently, one of my writing students emailed me to say:

> There are those days when I know I've gained 35 pounds overnight. There will be no hike, not even a walk, no leaving the house, no getting dressed and probably not even any getting out of bed. And then, I think, I can write in bed. I don't even have to wash my face, not even brush my teeth. I can scratch away at some exercise with abandon and I have to say sometimes I can't get over how funny and cute I think I am. After an hour or so, I often feel I've lost enough weight to get dressed! And maybe, MAYBE even leave the house.

She's talking about the sheer fun of putting words on paper, of watching amazing words come out of your fingertips, words that were never in the world before.

My friend Fiona Johnson woke in the night with an idea for a whole new approach to the biography she was working on. "I jotted on a notepad something that may be the opening paragraph of a totally different book: 'I first met Isaac in the roller skating rink in San Rafael in 1967.' I lay awake for most of the night mentally writing pieces of this new story and I was utterly happy, just because I had discovered what it was I was going to write." Another woman who came to see me recently said that she'd been getting up at 4:30 am, giddy at the thought that she was writing again. My friend Lynn Freed, a novelist, said, "Often, as I wrote, I laughed aloud. I screamed with laughter — the entomologist skewering to the board his prize beetles — those I adored and those I despised, both."

All these writers know that putting words on paper charges up every part of you, makes you feel alive, important, satisfied. You feel enlarged, fed, painted in brighter colors by what you have chosen to write down about yourself. You feel lucky to be doing something so valuable, interesting, and worthwhile, if only as a private record. Writing is hard, yes, but so are diamonds. That's why they give off that unearthly light. A friend said to me, "I realized after writing my book — which took five years — that I've done what I always wanted to do."

No matter what has happened to you, when you pin that misery to the page, turn it into little black marks that you invent and put in order, you rob it of its power. Once when I picked up Morgan the Bad at the police station, I noticed how the vending machine in the lobby kept flashing "Have a Nice Day" in red digital letters while they were fetching her for me. I was crying, but I was also, at the back of my mind, taking note of that ironic detail, the flashing vending machine. Being a writer helped that night. It helps on many days and nights. (And it's lot cheaper than therapy.)

Isabel Allende, who wrote a memoir about the death of her daughter called *Paula: A Memoir*, told me, "Writing is always a joyful process. You go into a quiet place inside you, and you transform something that may be very painful into words. It gives boundary to the pain. It sorts out the confusion. It helps you to understand, and, finally, to accept."

Writing can literally save your life. Tim O'Brien, author of *The Things They Carried*, was contemplating suicide one night, and as he thought about it, he wrote about it. "I'd literally leave the typewriter and go to the balcony, and think about jumping off, and go back and type another sentence."

You have to think about relatives as characters, with secret thoughts and passions of their own. It makes them hard to hate. My student Sharon said that she had been inclined to portray her ex-husband and others in her book as villains (twirling mustaches and train tracks), but the demands of good writing gave her, she said, "a real story of a family tragedy, not the melodrama the story might have been."

Real life is just one thing after another — sprinklers left on, a pain in the chest, a death, getting stuck in jobs and relationships. But viewed through binoculars from the hilltop — that is, with the perspective that writing can bestow — random cruel events are shown to be neither random nor cruel but understandable, and perhaps even the very events that made you strong.

When you write about the events of your life you give them order and coherence. The result is not life faithfully recorded, but life made sense of, redeemed, given meaning. "Life is a hopelessly meager thing," my father said. "What counts is what we dream into it, the words we find to describe it when we arrange jarring details to make a pleasing whole." As writers we impose order on our lives, and that allows us to think we're making progress.

Once the writing has helped you figure things out, you share your insights with others who might need it. William Styron discovered this when he wrote an article about the pain of severe depression that turned into the memoir *Darkness Visible*. "The overwhelming reactions made me feel that I had helped unlock a closet from which many souls were eager to come out and proclaim that they, too, had experienced the feelings I had described." Styron concluded that to educate his audience about depression represented a worthwhile reason to have invaded his own privacy.

Kirk Read, author of *How I Learned to Snap*, told me it's not easy to go home again when your home is Lexington, Kentucky and you've written a candid gay memoir. "But it all boils down to gay 14-year-olds in small towns," he went on. "If they can get their hands on the book, and it helps them even a little bit, then my being uncomfortable at my church's Christmas Eve service is a tiny matter."

After *Hold Me Close* came out, I got mail from mothers going through what I had, and those letters mattered to me. A woman named Louise Seeley said, "You've reminded me that the only thing I can do is the best I can, love my son, and never give up."(Admittedly, another reader called *Hold Me Close* a powerful birth control device.)

Write it down. Whatever it is, write it down. Chip it into marble. Type it into Microsoft Word. Spell it out in seaweeds on the shore. We are each of us an endangered species, delicate as unicorns.

APPENDIX

Reading List
Useful Texts
Suggestions for Writing
Writers' Resources

READING LIST

The Only Girl in the Car by Kathy Dobie

Bad Blood by Lorna Sage

The Color of Water: A Black Man's Tribute to his White Mother by James McBride

Angela's Ashes by Frank McCourt

This Boy's Life by Tobias Wolff

Don't Let's Go to the Dogs Tonight by Alexandra Fuller

Growing Up by Russell Baker

Memoirs of a Catholic Girlhood by Mary McCarthy

Borstal Boy by Brendan Behan

The Duke of Deception by Geoffrey Wolff

The Liars' Club by Mary Karr

And When Did You Last See Your Father? by Blake Morrison

USEFUL TEXTS

Writing Fiction A Guide to Narrative Craft by Janet Burroway (any edition)
Addison, Wesley Longman, Inc. (find it secondhand or it'll cost the earth)

Putting Your Passion into Print by Arielle Eckstut and David Henry Sterry

The Art of Time in Memoir by Sven Birkerts

Unreliable Truth: On Memoir and Memory by Maureen Murdock

Your Life as Story by Tristine Rainer

The Situation and the Story by Vivian Gornick

The Art of the Personal Essay by Philip Lopate

Bird by Bird by Anne Lamott

SUGGESTIONS FOR WRITING

Write a piece that takes place in a single time period: washing a car, packing a suitcase, cleaning a refrigerator, choosing an outfit for work, or a date, or a job interview.
—

Write a list of things that annoy or irritate you generally or in any particular situation. It could be a list of things that annoy you at parties, or in elevators or at the hairdresser's. Write a paragraph on each and see if they join up to become an essay on the minor difficulties of being human.
—

Jot down the events of your life under categories: events, people, secret thoughts, familiar objects. Which of those still haunt you?
—

Write about your mother's jewelry.
—

Write twenty things you love about your life
—

Where is home for you?
—

Write a list of ten things you will never write about. Write a paragraph on each. (You can begin, "It's hard for me to talk about the day when…")
—

Write about a time you slept outdoors.

—

Write about a time you deliberately kept yourself ignorant of what was going on around you.

—

Start every sentence with: "I remember" or "I don't remember" or "I wish"

—

Write a series of alternating sentences beginning "Once I was," "Then," "Now I am"

—

Begin a free write with this phrase: "Everything was fine until . . ."

—

Write about the worst thing that has ever happened to you.

—

What don't you know?

—

Write about a memory until you understand why you still remember it after all these years.

—

Write about your worst Valentine's Day.

—

Tell family stories through Christmas ornaments.

—

Write about your father's car.

—

Write down the rules your family lived by.

—

Begin your piece with the sentence, "I fell in love with my life one Tuesday in August" (you can change the day and the month, of course).

—

Tell a story that takes place within a larger public story: September 11, a blackout, Obama's inauguration, an earthquake. Invent the details that you don't remember.

—

Write about a procedure from start to finish, something you do at work or at home. Be precise, but don't be afraid to mix in other elements (memories, stories, and anecdotes).

—

You wanted it bad, and then you got it, and it was worth the wait ... or was it?

—

Write about something you decided you would never do again, and did anyway.

—

Free write for ten minutes, allowing whatever images and subjects that come up. When you finish, go back over your free write and highlight four key words or images. Now do four more ten-minute free writes using the highlighted words and images as springboards. Again, let the writing go where it will. When you finish, read back over all five drafts. Cut and paste them together into a single piece.

—

Write about something you've just discovered a passion for that's unlike you: roses, or investing, or shooting a gun

—

Write a letter to someone who is dead. In it, make a confession.

—

Describe making love in an unconventional place.

—

Describe a journey you took. Tell where you broke down, where you slept, ate, and visited. Make the story evocative of your mood at the time.

—

Tell us about something you don't understand.

—

Tell us why you've always been such a scum-sucking worm where men (or women) are concerned.

—

In thinking about a piece, tell us everything you will certainly not be putting in.

—

Write a piece called "What I Believe."

—

Describe a ritual in your family.

—

Describe your first experience of death.

—

Write about the moment you found out what men and women do together in bed.

—

Write about an object you lost and then found, or just lost. Describe it, and show the moment you discovered it was missing. Talk about the period of adjustment, moments of forgetting the object is lost, and then experiencing the loss over again.

——

What skill did you never learn (my ex-husband never learned to ride a bicycle; I never learned to put on eyeliner)?

——

Start with a surprising remark your friend made. (A woman friend of mine once said, "I like being lost. It makes me feel feminine.")

——

Write about your relationship to paperwork.

——

How has your relationship with your mother changed over the years?

——

Write a story about how another point of view was imposed on you. This is often something that one of your parents (or teacher) said repeatedly about you, or about your family, that hampered the direction you took or made you angry. My sister Adrian might say that she didn't get to college until her forties, when it took her six years in night school to get a diploma, because our mother believed in having a good job instead.

——

List all the presents your mother has given you over the years. Who the heck is she buying those presents for?

——

Your name wasn't on the list.

——

Write a piece about cleaning something out: a fridge, a drawer, a room, a garage. Show that you're not just physically making space, that you're also making mental space, letting go of an old self and making room for who you are now, and who you want to be.

——

Write a holiday newsletter. Make it terse, funny, with lots of ironic self-deprecating detail.

——

Review your education. In light of what you know now, and who you became, what would you do differently to prepare yourself for life?

——

If you have lost a parent, write on this subject:
I forgot to tell my mother …
I forgot to tell my father …

—

Compile a list of as many incidents and experiences from your life as you can recall. Next, review this list and ask yourself about each item on it: Is the story interesting enough to be a stand-alone piece? Can it sustain a length of 1,000 or more words? And if not, might it instead be a brief anecdote that could serve as a starting point, a launching pad for another idea?

—

Use a favorite passage of writing as a model, sentence by sentence, copying the writer's rhythms but putting in your own content.

Example from Joan Didion: "To be married in Las Vegas, Clark County, Nevada, a bride must swear that she is eighteen or has parental permission. Someone must put up five dollars for the license."

Imitation: To backpack in the High Sierra, a person must obtain a wilderness permit and he or she must file a schedule of travel. Someone must contact the ranger.

—

Choose a favorite essay and type it into your computer word for word. You will see that the exalted author is just a person typing words, like you. You'll see how he or she did it.

—

Start with this quote by Wendell Berry: "You have throwed in your lot with them sons a' bitches against me."

—

Write a letter of complaint (Your rental car is insufficient for any pursuit situation. Cornering in city streets at any speed over 50 miles per hour results in excessive tire slippage.)

—

Write about how to be you in a primer written like a how-to book.

—

Describe an activity — cleaning the house, driving, fishing, dancing, or cooking — that could serve as a metaphor for your approach to things.

—

Take a very small incident, such as your flapping shoelace, the failure of your coworkers to notice your stunning ten-pound weight loss, or your husband's insistence of going for a bracing walk in the sunshine when you want to slouch on the couch and make a huge deal of it.

—

Write one page about an area in which you have bad taste but don't care.

—

Pretend to admire something to reveal its flaws. You can admire the wisdom of the city fathers for tearing down a freeway, admire your teenage daughter's scanty outfit (so sensible for a hot climate, if only you lived in one).

—

Write about something you love, but be annoyed with it. For example, ferry rides are cold and they're over in 35 minutes. For example:
"I hate walking in San Francisco. You are always on a hill, near a hill, coming down a hill, so that the view is always shifting. And the people! Sidewalks are for going somewhere. San Franciscans think they're long, narrow patios."

—

Take any commonly accepted idea and reverse it. Write about the benefits of being mugged, fired, sick, divorced, broke, stood up.

—

Write ten cranky, specific tips for buying presents.

—

 Write a list of 10-20 ways in which you do something odd: in dress, in eating, in driving, in thinking, in hobbies, superstitious behavior, anything. Would you drive two hours to buy a mango? Put that in.

—

Tell us, in one page, why you are so delightful to live with (irony here, please).

—

Write three apologies. Example:
To Gabrielle:
I'm sorry that I stepped on your hamster. I was too embarrassed to tell you how he died that night. I was only seven. It was like stepping on a warm beanbag, a small crunch of softness.

—

Pick a single sense other than sight to write about. Walk around your neighborhood, or house, and take notes about everything you can identify using that single sense.

—

Write a character sketch by examining someone's wastebasket.

—

Write down thirty images from a typical day. Include anything that strikes you: overheard snatches of conversation, graffiti, the sights and smells and textures of your day.

—

Write a piece that begins with a foreboding smell.

—

Go somewhere you've never been and where you would never ordinarily go. Let us learn something about you by your response to it (for example, a biker bar, a library, a hardware store, a baby shower, a church).

—

Use a succession of objects to tell your life story: cars, houses, t-shirts, coffee cups, couches.

—

Draw the floor plan of a house you lived in. Or of your childhood neighborhood, the streets, houses, and so on, putting in notes about incidents as you remember them. I draw my neighborhood, and soon those penciled lines bring back images of chasing a doughnut truck down Lagunitas Road, the delicious hot scorched tortillas made by the Villeneneuvas up on the hill. I draw the spot where St. Cecelia's Church fronts on Sir Francis Drake Boulevard and remember the day a man asked me to duck under a counter and put a dime on a plate, and how I did it and felt such a fool when he walked off with a giant pink poodle.

—

Tell your life story in quotes.

EXAMPLE:
1. "Go to your room," my mother said.
2. "You have to put your face underwater so you can swim," she said, shoving my head into the enamel dishpan.

—

Write a complete, but short, piece (1,000 words maximum) that spans a large amount of time (at least 10 years) in your life. Avoid generalization and abstraction.

—

Write a half- page about what you are most afraid of.

—

Get out your photograph albums. Pick out a number of photographs, one or two from each period of your life, arrange them in a stack like a deck of cards, with the earliest photo on top and the latest on the bottom. Pick up the first and start writing. Tell your reader what's in the photograph, what it doesn't show, what happened just before or just after it was taken. Mark Senak, author of *A Fragile Circle: A Memoir,* says he tries to remember his life as a series of snapshots. "Writing about my life started out like looking at a big, friendly stack of Polaroids," he said "But after a couple of weeks, it was like an endless motion picture."

———

List specific images and details about an event, then pick the best ones and add new ones if they occur. Order the specifics to reveal meaning and continue to add new ones and cut old ones. Don't state the meaning, but allow the details to reveal it.

———

Write a self-portrait from the perspective of your worst enemy at a particular time in your life. Or begin this way: "I know what Bill is about. The thing about Bill that nobody else knows is …"

———

Think of a place you go to regularly: a library, coffee joint, exercise class, gas station, dry cleaner. Write one to two pages about you from the point of view of whomever waits on you, trying to figure out who you are and what's going on with you from what he or she glimpses of you. The person is not important. The idea is to learn something about you as seen by somebody else.

———

Write a scene with two characters in which one wants something that the other does not want to give.

———

Write a how-to guide for someone undertaking an impersonation of the character, i.e. how to be Dad. What are their characteristic physical gestures?

WRITERS' RESOURCES

All the information you need is on the Internet, from writers' guidelines to media kits to editorial calendars.

Bacons.com

Matchwriters.com

mediabistro.com

National Writers Union (US) www.nwu.org

www.writemarket.com

www.writersdigest.com

writerswrite.com

redroom.com

freelancewriting.com

elance.com

creativecaffiene.com